Rupert B. Vance
University of North Carolina
1930.

STUDIES IN HISTORY, ECONOMICS AND PUBLIC LAW

EDITED BY THE FACULTY OF POLITICAL SCIENCE OF
COLUMBIA UNIVERSITY

Number 323

THE DEVELOPMENT OF THE FEDERAL PROGRAM OF FLOOD CONTROL ON THE MISSISSIPPI RIVER

THE DEVELOPMENT OF THE FEDERAL PROGRAM OF FLOOD CONTROL ON THE MISSISSIPPI RIVER

BY

ARTHUR DeWITT FRANK, Ph.D.

NEW YORK
COLUMBIA UNIVERSITY PRESS
LONDON: P. S. KING & SON, LTD.
1930

Copyright, 1930

BY

COLUMBIA UNIVERSITY PRESS

PRINTED IN THE UNITED STATES OF AMERICA

ACKNOWLEDGMENTS

This opportunity is taken to express my gratitude to Professor David S. Muzzey, under whose direction this study was made, for his valuable criticism and his generous aid.

I also wish to express my thanks to the members of the Staff of the Library of Congress and to Edith Pierce Frank for their most helpful services.

A. D. F.

5

PREFACE

Floods of the Mississippi river have been one of the greatest natural enemies that the people of any section of the United States have ever encountered. The tremendously fertile delta area constitutes one of the potential garden spots of the world. The lure of such valuable land has been the leading factor in keeping up the morale of the men who have fought the river, so that they have willingly faced numerous almost insurmountable difficulties.

For many years the riparian owners carried on the struggle unaided by any government. Then, parishes and counties began to help. States and, finally, the United States came to the rescue when it became evident that the burden was too heavy for the local communities. The program of the Federal government has continuously expanded until at present it assumes practically all of the responsibility.

This volume attempts to trace the development of the ever increasing program of the Federal government. Special attention has been given to the forces that have aided or hindered the growth of such a colossal system of internal improvement.

Many theories of control have been advanced and considered. Numerous bitter controversies have occurred both among hydraulic engineers and among laymen concerning the various methods of flood control. This volume has neither attempted to solve technical engineering problems nor to settle controversies. It has only stated the outstanding ones as they have affected the development of the program of the Federal government.

A. D. F.

Greenville, N. C., March, 1930.

TABLE OF CONTENTS

CHAPTER I

BEGINNINGS OF FEDERAL CONTROL OF FLOODS ON THE MISSISSIPPI RIVER

THE exact date of the beginning of the national interest in the control of the floods on the Mississippi river cannot be established. The growth of that interest represents an evolutionary process that extends back into our history until it finally loses itself in broader interests in the Mississippi valley. From the very birth of our nation, there has existed a widespread general interest in the Mississippi river.[1] The disposition of the lower Mississippi valley furnished one of the difficult problems during the negotiations at Paris in making the treaty that recognized the independence of the United States. England, France, Spain and the United States figured prominently in the various moves to secure control of that important stream, which all seemed to recognize would play a most important role in the future history of the world.[2] The success of our peace commissioners in gaining possession of the east bank of the Mississippi from its source to within a short distance of the Gulf of Mexico represented an outstanding accomplishment for the diplomacy of a new nation.

The question of the control of the Mississippi, however, was not settled at Paris. England, Spain and France continued to give evidence of great interest in the valley. Intrigue of these European nations among the inhabitants of the West, especially in Kentucky and Tennessee, and with the

[1] *Cong. Record*, 47th Cong., 1st Sess., pt. 4, 1882, p. 3033.

[2] Frederic A. Ogg, *The Opening of the Mississippi*, p. 396.

Indians of the valley showed that they were willing to take great risks to secure a foothold there. During the early years of the United States, this situation offered a serious problem. The attitude of the inhabitants of these Western settlements added gravity to the problem. They showed very clearly by words and acts that they deemed the control of the Mississippi as absolutely essential to their welfare, and that they might even go so far as to withdraw from the Union and ally themselves with whatever nation was in control of this important waterway.[1]

Navigation of the river furnished the most mooted question in the negotiation of the Jay-Gardoqui treaty, which was never ratified.[2] The dispute extended over a period of years. It was settled temporarily by Spain's grant of the right of deposit at New Orleans by the Pinckney treaty of 1795.[3] But the attitude of the people of the United States toward the transfer of Louisiana from Spain to France in 1800 showed convincing evidence of a national interest in the valley far beyond that of the mere question of navigation. It furnished proof that the people of the United States regarded the Mississippi and its wonderful valley as a very splendid territory for future development, and that they wanted no strong and aggressive power for a neighbor. On May 26, 1801, Thomas Jefferson wrote to James Madison that the transfer of Louisiana to France would prove " very ominous to us ".[4] In his annual message to Congress in 1802, Jefferson stated that the transfer of Louisiana by the treaty of San Ildefonso seriously affected the interests of the United States.[5] In the meantime, the people of the United

---

[1] John B. McMaster, *History of the People of the U. S.*, vol. ii, p. 143.

[2] Frederic A. Ogg, *The Opening of the Mississippi*, p. 423.

[3] Edward Channing, *The Jeffersonian System*, p. 56.

[4] *Ibid.*, p. 60.

[5] Henry S. Randall, *Life of Thomas Jefferson*, vol. iii, p. 6.

States had talked and written much about the natural right of free navigation on the Mississippi, and they had repeatedly pointed out the grave dangers of permitting a European nation to establish a strong colony in the lower valley.[1] This great interest in the problem created a sentiment so strong that Jefferson determined to secure control of at least the east bank of the river. Then, when the opportunity presented itself, he committed an act " beyond the Constitution " by purchasing the whole of the Louisiana territory. A public demand that could induce Jefferson to take such a step furnishes ample proof that the people of the United States were giving serious consideration to the Mississippi.[2]

The purchase of Louisiana did not indicate an interest in flood control but it did indicate a condition out of which a favorable attitude toward flood control might easily grow. And those in authority in the Federal government appeared to take an interest in the problem of floods from the date the territory was acquired. The problem had been from the beginning of the settlement of Louisiana the major difficulty of the people of the lower valley. They had given much time, effort and money in attempting to solve it. This situation naturally attracted the attention of the officials of the United States, who placed high value on this section. History offers ample proof that the flood problem extended back of the first settlements of white men to the native Indians of the lower valley. An early account of De Soto's expedition tells us that the great inundations in the Mississippi valley forced the Indians to use only the highest ground on which to build their homes and, in places where no high ground could be found, compelled them to build huge earth mounds with flat tops on which they could live during the flood season.[3]

[1] John B. McMaster, *History of the People of the U. S.*, vol. ii, p. 803.

[2] Henry S. Randall, *Life of Thomas Jefferson*, vol. iii, p. 70.

[3] *Literary Digest*, vol. 94, July 30, 1927, p. 22. Translation of account by De la Vega.

Anthropologists have verified this account of the use of mounds for protection against floods.[1]   These mounds are, to this day numerous in the delta.   They show convincing evidence of having been used in times of inundation. Many of them have connecting ridges or elevated runways apparently for the purpose of communication during floods.[2] De Soto's men tell about finding a chief's house surrounded by palisades on one of these gigantic mounds with a village of huts surrounding the foot of the mound.[3]

La Salle found the lower Mississippi out of its banks in 1684.[4]   Accounts of his expedition graphically describe the sufferings of vast portions of the lower valley from inundations.[5]   Bienville selected the site for New Orleans because the land there was above water when he arrived, while all of the surrounding territory had been inundated by the flood on the Mississippi.[6]   This settlement at New Orleans suffered very heavily from the annual spring floods.[7]   And the other settlements of white men fared even worse.   They " were almost destroyed " by the mighty floods that " came sweeping down upon them in early spring ".[8]

The first white men learned from the natives that floods made yearly appearances and at intervals proved highly destructive.   But the white men showed no inclination to surrender such a promising territory to the river and soon gave evidence that they would defend themselves against

[1] *Science*, N. S., vol. 65, supplement, p. xiv.

[2] Lyle Saxon, *Father Mississippi*, p. 65.

[3] *Ibid.*

[4] Tompkins, *Riparian Lands of the Mississippi River*, p. 121.

[5] Lyle Saxon, *Father Mississippi*, p. 253.

[6] Rightor, *Standard History of New Orleans*, p. 171.

[7] Tompkins, *Riparian Lands of the Mississippi River*, p. 20.

[8] Lyle Saxon, *Father Mississippi*, p. 66.

their great natural enemy.[1] The river took a heavy toll while they prepared plans for defense against the inundations.[2] But the men from Europe knew a better way to fight the river than to build mounds of earth for temporary habitation while the muddy waters swept over their fields and submerged their homes. They knew the value of levees.

The Pharoahs built levees along the banks of the Nile four thousand years before the white man came to fight the floods of the Mississippi.[3] However, Europeans did not have to go to Egypt for examples of the use of levees to protect against floods. The Po had been controlled by levees before 1300 A. D. Holland had made extensive use of levees prior to the white man's coming to America. The Danube, the Rhine, the Rhone, the Volga and many other European rivers had levees for protection against floods before 1700 A. D.[4] Thus, the white men from Europe had the advantages of an experience in flood control that served as an excellent example for their work in America.

The settlers at New Orleans began the construction of the first levees on the banks of the Mississippi in 1717.[5] Ten years later, Governor Perrier proudly announced that New Orleans had a levee a mile long and eighteen feet wide. He further stated that within another year the embankment would be extended above and below the city for a total distance of eighteen miles.[6] By 1735 the protective embankments had been extended twelve miles below and thirty miles above New Orleans on both banks of the river.[7] In 1812,

[1] Amos Stoddard, *Sketches of Louisiana*, p. 166.

[2] B. G. Humphreys, *Floods and Levees of the Mississippi River*, p. 16.

[3] *Ibid.*

[4] *Ibid.*, p. 19.

[5] Humphreys and Abbott, *Physics and Hydraulics of the Mississippi River*, p. 150.

[6] Lyle Saxon, *Father Mississippi*, p. 253.

[7] Tompkins, *Riparian Lands of the Mississippi River*, p. 22.

when Louisiana became a state, the levees extended 155 miles on the east bank and 185 miles on the west bank of the Mississippi. The cost of those 340 miles of levee can never be reliably established, but it has been estimated at $6,000,000.[1]

Each planter constructed his share of the levee by his own labor and his own resources. The government under which he lived likewise showed much interest in the levee which he was constructing. One of the conditions of the grants by which the people received the land from the King of France obliged the planters to build levees.[2] Throughout the early history of Louisiana the police juries compelled all who lived within seven miles of the river to work on the levees.[3] Although the work was done by individual planters, the local governments exercised considerable supervision so that the planters would not neglect their tasks. In 1743, the Governor of the territory promulgated an ordinance that required the inhabitants to complete their portions of the levees by January 1, 1744, or forfeit their grants as penalties.[4] These facts furnish proof that a governmental interest in protecting the lower valley from floods existed long before Louisiana became a part of the United States, and exerted a powerful influence among the inhabitants of the lower delta when we purchased the territory.

However, the national interest in the Mississippi river during the first half of the nineteenth century was directed toward the improvement of navigation, rather than flood control. The earliest demands of the people of the West for free navigation of the Mississippi, which resulted in the purchase of Louisiana, did not create any movement for the improvement of navigation because the type of boats in use at

[1] Tompkins, *Riparian Lands of the Mississippi River*, p. 139.
[2] Lyle Saxon, *Father Mississippi*, p. 257.
[3] Rightor, *Standard History of New Orleans*, p. 174.
[4] Tompkins, *Riparian Lands of the Mississippi River*, p. 22.

that time did not need an improved river. The people merely insisted on free navigation. The development of the steamboat furnished ample stimulus for the creation of a widespread demand for the improvement of navigation on many rivers, especially on the Mississippi. Congress could not easily avoid the issue. In 1820, it appropriated $5,000 for a survey of the Ohio and Mississippi rivers for the purpose of determining the most practicable way of improving navigation.[1] Protection against floods attracted no attention in the discussion of that appropriation. Two young army engineers, S. Bernard and Joseph G. Totten were designated to make the survey provided for by the appropriation.[2] These two engineers gave us our first important official report on the Mississippi river in 1822.[3] Although the survey primarily concerned itself with navigation it also involved the question of flood control. Snags offered the greatest hazard to the river boats. The report of 1822 concluded that the accumulation of snags in the main channel of the river resulted very largely from the effects of the many lateral currents.[4] The engineers concluded that the only way to prevent the accumulation of snags was to construct dykes to prevent the lateral currents. "When the whole river shall be dyked . . . then will these snags cease to accumulate ".[5] They had observed that the levees on the lower river served both as protective works against floods and as preventive works against lateral currents. While these levees had been built for the purpose of protection against floods, the engineers believed they were improving

[1] *House Doc.*, no. 35, 17th Cong., 2nd Sess., 1823, p. 3.

[2] *House Report*, no. 300, pt. 2, 63rd Cong., 2nd Sess., 1914, p. 21.

[3] *House Doc.*, no. 35, 17th Cong., 2nd Sess., 1823, p 1

[4] *Ibid.*, p. 22.

[5] *Ibid*, p 21.

navigation.[1]   This conclusion and the recommendation for the construction of more levees definitely connected flood control with the improvement of navigation.   Thus, flood control became a secondary interest while navigation improvement remained the chief consideration of those interested in the welfare of the valley.

The navigation interests made a very strong appeal for river improvement before Congressional Committees in 1827.   Several witnesses gave graphic accounts of the exceedingly heavy losses from wrecks of river boats due to the boats striking snags.[2]   The Federal government began to do some work in the improvement of the river by detailing members of the Corps of Engineers for the task.   The report of the progress of this work of improving navigation which was submitted to Congress in 1831 urged the Federal government to remedy the very unfavorable conditions that were seriously hindering the development of river commerce.[3]   In 1843, the Senate Committee on Commerce and Navigation of the Mississippi River reported the vast importance of commerce by the steamboats on the Mississippi and urged improvement of the river by the Federal government.[4]   No mention was made of flood control in this report.   In 1846, John C. Calhoun introduced a bill for the general improvement of the Mississippi.[5]   Navigation received special consideration but flood control entered incidentally by the back door through an "etc."[6]   The reference of the bill to the Committees on Roads and Canals indicated the

[1] *House Report*, no. 300, pt. 2, 63rd Cong., 2nd Sess., 1914, p. 21.
[2] *House Doc.*, no. 11, 20th Cong., 1st Sess., 1827, p. 5.
[3] *Senate Doc.*, no. 72, 21st Cong., 2nd Sess., 1831, p. 7.
[4] *Senate Doc.*, no. 137, 27th Cong., 1st Sess., 1843, p. 3.
[5] *Cong. Globe*, 29th Cong., 1st Sess., 1846, p. 1028.
[6] *Ibid.*

major interests behind it.[1] As late as 1855 the Senate engaged in a lengthy debate over the improvement of the Mississippi without mentioning floods.   Improvement of navigation seemed to be the only phase of the problem worthy of consideration.[2] However, one does not have much difficulty in locating the cause for the neglect of the flood situation. Practically all of the complaints in regard to conditions on the river had come from merchants and owners of boats, a powerful group of business men who were demanding river improvement in aid of navigation. The landowners had said practically nothing. But they were fortunate because every movement for improving navigation looked toward the construction of levees, which would protect their lands from inundation.

The general movement for internal improvements throughout the Mississippi valley during this period gave those who favored flood control by the Federal government another impetus in creating a favorable public attitude. In 1845, a powerful convention of the leaders of all the valley states known as " a Convention of Southern and Western States " assembled at Memphis for the purpose of considering means of improvement of the entire section.[3] John C. Calhoun presided over that very important meeting. He made a strong plea for control of Mississippi floods by the Federal government, but he took particular caution to say that flood control was not internal improvement.[4] The speeches, however, before the convention showed that many of those present, practically all of whom strongly favored Federal expenditures in their section, thought that flood control was

---

[1] *Cong. Globe*, 29th Cong., 1st Sess., 1846, p. 171.

[2] *Cong. Globe*, 34th Cong., 1st Sess., 1855, p. 1908.

[3] *House Report*, no. 300, pt. 2, 63rd Cong., 2nd Sess., 1914, p. 22.

[4] *House Committee on Flood Control, Hearings 1916*, p. 12.

a type of internal improvement.   Ten years prior to this convention Henry Clay had proposed a measure in Congress which seemed to many to place flood control in the category of internal improvements.[1]   He introduced a resolution directing the Secretary of the Treasury to have an estimate made " of the probable expense of constructing a levee on the public land on the western bank of the Mississippi, and the southern bank of the Red river."   The resolution also called for an estimate of the " probable effects upon the health and prosperity of the country in which any such works may be constructed " and the probable quantity and quality of public land that might be reclaimed by such works.   The consideration of the increase in the value of the lands that could be drained and reclaimed furnished much inducement to those who favored internal improvements for voting for the resolution.[2]   In 1848, Abraham Lincoln argued in the House that the fact that improvement of the Mississippi would benefit certain individuals along its banks was no reason why the improvement should not be made.[3]   He was plainly presenting argument in rebuttal to the opponents of internal improvements.   In 1855, considerable discussion on internal improvement took place in the Senate in a debate over a bill to improve the Mississippi.   Senator Robert Toombs made a very strong argument against internal improvements by the Federal government condemning the proposed project for that reason.[4]   Such discussion tended to give those who favored Federal flood control definite connection with the powerful faction that favored Federal expenditure for internal improvements and, thus, helped to create favorable public sentiment for the project.

[1] *House Doc.*, no. 11, 24th Cong., 1st Sess., 1835, p. 3.

[2] *Ibid.*, p. 11.

[3] *House Committee on Flood Control, Hearings 1916*, p. 17.

[4] *Congressional Globe*, 34th Cong., 1st Sess., pt. 3, 1855, p. 1908.

While the movement for flood control by the Federal government developed, the levees grew in length and in strength through the efforts of the individual riparian proprietors, or, in the later years, with the aid of counties or parishes.[1] As the various states in the lower valley came into the Union they enacted statutes for regulation and supervision of levee building.[2] But the actual work of construction under these statutes remained to be done by the riparian owners and the actual supervision was placed in the hands of the counties and parishes. Slave labor enabled the planters to build most of the levees at the least possible cost because most of the work could be done at odd times and during seasons when there was little farm-work.[3] And some counties and parishes went so far as to make appropriations for levees, as it became apparent that the riparian owners could not cope with the task. But this aid did not amount to much.[4]

The agitation in behalf of flood control by the Federal government grew very rapidly during the period from 1840 to 1860. A series of bad floods made it evident that the problem was too large for the planters, that it had already gone beyond the capacity of the counties and parishes and that it was perhaps too great even for the State governments.[5] The time had come when the " unoccupied links of the chain " had to be constructed to protect the sections that had built levees.[6] Much of the unoccupied territory was in the public domain of the United States. This fact caused a widespread demand for the United States government to

[1] *Cong. Record*, 43rd Cong., 1st Sess., pt. 5, 1874, p. 4653.

[2] *House Committee on Flood Control*, 70th Cong., 1st Sess., 1927-8, *Comm. Doc.*, no. 5, p. 94.

[3] *Cong. Record*, 43rd Cong., 1st Sess., pt. 5, 1874, p. 4653.

[4] *De Bow's Review*, vol. viii, Feb., 1850, p. 101.

[5] *Cong. Record*, 43rd Cong., 1st Sess., pt. 4, 1874, p. 3243.

[6] *Ibid.*, p. 3243.

aid in building levees that would protect the public domain as well as private property.[1]

The conventions that had met on several occasions in the valley states for the purpose of advancing the interests of the Mississippi valley certainly had much to do with creating public sentiment favorable to flood control. These conventions were composed of leading business men and of leading politicians. The one at Memphis in 1845 had over five hundred delegates from twelve states.[2]   Another fully as large met at Chicago in 1847. Such men as Thomas H. Benton, Abraham Lincoln, John C. Calhoun and Horace Greeley attended these conventions.[3]   The memorials of these organizations urging flood control by the construction of levees by the Federal government had much weight with members of Congress.[4]

Congress followed its practice of requiring all such problems to be investigated.   Two army engineers, James Gadsden and James Guthrie, made a superficial survey and reported but nothing developed from this report except perhaps a little increase in the public interest in flood control.

As early as 1845, John C. Calhoun suggested the assigning of certain public lands to the states concerned to be used for the purpose of flood protection.[5]   This system seemed to many to offer a means whereby the Federal government could aid the states without incurring any financial burden. Two severe floods in 1849 and 1850 hastened the decision to give the first Federal aid to levee building.[6]   These two great

[1] Cong. Globe, 28th Cong., 1st Sess., 1843-4, p. 267.

[2] Proceedings of the Miss. River Improvement Convention, St. Louis, 1881, p. 12.

[3] House Report, no. 300, pt. 2, 63rd Cong., 2nd Sess., 1914, p. 22.

[4] B. G. Humphreys, Floods and Levees of Miss. River, p. 29.

[5] Ibid., p. 31.

[6] House Committee on Flood Control, 70th Cong., 1st Sess., 1927-8, Committee Doc., no. 1, p. 20.

floods caused much damage and created considerable complaint among the delta people. *De Bow's Review* in 1850 concluded that " the levees on this portion have not within a few years past offered the same protection that they formerly did ".[1] The great destruction of the floods of 1849 and 1850 showed the inadequacy of the existing levees and convinced a large number of the members of Congress that the time had come when the Federal government should give some aid to the people of the Mississippi delta.

The first aid from the Federal government in the control of floods on the Mississippi came in two acts in 1849 and 1850, the first one applying only to Louisiana and the other to several states. By these acts Congress granted to the several states the swamp and overflowed lands within their borders unfit for cultivation and provided that the proceeds from the sale of the lands must be spent for drainage and for flood protection.[2] Although flood control was the chief actuating cause for the donation of the swamp lands to the States, drainage and reclamation were also important considerations. Several states that had no serious flood problems received donations of large acreages.[3] Alabama, Iowa and Oregon received some lands. Illinois, Minnesota and Wisconsin were among the large beneficiaries, each receiving more than Mississippi. Louisiana received the largest share, with Arkansas next.[4] Although the swamp and overflowed land acts of 1849 and 1850 could not be considered strictly as flood-control legislation, they did represent the actual beginning of Federal aid for flood control. Perhaps Daniel Webster foresaw the results that would follow when he ex-

---

[1] *De Bow's Review*, vol. viii, Feb., 1850, p. 101.

[2] Rightor, *Standard History of New Orleans*, p. 173.

[3] *House Committee on Flood Control*, 70th Cong., 1st Sess., 1927-8, Report to Accompany House Bill 8219, p. 13.

[4] *House Miscellaneous Doc.*, no. 13, 45th Cong., 3rd Sess., 1879, p. 12.

claimed in 1850 that " ere long the strength of America will
be in the valley of the Mississippi ".[1]   The fulfilment of this
prophecy was hastened by the decision of the Federal government to aid in the construction of flood-control works.

Congress passed another act in 1850 that must be given an
important place in any consideration of the problems of the
lower Mississippi valley.   This act " directed a topographi-
cal and hydrographical survey of the delta of the Mississippi
River, with such investigation as might lead to determine the
most practical plan for securing it from inundation ".[2]
Then, Congress appropriated the sum of fifty thousand
dollars to carry out the provisions of the act.   This appropriation was increased by another of the same amount two
years later.[3]   The $100,000 thus appropriated resulted in
two surveys and two reports.   The report made by A. A.
Humphreys and H. S. Abbott, engineers of the United States
army, under the title of the " Physics and Hydraulics of the
Mississippi River " still remains one of the most weighty
authorities on any of the Mississippi river problems.[4]   The
other report, which never reached nor deserved the prominence of that by Humphreys and Abbott, resulted from a
survey by Charles Ellet, a civil engineer working for the
Corps of Engineers of the United States army.[5]   The report
by Ellet preceded the scholarly and detailed report of Humphreys and Abbott by ten years.   It gave a rather comprehensive statement of the problem but often lacked verified
data.   Humphreys began the work with Ellet but became ill
and had to return to the North to regain his health.[6]

[1] *Manufacturers Record*, vol. 91, June 2, 1927, p. 69.

[2] *House Committee on Flood Control, Hearings 1922*, p. 180.

[3] *Cong. Record*, 43rd Cong., 1st Sess., pt. 4, 1874, p. 2243.

[4] *House Committee on Flood Control, Hearings 1922*, p. 180.

[5] *Senate Executive Doc.*, no. 49, 32nd Cong., 1st Sess., 1852 (the report).

[6] *House Committee on Flood Control*, 70th Cong., 1st Sess., 1927-8,
Committee Doc., no. 17, p. 17.

The Ellet report of 1852 was the result of the first official study by the Federal government for the purpose of determining how to control or to prevent destructive floods on the Mississippi river.[1] Ellet concluded that the control of the floods on the Mississippi was the nation's duty and that it was a question that "must be decided by the justice and humanity of the nation ".[2] That statement showed a definite trend in official thinking. Prior to 1849 the Federal government had not taken cognizance in any material way of the responsibility that might rest upon it to aid the local governments and individuals in fighting floods.[3] Ellet contended that fairness dictated that the first Congressional aid should be extended to the area from the Red river to the Gulf of Mexico.[4] His statement that increased cultivation and improved drainage in the upper valley areas had caused the increased flood heights has been widely quoted ever since his time. "The process by which the country above is relieved is that by which the country below is ruined ".[5] As a result of these conclusions he recommended that Congress should not only aid in building levees but that it also should investigate the advisability of constructing reservoirs and diversion channels.[6] Thus, Ellet seemed to favor a rather comprehensive plan of control. His position becomes very interesting in the light of later developments.[7]

The report by Humphreys and Abbott, which resulted from the appropriations of 1850 and 1852, came in 1861

[1] *Senate Executive Document*, no. 20, 32nd Cong., 1st Sess., 1852, p. 2.

[2] *House Committee on Flood Control*, 70th Cong., 1st Sess., 1927-8, *Committee Doc.*, no. 5, p. 107.

[3] *Ibid.*, p. 94.

[4] *Ibid.*, p. 98.

[5] *Ibid.*, p. 54.

[6] *Ibid.*, p. 67.

[7] *House Committee on Flood Control, Hearings 1916*, p. 8.

after almost ten years of painstaking research and profound study. This report thoroughly covered every phase of the problem in a very scientific manner.

The acts of Congress in 1849, 1850 and 1852 represented the beginning of actual Federal participation in the control of floods on the Mississippi. In the meantime, the states of the lower valley had showed increased interests in the problem. They had rapidly revised their laws to make them more uniform and to meet more effectively the difficulties in solving such a great problem.[1] Many situations arose in which the needed protective works overlapped county or parish lines, or where protective works had to be constructed in some places for the protection of areas in other counties or parishes. To meet such conditions, the states created levee districts and levee boards, which agencies have borne the brunt of the fight against floods for the past seventy-five years.[2] The first of the levee boards were created almost immediately following the swamp and overflowed land act of 1850.

The fact that the actual beginning of activity by the Federal government in the control of floods came during the administration of Zachary Taylor may suggest the importance of a friendly President in advancing the interests of any great movement. President Taylor came from Louisiana, where he owned a large plantation which had suffered from inundations. His knowledge of actual conditions gave him an insight to the problem that must have had much influence on his ideas concerning it.[3]

By 1858 the two banks of the Mississippi had levees for a total of two thousand miles. The average height had

[1] *American Railway Engineering Association Bulletin*, vol. 29, July, 1927, p. 11.

[2] *Ibid.*, p. 10.

[3] *Cong. Record*, 45th Cong., 3rd Sess., pt. 1, 1879, p. 503.

reached eight or ten feet and the width at the base from fifty to seventy feet. The people of the lower valley had spent more than $40,000,000 in building that levee line.[1]   Louisiana had spent more than all other states together and had most of the levees. The people of the delta by 1858 had come to feel rather secure behind their magnificent line of defense, which they thought would protect them against any probable flood.   However, in 1858 and 1859 they had their eyes opened to the serious need for a more powerful agency to deal with the colossal problem. During the fall, winter, and spring of 1858 and 1859 occurred the worst flood in the history of the Mississippi valley. Just at the time when the builders had begun to consider their protective works powerful enough to cope with the floods that great inundation tore through the levees by numerous crevasses and devastated most of the delta area.[2]   The general breakdown in the levee system at the time when the people confidently expected it to hold offered conclusive evidence that flood-control works had to be built higher and stronger in order to protect the delta area.[3]   This meant that the local governments would naturally turn to the Federal government with a problem that had evidently become too great for them.

[1] *Cong. Record*, 43rd Cong., 1st Sess., pt. 5, 1875, p. 4654.

[2] *American Railway Engineering Association Bulletin*, vol. 29, July 1927, p. 11.

[3] *House Committee on Flood Control*, 70th Cong., 1st Sess., 1927-8, *Committee Doc.*, no. 1, p. 20.

CHAPTER II

CHAOTIC CONDITIONS AND THE CREATION OF THE MISSISSIPPI RIVER COMMISSION

THE great flood in the spring of 1859 severely damaged the levees and left the people of the delta in an impoverished condition. But the victims courageously began the burdensome task of repairing their levees as they had done many times before, only showing greater disappointment than they had ever shown before.[1] The years from 1850 to 1857 had been prosperous ones for the lower valley states. The period of prosperity largely resulted from increased returns from the cotton crops, the general prosperity of the section and land grants from Congress under the swamp and overflowed land acts of 1849 and 1850.[2] The planters along the river used much of their increased funds for building protective works, which expenditure caused the levees to be more rapidly extended than in any similar period prior to that time. The embankments were very rapidly and often poorly constructed. Such new and unset works could not be depended upon until they had been severely tested. No opportunity was offered for thoroughly testing the new levees until the great flood came in the spring of 1859.[3] Yet, the people who had built them expected them to hold and were quite naturally much disappointed when the flood waters poured upon them through twenty-five miles of crevasses. How-

[1] B. G. Humphreys, *Floods and Levees of the Mississippi River*, p. 22.
[2] R. S. Taylor, *Mississippi River Improvement*, p. 30.
[3] Lyle Saxon, *Father Mississippi*, p. 263.

ever, the builders would not be defeated and returned to the task with more determination than ever.[1]

The determination to continue to fight the enemy did not mean that the people of the delta would not seek allies. In fact they really expected to get assistance from the Federal treasury and began to make very strong appeals for funds from that source.[2] By 1861 their case appeared to be in a good position before the select committees of the House and the Senate which had been appointed to consider the problem.[3]

But all chances for success suddenly collapsed with the approach of the greatest catastrophe that ever befell this nation. The Civil War turned the people from progress and construction to stagnation and destruction. That horrible calamity struck the delta section a staggering blow which naturally stopped all work of rebuilding and extending the levees.[4] The riparian owners had other business for themselves and other occupations for their slaves in their efforts to serve their states.

Levees must have constant care and repairs to keep them in satisfactory condition. If they are left alone they deteriorate very rapidly.[5] When the war came the owners of the lands simply abandoned them. The general neglect for four years would have caused serious loss from natural deterioration, if no other forces of destruction had been at work. But other destructive forces were there. The contending armies proved as destructive to levees as they did to other property. Apparently both armies destroyed them when there appeared to be any military advantage in doing so.[6]

[1] Lyle Saxon, *Father Mississippi*, p. 263.

[2] *Rand-McNally Bankers' Monthly*, vol. 32, Feb., 1915, p. 15.

[3] B. G. Humphreys, *Floods and Levees of the Mississippi River*, p. 35.

[4] Lyle Saxon, *Father Mississippi*, p. 264.

[5] R. S. Taylor, *Mississippi River Improvement*, pt. 6, p. 1.

[6] *Engineering and Contracting*, vol. 53, Jan. 14, 1920, p. 36.

In the name of military necessity, the delta people saw the
destruction of much of their work for the peaceful defense
of their homes.[1]   The Union army destroyed the great
Yazoo and Huspuckena levees in an effort to reach Vicksburg from the rear.[2] They represented the finest in the delta,
the Yazoo Pass embankment being thirty-eight feet high,
and had been constructed at an enormous cost for resources
at the command of the people who constructed them.[3]

During the Civil War and the period of reconstruction
there occurred one of the most remarkable series of floods
ever recorded in our history.   Great floods came in 1858,
1859, 1862, 1865, 1867, 1874 and 1882.[4]   Each flood found
the levees in worse condition than the previous one; and
each flood, therefore, wrought greater havoc to protective
works than the previous one had wrought.   Crevasse after
crevasse appeared and mile after mile of levee fell into the
river with the caving banks.[5]   By 1878 hundreds of miles
of the main line had disappeared or had been abandoned.[6]
The value of the levees for defense against floods in 1878
represented only a small fraction of their value for such a
purpose in 1858.   For two decades their conditions grew
worse and worse until great floods went " through them
and over them without restraint ".[7]

Although the agencies of destruction wrought havoc with
the levees, the people of the delta began as soon as the war had

[1] *Cong. Record*, 47th Cong., 1st Sess., 1882, pt. 4, p. 3215.

[2] *Cong. Record*, 70th Cong., 1st Sess., 1928, pt. 6, p. 4247.

[3] Barbour Lewis, M. C., *Speech on Levees of the Miss.*, House June 6,
1874, p. 5.

[4] I. M. Cline, *Floods in the Lower Mississippi Valley*, p. 5.

[5] *House Committee on Flood Control*, 70th Cong., 1st Sess., 1927-8,
Comm. Doc., no. 1, p. 21.

[6] *Cong. Record*, 43rd Cong., 1st Sess., pt. 4, 1874, p. 3243.

[7] R. S. Taylor, *Mississippi River Improvement*, pt. 1, p. 6.

ended a half-hearted effort to repair and rebuild them. Under the circumstances their spasmodic attempts deserve much commendation.[1] Money had to be raised to carry on construction. This task was doubly hard as the economic disaster that the war and reconstruction visited upon the delta could harly be exaggerated. Farm lands in Arkansas, Louisiana and Mississippi were valued at almost four times as much in 1860 as they were in 1870.[2] And farm lands had to bear most of the burden of replacing the levees. In an effort to protect themsedves against floods the people of the delta taxed a large part of their lands to such a degree that they passed out of their possession and back into the possession of the States where they yielded no revenue.[3] By 1870, more than half of the lands of the fertile Yazoo basin, which in 1861 had been valued by Humphreys and Abbott at $100 per acre for cleared lands and $25 per acre for woodlands, had been forfeited by the owners to the States because the taxes could not be paid.[4] That process simply helped to make the burden for those who retained their lands impossible to bear. The owners in many localities called conventions to discuss the problem and to plan its solution if possible. They seriously considered the advisability of abandoning the whole fight and permitting the river to run wild over their formerly productive fields.[5] Yet, in spite of their great losses and their great economic disaster the delta people were reluctant to surrender. They had never known the time when the enemy river did not menace their lives and property. They had apparently come to consider an eternal fight with it as a necessity. But it now appeared that they would be com-

[1] *Engineering and Contracting*, vol. 53, Jan. 14, 1920, p. 36.

[2] *House Report*, no. 300, pt. 2, 63rd Cong., 2nd Sess., 1914, p. 19.

[3] *Ibid.*

[4] B. G. Humphreys, *Floods and Levees of the Mississippi River*, p. 19.

[5] *House Committee on Flood Control, Hearings 1916*, p. 12.

pelled to surrender to the river on the one hand or to general poverty on the other hand.[1]

During this period of stress the Federal government dealt the people of the lower Mississippi a severe blow.[2] Congress during the years 1866, 1867 and 1868 levied a tax of three cents per pound on cotton.[3] The funds for levee construction had to come very largely from the cotton lands. A tax on cotton of three cents per pound created a burden that was almost unbearable for the people of the delta. Fortunately, at the special request of the Secretary of the Treasury Congress repealed the tax, which had been levied at a most inopportune time.[4]

Under such conditions the people of the delta were waging a losing fight. But they accomplished something. Prior to the Civil War, flood protective works had been constructed by poorly managed organizations.[5] Legislation on the eve of the outbreak of the war had paved the way for the organization of levee boards, and as soon as the war ended the people developed the organization of the boards as a part of their plans for renewing the fight.[6] The state of Louisiana tried an interesting experiment in organization for levee construction. The State granted a charter to the Louisiana Levee Company, and then contracted with that company to build and repair levees. The prices agreed upon would now appear exorbitant, but they were perhaps reasonable enough in 1871.[7] The law provided for the location of all levees by

[1] Lyle Saxon, *Father Mississippi*, p. 264.

[2] *Cong. Record*, 45th Cong., 3rd Sess., pt. 2, 1879, p. 980.

[3] B. G. Humphreys, *Floods and Levees of the Mississippi River*, p. 23.

[4] James L. Alcorn, *Speech on Mississippi Levees*, Senate, Jan. 21, 1873, p. 7.

[5] *Cong. Record*, 43rd Cong., 1st Sess., pt. 4, 1874, p. 3243.

[6] *Cong. Record*, 70th Cong., 1st Sess., pt. 6, 1928, p. 4247.

[7] *Cong. Globe*, 42nd Cong., 1st Sess., pt. 2, 1871, p. 753.

a Commission of three engineers. One member of this Commission was to be selected by Louisiana and one was to be detailed from the Corps of Engineers of the United States army by the President of the United States. The third member was an employee of the corporation.[1] That appears to have been the first official participation of a representative of the Federal government in the actual construction of flood-control works.

Fortunately for the people of the delta, the movement for the participation of the Federal government in flood control had been growing. That movement had developed rapidly during the decade preceding the war.[2] In 1861 the remarkable report of Humphreys and Abbott, officially called the Delta Survey, was published. While the report did not make as many recommendations as others had often done it plainly urged the duty of the Federal government to aid in the control of floods on the Mississippi and it included so much scientific data, compiled in such a convincing manner, that it stood as a great bulwark for those who presented the case of the delta.[3] The war naturally turned the minds of the people away from all civil activities, but it only retarded the movement for expenditure of Federal funds for the control of floods. The war had been over only a short while when the Secretary of War, Edwin M. Stanton, showed an active interest in repairing and rebuilding the levees.[4] On December 1, 1865, he directed General A. A. Humphreys to investigate and to report the repairs to the levees necessary to prevent great injury to agriculture in the delta.[5] Congress also took

---

[1] *Cong. Globe*, 42nd Cong., 1st Sess., pt. 2, 1871, p. 753.

[2] *House Committee on Flood Control, Hearings 1916*, p. 256.

[3] Weather Bureau Bulletin, no. 143, *Floods of the Mississippi River*, p. 3.

[4] Tompkins, *Riparian Lands of the Mississippi River*, p. 212.

[5] *Cong. Record*, 47th Cong., 1st Sess., pt. 4, 1882, p. 3034.

cognizance of that investigation when it directed by resolution on June 11, 1866 the Chief of Engineers to report the results and to furnish an estimate of the amount of money that would be required to repair the breaks.[1]   The report was made by General Humphreys in 1866.[2]   The short document was a welcome message to the people of the delta and renewed hope for help from the Federal government.   General Humphreys stated frankly that he found many miles of levee line missing and many more miles in such condition that repairing them " would be practically the rebuilding of the levees ".[3]   He very strongly suggested the necessity of the Federal government's giving aid when he said, " The proper establishment and maintenance of the first order of levees requires some authority entirely beyond the influence of local interests ".[4]

The second annual message of President Johnson greatly pleased the flood-control interests.   In it, the President urged Congress to pass whatever legislation seemed necessary " for the preservation of the levees of the Mississippi River ".[5] He stressed the great national importance to both production and commerce of maintaining strong barriers against the floods on the Mississippi, and incidentally, he mentioned the necessity of removing all obstructions to " free and safe navigation " of the river.[6]   However, he put the emphasis upon the flood-control phase of the problem.

The three years immediately following the war furnished much activity for Federal flood control in both houses of

---

[1] B. G. Humphreys, *Floods and Levees of the Mississippi River,* p. 35.

[2] *Senate Executive Doc.,* no. 8, 40th Cong., 1st Sess., 1866, The Official Report.

[3] *Senate Executive Doc.,* no. 8, 40th Cong., 1st Sess., 1866, p. 2.

[4] *Ibid.,* p. 12.

[5] J. D. Richardson, *Messages and Papers of the Presidents,* p. 3652.

[6] *Ibid.*

Congress in the nature of committee reports, the introduction of bills and the passing of resolutions. On July 2, 1866, the Senate Select Committee reported that it believed that the Federal government would have to aid in rebuilding the levees in order to prevent serious damage to the delta.[1] On March 27, 1867, the Senate Committee on Finance reported that it was satisfied of the " constitutional power and the expediency and good policy " of granting aid in the construction of levees along the banks of the lower Mississippi.[2] That Committee report went so far as to recommend the expenditure of three million dollars for the construction of levees.[3] The House of Representatives on July 22, 1868, passed a resolution instructing the Committee on Roads and Canals to " inquire into the propriety of making the levees of the Mississippi a national highway or otherwise so improving them as to protect them at the expense and to the advantage of the public ".[4] Three days later, the Senate resolved to instruct the Committee on Commerce to make inquiry concerning the " expediency of taking measures by the General Government to rebuild the levees upon the lower Mississippi which were destroyed during the late war ". The resolution further instructed the Committee to report by bill or otherwise at the next session of Congress.[5] In the meantime, the friends of flood control in Congress introduced bills by the dozen. Although the bills invariably died in committees, they caused much discussion and created much favorable sentiment. Some of the bills simply provided that the Federal government should participate in the construction of

---

[1] *Cong. Record*, 43rd Cong., 1st Sess., pt. 4, 1874, p. 3243.

[2] *Ibid.*

[6] *Cong. Record*, 45th Cong., 3rd Sess., pt. 2, 1879, p. 980.

[4] *Cong. Globe*, 40th Cong., 2nd Sess., pt. 5, 1868, p. 4335.

[5] *Ibid.*, p. 4450.

levees.[1] Several members presented plans for construction and financing. One method of financing that received considerable attention was to have the Federal government guarantee State bonds, the proceeds from which would be used in building levees.[2]

Following this very enthusiastic display by Congress, there came a period of about five years in which little interest in the problem was shown. The drab days of reconstruction killed all enthusiasm for the project. However, a few bills were introduced each year proposing to protect the delta by a " uniform and permanent " system of levees.[3] Representative L. A. Sheldon of Louisiana introduced an interesting bill in 1871, proposing to charter a corporation of private capital to build a levee from Cape Girardeau, Missouri to Fort Jackson, Louisiana.[4] The corporation would also build a telegraph line on the levee and a railway along the side of it. The supervision of both construction and maintenance was to be under the engineers of the United States army, but ownership and management were to remain with the corporation. The original investment of the United States under that plan would have been a subsidy of $16,000 per mile, in all a total of about $18,000,000.[5]

In 1870, Congress established an agency that could not be considered as an act for the control of floods, but must be listed as an important one in developing the Federal program for flood control. This agency was the United States Weather Bureau, which long ago proved its value as a source of data on floods.[6] Its publications and the information

[1] *Cong. Globe*, 40th Cong., 1st Sess., pt. 5, 1868, p. 1670.

[2] *Ibid.*, 40th Cong., 2nd Sess., pt. 5, 1868, p. 4450.

[3] *Ibid.*, 42nd Cong., 2nd Sess., pt. 1, 1871, p. 68.

[4] *Ibid.*, 42nd Cong., 2nd Sess., pt. 1, 1871, p. 823.

[5] *Ibid.*, 42nd Cong., 2nd Sess., pt. 1, 1871, p. 283.

[6] Morrill Park, Weather Bureau, no. 143, *Floods of the Mississippi River*, p. 4.

give to the public served to create a sentiment for flood control that was firmly based on scientific data.[1]

After a lapse of about five years, Congress again showed considerable interest in Mississippi floods. In 1873, Senator James L. Alcorn of Mississippi introduced a bill designed to carry out the recommendations of the report made by General A. A. Humphreys in 1866.[2] The bill provided for an issue of United States bonds for $36,000,000 to be spent in the construction of levees on the banks of the Mississippi for " the reclamation of twenty million acres ".[3]

Following the Civil War the people of the delta resorted to frequent use of their constitutional right of petition in an effort to get their problem before Congress. Memorials and petitions from various sections and organizations of the South were frequently presented before Committees, in bulletins and on the floors of Congress. The citizens of Louisiana sent up a strong memorial in 1873.[4] It contained strong arguments for control by the Federal government and maintained that states and local units could not possibly subdue the river. " No power but that of the General Government can reach a case so ramified and touching the interests of the people of so many states ".[5] Such petitions were prominently displayed by members of Congress from delta states.

A serious flood, the first one since 1868, inundated most of the delta in the spring 1874 and caused great losses and widespread suffering. During the flood Congress moved one step nearer control by the Federal government by appropriating $90,000 for the relief of flood sufferers. The act,

[1] I. M. Cline, *Floods in the Lower Mississippi Valley*.

[2] James L. Alcorn, *Speech on the Mississippi Levees*, Jan. 21, 1873, p. 1.

[3] *Ibid.*, p. 15.

[4] *House Miscellaneous Doc.*, no. 41, 42nd Cong., 3rd Sess., 1873, p. 15.

[5] *Ibid.*, p. 25.

which was introduced by James A. Garfield, started the Federal government into a new line of activity in regard to floods and created strong interest in the losses and suffering caused by floods.[1]   Serious floods practically always moved Congress to feel the necessity for an investigation into the causes and remedies, and often caused an official report.   The Federal appropriation of $90,000 impressed upon Congress the necessity of a thorough study.   Immediately following the flood, on June 22, 1874, the President approved an act creating a commission of engineers " to investigate and report a permanent plan for the reclamation of the alluvial basin of the Mississippi River subject to inundation ".[2]   This commission was composed of three engineers from the Corps of Engineers of the United States army and two eminent civil engineers actively engaged in the profession.   The President soon appointed the commission with General G. K. Warren as chairman, and the sum of $25,000 was appropriated for its use.[3]   The preamble to the act that created the commission sounded as if Congress fully believed that the Federal government should assume the obligation of controlling Mississippi floods.   It said, ". . . whereas the Mississippi river is national in character, is fed by over fifteen hundred streams . . . ; and whereas all improvements looking to the reclamation of the delta must conduce to the general welfare of the whole Union, and should be undertaken and accomplished by the General Government; and whereas all systems for the redemption and protection of the alluvial lands of the Mississippi should be general and uniform in their character " the commission should be provided to study the problem and report its findings.[4]   Members of Congress in discussing the

[1] *Cong. Record*, 43rd Cong., 1st Sess., pt. 4, 1874, p. 3171.

[2] *Ibid.*, p. 3151.

[3] *House Executive Doc.*, no. 127, 43rd Cong., 2nd Sess., 1875, p. 1.

[4] *Cong. Record*, 43rd Cong., 1st Sess., pt. 4, 1874, p. 3242.

bill made many strong arguments in behalf of control by the United States.[1] That members of Congress understood that the creation of the commission was a forerunner of a program of large expenditures and that it certainly meant the inauguration of a " new policy in respect to the levees of the Mississippi river" were clearly shown by the debate.[2] Some predicted that the new policy would mean the expenditure of many millions of federal funds.

The report of the Warren Commission, made in 1875, showed considerable study of conditions in the delta and of the problem of floods.[3] It did much to hasten the trend toward control by the Federal government. It openly criticized the efforts and methods of the local organization with the statement, " It is a common and apt figure of speech to personify the Mississippi; and to speak of the conflict waged to protect the country against the inroads of a terrible enemy, and yet the army of defense has always been content to remain a simple aggregation of independent companies, with here and there a battalion under the command of a board of officers. That victory has not more frequently perched upon their banners is surely not surprising ".[4] Then, the report proceeded to give reasons why the Federal government should engage in the control of the Mississippi flood situation.[5] General Warren further stressed the very poor condition of the levees after the flood of 1874, estimating that in some states the gaps in the levees equaled from one-third to one-half of the entire length of the levees.[6] Then, he concluded

[1] Barbour Lewis, *Speech on Levees of the Mississippi*, House, June 6, 1874, p. 10.

[2] *Cong. Record*, 43rd Cong., 1st Sess., pt. 4, 1874, p. 3246.

[3] *House Executive Document*, no. 127, 43rd Cong., 2nd Sess., 1875.

[4] B. G. Humphreys, *Floods and Levees of the Mississippi River*, p. 37.

[5] *House Committee on Flood Control, Hearings 1916*, p. 13.

[6] *House Executive Document*, no. 127, 43rd Cong., 2nd Sess., 1875, p. 30.

that the Southern states were so impoverished that neither the local riparian proprietors nor the states could do much toward solving the problem " unaided by the General government ".[1]   The strong support for Federal control from the Warren report greatly encouraged members of Congress from the delta states and stimulated the growth of favorable sentiment both in Congress and among the general public, although no important action followed immediately.

During the period of reconstruction Captain James B. Eads came into great national prominence as an authority on hydraulics.   The Eads bridge at St. Louis and the jetties at the mouth of the Mississippi gave him a popular fame rarely equaled in this country.[2]   Friends of control by the Federal government fully appreciated the effect that his opinion would have upon the public mind.   Therefore, he was asked many questions before Congressional Committees.   He stated that he believed that it was entirely feasible and practical for the Federal government to improve the Mississippi river and to control its floods at a reasonable cost. His position added much prestige to the movement for Federal control.

This demonstration of interest lasted only about two years, after which for a short time the problem attracted little attention.   However, bills continued to appear and to perish quietly in Committees; and members of Congress from the delta states continued to talk on the question in a determined effort to keep the movement for Federal control alive until the next flood aroused the public again.[3]

During the period covered by this chapter the flood-control interests had strong allies among those who for various reasons favored the improvement of navigation on the Mis-

[1] *House Executive Document*, no. 127, 43rd Cong., 2nd Sess., 1875, p. 33.

[2] *House Report*, no. 300, pt. 2, 63rd Cong., 2nd Sess., 1914, p. 27.

[3] *Congressional Record*, 44th Cong., 1st Sess., pt. 2, 1876, p. 1374.

sissippi. The navigation interests and the flood-control interests had quite different objects in view, but they both wanted levees in the same locations, which, after all, made their causes inseparable. The official reports on the Mississippi had frequently pointed out that flood control and the improvement of navigation both demanded levees. Members of Congress often argued the right and duty of the Federal Government to build levees on the banks of the Mississippi to improve navigation, but at the same time denied the right or duty to build the same levees in the same places to protect against floods.[1] However, other members of Congress who favored flood control on the one hand or improvement in the aid of navigation on the other took the position that, since levees built for one purpose would serve for the other, they should not be so particular in defining the exact purpose for which the levees should be built.[2]

The recommendation of the engineers for the construction of levees for improving the river to aid navigation was very fortunate for the delta people, because those interested in navigation had enough influence of their own to cause Congress to appropriate money for the improvement of the river. In 1878 the rivers and harbors bill provided one million dollars for aiding navigation of the Mississippi.[3] The money was spent by the Board on the Improvement of the Mississippi river under the supervision of the Corps of Engineers of the United States army. The membership of that board was composed of army engineers who favored levees for improving navigation.[4] Thus, the engineers of the United States army, who were actually improving the river, by favoring levees for the aid of navigation gave much

[1] *Cong. Record*, 43rd Cong., 1st Sess., pt. 4, 1874, p. 3246.

[2] *Ibid.*, 45th Cong., 3rd Sess., pt. 2, 1879, p. 1031.

[3] *Ibid.*, p. 1033.

[4] B. G. Humphreys, *Floods and Levees of the Mississippi River*, p. 221.

support to those who wanted levees to control floods. And the opinions of the army engineers generally were held in high regard by members of Congress.

The combining of the groups desiring flood control and the groups interested in navigation was very plainly evidenced in the formation and in the debate on the bill creating the Mississippi River Commission in 1879, which put the United States definitely into flood-control work, and which probably stands as the most important piece of flood-control legislation in all of our history.[1] In that combination the groups primarily interested in navigation probably dominated in framing the law that has since developed into an act very largely for the control of floods. The act made it the duty of the Commission " to take into consideration and mature such a plan or plans and estimates as will correct, permanently locate, and deepen the channel and protect the banks of the Mississippi River, improve and give safety and ease to the navigation thereof, prevent destructive floods and promote and facilitate commerce, trade, and the postal service ".[2] This statement in the preamble of the act of the purpose and duty of the Mississippi River Commission plainly showed the influence of the forces primarily interested in navigation.

The debate on the bill in Congress not only showed that the navigation interests dominated but also that the apparent yielding of the flood-control people merely camouflaged their efforts in behalf of their plans to use the Commission for the purpose of controlling floods. Representative R. L. Gibson, who loyally and enthusiastically supported any and all legislation for flood control, made a strong appeal for the improvement of navigation on that " national river, the grandest highway of commerce in the world ".[3] He supported the bill

[1] House Committee on Flood Control, *Hearings 1916*, p. 8.

[2] *Ibid.*, p. 8.

[3] *Cong. Record*, 46th Cong., 1st Sess., pt. 2, 1879, p. 2282.

solely as a flood-control measure, but his speech urged it as a means to improve navigation. Such an attitude drew heavy fire from the opponents of the bill, who proclaimed that it was only a ruse to rob the Treasury of the United States to secure reclamation under the pretense of aiding navigation.[1] Some frankly supported or opposed the bill as a flood-control measure.[2] Still others paid attention only to the phase of the bill that dealt strictly with navigation.[3] And some, like James A. Garfield, supported the bill and openly espoused the expenditure of money both for flood control and for the improvement of navigation.[4] The engineers of the United States army aided the passage of the bill by maintaining that levees would aid commerce on the river.[5] Those who stressed the navigation phases of the bill presented arguments to show the great need for better transportation as a means of lowering freight rates and of breaking the monopoly of the railways.[6] Those who stressed the flood-control features urged the national interest in the delta. Senator W. W. Eaton of Connecticut said that the valley of the Mississippi belonged to him as well as to those who lived there, and that he and his state had great interest in the welfare and prosperity of the delta, which would be increased by protection against floods.[7] The administration forces favored the bill apparently in behalf of both flood control and navigation.

One very interesting feature of the very full and enthusiastic debate was the charge that the Commission created by

[1] *Cong. Record*, 46th Cong., 1st Sess., pt. 2, 1879, p. 2282.

[2] *Ibid.*, 45th Cong., 3rd Sess., pt. 2, 1879, p. 979.

[3] *Ibid.*, p. 978.

[4] *Ibid.*, 46th Cong., 1st Sess., pt. 2, 1879, p. 2283.

[5] *Ibid.*, 45th Cong., 3rd Sess., pt. 2, 1879, p. 985.

[6] *Ibid.*, p. 990.

[7] *Ibid.*, 45th Cong., 3rd Sess., pt. 3, 1879, p. 2306.

the bill would reflect the opinions of the Corps of Engineers of the United States army, which meant that levees would be the only means of flood control with any chance of adoption. Representative John H. Reagan of Texas led a hard but successful fight to secure an amendment that compelled the Commission to consider other systems of control.[1] The Amendment simply made it a duty of the Commission to give due consideration to reservoirs, outlets and other means of flood-control.

Thus, two factions of people, seeking different ends by the same means, combined to pass the act that created the Mississippi River Commission, an agency that has carried out the flood-control program of the Federal government to the present time and seemingly will continue to do so. This act, which has proved by far the greatest milestone reached thus far in the development of a Federal program for flood control, began under the guise of an agency largely for the purpose of improving navigation.

[1] *Cong. Rec.*, 45th Cong., 3rd Sess., pt. 3, 1879, supplement, p. 74.

CHAPTER III

ARGUMENTS FOR FEDERAL CONTROL

ONE of the strongest arguments generally advanced for flood control by the Federal government is that the United States owns the river and has paramount jurisdiction over it. The conclusion that the United States should not permit its property to damage the citizens of any section is the natural outgrowth of ownership. Two reasons are offered as proof that the Federal government owns the Mississippi. The basis most frequently used for such an assumption rests on the authority and duty of the Federal government under the constitution and from court decisions in regard to navigable streams. On that basis, President Arthur in 1882 wrote to the Senate that " having possession and jurisdiction over the river " it became the duty of the Federal government to improve its navigation and to protect the people of its valley against floods.[1] In the same year, several Senators pressed the argument of ownership and jurisdiction under the constitution in supporting an appropriation for the improvement of the river.[2]

The second reason given that the United States owns the river rests on the assumption that it was acquired through right of purchase. This conclusion assumes that the Federal government acquired the river as a part of the Louisiana Purchase and that ownership of the river has never been alien-

[1] J. D. Richardson, *Messages and Papers of the Presidents*, vol. vi, p. 4682.

[2] *New Orleans Times-Democrat*, April 22, 1882.

45

ated.[1]   In fact, many members of Congress have maintained
that Thomas Jefferson purchased the Louisiana territory
mainly to get control of the river for the Federal government.[2]   The payment out of the Federal Treasury attracted
the attention of Senator Thomas A. Hendricks of Indiana in
1866 when he declared that the United States bought the
river under doubtful legal rights and had since its purchase
controlled it " for almost every purpose ".[3]

The statement that the United States owns the river has
frequently been made without any reason being assigned.
And many times ownership has not been mentioned when it
was plainly implied.   Members of Congress have often
pointed out that neither individuals nor the states could in-
terfere with navigable streams in any way without the consent of the Federal government.[4]   Witnesses before congressional committees have made repeated use of such general
statements in their appeals for aid.[5]   Testimony has been
offered as proof that the people of the lower valley have
almost unanimously maintained that the United States owns
the river.[6]   One phase of this controversy is the demand of
the delta citizens that the Federal government should keep its
water from inundating their lands.   They turned to the old
common law to find a basis for such a contention.   Under
this law the owners of property assume the obligation of ad-
ministering it in such a manner as not to injure the person
or property of others.[7]   The proponents of flood control

[1] Senate Committee on Commerce, *Hearings 1904*, p. 66.

[2] *Cong. Record*, 47th Cong., 1st Sess., pt. 4, 1882, p. 3033.

[3] *Ibid.*

[4] Senate Committee on Commerce, *Report on Hearings on Improvement
of Miss. River*, 1904, p. 21.

[5] *House Report*, no. 300, pt. 2, 63rd Cong., 2nd Sess., 1914, p. 301.

[6] House Committee on Flood Control, *Hearings 1916*, p. 96.

[7] *Ibid., Hearings 1922*, p. 107.

maintained that if a citizen cannot permit his property to damage others, then the Federal government should not be given such a right.[1] That point has been stressed many times in debates in Congress.[2] Some have carried the argument a step further and have maintained that if the United States would not permit a damage suit against it, then the states of the lower valley in self-defense certainly should have a case against the states of the upper valley. The Memphis Commercial Appeal in an editorial in 1913 took the position that flood control was so clearly a national problem that the South should have a case in equity for an injunction preventing the upper valley states from clearing land of making any improvement that would increase floods.[3] Recently the right of the riparian owners of the lower valley to recover for injuries from those of the upper valley or from the owner of the river has received considerable attention.[4]

The interstate nature of the flood-control problem has furnished one of the bulwarks for the proponents of the construction of protective works by the Federal government. A glance at the drainage map of this region gives two very definite impressions. The gigantic size of the drainage area of the Mississippi river and the small territory drained by the lower valley, a region suffering most from floods, stand out strikingly.[5] The basin drained by the Mississippi extends from New York and Pennsylvania to Montana and Colorado; from North Carolina and Georgia to Texas and New Mexico.[6] This area covers fifteen hundred miles of latitude and eighteen hundred miles of longitude. It contains about

[1] Senate Committee on Commerce, *Hearings 1904*, p. 21.

[2] *Cong. Record*, 45th Cong., 3rd Sess., pt. 2, 1879, p. 980.

[3] *The Memphis Commercial Appeal*, April 20, 1913.

[4] *Cong. Record*, 70th Cong., 1st Sess., pt. 11, 1928, p. 8692.

[5] *The New York World*, April 24, 1927, Section E, p. 2.

[6] House Committee on Flood Control, *Hearings 1916*, p. 252.

one million and a quarter square miles of territory, which is forty-one per cent of the area of the United States. The river system spreads across the borders of thirty-one states, whose combined area equals about two-thirds of that of the whole nation. This colossal system has fifteen thousand miles of navigable streams and many thousands of miles of non-navigable ones that extend over a territory as large as the combined area of a dozen European nations.[1] The states that contribute waters to the Mississippi contain half of the people of the entire nation.[2] The *Scientific American* in an editorial in 1913 remarked that if anyone doubted that the control of floods on the Mississippi constituted a national problem an examination of a map of the region drained by that mighy stream would be sufficiently convincing.[3] The people of Louisiana have frequently complained that water from other states rolled down upon them and created their flood problems.[4] The interstate aspects of the question appealed very strongly to Secretary of War Dwight Davis when he acted as the spokesman of President Coolidge at Chicago.[5] These same phases also made an indelible impression upon " the intensely practical engineer ", Herbert Hoover, when he spoke of holding " accountable " the various states that had suffered little or no loss but had contributed mightily in the aggregate to the overflow of the Mississippi and its main tributaries.[6] Thus, interstate drainage furnishes a very logical argument for control by the Federal government, especially in view of the large number of states and vast territory affected directly.[7]

[1] House Committee on Flood Control, *Hearings 1916*, p. 252.
[2] *A. A. A. of Political and Social Science*, vol. 135, Jan., 1928, p. 7.
[3] *Scientific American*, April 12, 1913, vol. 108, p. 336.
[4] *The New Orleans Daily Picayune*, April 6, 1912.
[5] *United States Daily*, June 4, 1927, p. 4.
[6] *Kansas City Daily Star*, April 29, 1927.
[7] *United States Daily*, May 6, 1927, p. 8.

The contention that the interstate nature of the problem makes it a national one grows much stronger when it is understood that the areas that suffer most from floods contribute little or none of the water that causes them. The map shows that the drainage basin of the Mississippi spreads like a gigantic fan across central United States with the flared portion extending to the mountains on either side and into Canada and the handle resting at the mouth of the river. A very apt comparison calls the river system a collossal funnel with the huge top in the interior and the small mouth at New Orleans.[1] Certainly the water from the vast drainage basin piles up as it rushes into the main stream of the Mississippi and then spreads out over the lands of Mississippi and Louisiana which send most of their water directly to the Gulf of Mexico.

The area of causation lies both in navigable streams under the jurisdiction of the United States and in non-navigable streams under the jurisdiction of the various states, including portions of Canada.[2] But the region seriously affected by floods lies in the narrow lower valley, mainly in Arkansas, Mississippi and Louisiana, extending roughly about six hundred miles from near Cairo, Illinois to the Gulf of Mexico. This area, which bears practically all of the flood damages, totals less than thirty thousand square miles, or a little more than two per cent of the drainage basin of the Mississippi.[3] The state of Louisiana has the worst flood problem; yet, most of that state, including the fertile Atchafalaya basin, drains into the Gulf of Mexico. Thus, Louisiana cannot be accused of contributing to the floods that

[1] *The Survey*, vol. 58, July 1, 1927, p. 369.

[2] *House Committee on Flood Control*, 70th Cong., 1st Sess., 1927-8, *Comm. Doc.*, no. 24, p. 29.

[3] *Annals of the American Academy of Political and Social Science*, vol. 135, Jan., 1928, p. 2.

cause such great losses to its citizens.[1]   The people there
have long felt that unaided they should not have to receive
and to dispose of the vast volume of flood waters accumulated
in up-river states.[2]

The suggestion has frequently been made that the cost of
flood control should be borne by the various states in proportion to their responsibility for the floods.   The difficulties
of apportioning costs on such a basis appear insuper-
able.[3]   The state of North Dakota and the state of
New York have contributed water, but it would hardly be
possible to say how much that water contributed to the
floods.[4]   Members of Congress from various valley states
have not hesitated to admit that their states have helped to
create the floods, which have done no damage to their own
states but much damage to the down-river states.[5]   One can
imagine the hostile reception the people of Montana or of
New York would give to an effort to make them bear a part
of the cost of flood control, unless the distribution of the
cost were on a national basis.[6]

The problem becomes very complex when we consider the
natural causes of the floods.   But it becomes much more so
when the acts of states and individuals in regard to drainage
and flood-control are considered.   The trouble in West
Tennessee has been almost wholly caused by levees across the
river in Missouri.[7]   Works built for flood protection by

[1] James B. Aswell, *Speech before House*, April 9, 1928, p. 5.

[2] *New Orleans Times-Democrat*, April 17, 1882, p. 1.

[3] *Washington Post*, Feb. 17, 1928.

[4] *House Committee on Flood Control*, 70th Cong., 1st Sess., 1927-8,
Comm. Doc., no. 18, p. 3.

[5] *Ibid., Comm. Doc.*, no. 24, p. 29.

[6] *Cleveland Plain Dealer*, April 18, 1927, p. 8.

[7] *House Committee on Flood Control*, 70th Cong., 1st Sess., 1927-8,
Comm. Doc., no. 18, p. 43.

citizens of one state pile up the water and throw it over the lands of the citizens of another state. The trouble in the St. Francis basin in Arkansas in 1927 was caused by a break in the levee at Dorena, Missouri.[1] The break at Dorena made the people in Cairo, Illinois more secure.[2] Thus, a break in the levee in one state endangers the citizens of another and renders safer the citizens of a third one. The Tensas Basin Levee Board of Louisiana spends all of its money in Arkansas because the danger points for its citizens are all in Arkansas.[3] Such intricate interstate problems have puzzled the Mississippi River Commission and all others who have given them serious thought.[4] " The vigilant have often been inundated from the negligence of their neighbors " in other states and flood-protective works in one state have inundated property of the citizens of other states, thus creating a demand for Federal control.[5]

Anyone giving reasons for flood control by the government of the United States would very likely list as an outstanding one the general welfare. That most of our people believe that the Federal government " exists for practical purposes " has been demonstrated many times by the expenditure of money for various projects ranging all the way from fighting cattle ticks to building an interoceanic canal.[6] Under such circumstances, a problem that vitally affects the lives of millions of our people would naturally be connected with the general welfare, which touches both the humani-

---

[1] *House Committee on Flood Control, Hearings 1927*, p. 2593.

[2] *Ibid.*, p. 3277.

[3] *Ibid., Hearings 1922*, p. 124.

[4] *Ibid., Hearings 1927*, p. 2017.

[5] *House Miscellaneous Document*, no. 41, 42nd Cong., 3rd Sess., 1873, p. 13.

[6] *The Independent*, vol. 55, May 14, 1903, p. 1138.

tarian side and the economic side of our life, both of which are very definitely connected with great floods.[1]

The humanitarian aspects of life, although they may not be as influential in securing legislation as the economic aspects, have a strong universal appeal.   The awful loss in human life and the very widespread human suffering have attracted general attention, especially during and immediately following great floods.[2]   President Arthur in his annual message to Congress in 1882 stressed the great suffering of the people of the delta.[3]   John M. Parker, former Governor of Louisiana, maintained that it was entirely inhuman to permit three-quarters of a million of people to be driven from their homes and to " make them dependent upon the charity of their fellow Americans ".[4]   Editors of papers of the delta have maintained that the members of Congress would vote ample funds if they could only see the great human sorrow resulting from a great flood.[5]   Hon. Frank R. Reid, Chairman of the Flood Control Committee of the House of Representatives, in 1928 made a fervent appeal for our civilization to remove itself far enough from barbarism to prevent such suffering in the name of humanity.[6]   The American people have not yet lost interest in the prevention of human suffering and the loss of human life.

In considering the general welfare, the humanitarian phases and the economic phases of the problem cannot be

[1] Mississippi River Levee Association, *Letters from Prominent Bankers*, p. 7.

[2] *House Committee on Flood Control*, 70th Cong., 1st Sess., 1927, *Comm. Doc.*, no. 13, p. 3.

[3] *New Orleans Times-Democrat*, April 17, 1882, p. 1.

[4] *House Committee on Flood Control*, 70th Cong., 1st Sess., 1927, *Comm. Doc.*, no. 24, p. 2.

[5] *Memphis Commercial-Appeal*, May 7, 1927.

[6] *Cong. Record*, 70th Cong., 1st Sess., pt. 8, 1928, p. 5846.

entirely separated. One leading magazine editor suggested after the flood of 1927 that " Congress might provide that no little fellow should lose his place because the flood had made it impossible for him to meet the payments. . ." [1] President Coolidge spoke of restoring the people of the delta to " productivity and comfort ".[2] The great sacrifices, suffering, expenses and property losses of the inhabitants of the inundated region frequently received mention in the same sentence, which indicates the definite connection and inter-relationships of the humanitarian and the economic.[3]

However, if the amount of discussion can be taken as a criterion, the purely economic phases of the problem have received most consideration. Our government has not generally refused to listen to arguments based on good business principles. Secretary Hoover stated that the losses from the flood of 1927 touched the whole nation and subtracted something from the wage or income of every worker, whether he lived in a mill town of New England or tilled the soil in Kansas.[4] The economic indifference that has permitted such losses could hardly escape the attention either of the business men or of the legislators.[5] Since 1890, the Chamber of Commerce of the State of New York has been sending special representatives and resolutions to Congress to say that the merchants of that state have great economic interest in the purchasing power of the people of the delta and, therefore, in flood control by the Federal government.[6]

[1] *The Survey*, vol. 58, July 1, 1927, p. 363.

[2] *House Committee on Flood Control*, 70th Cong., 1st Sess., 1927, *Comm. Doc.*, no. 13, p. 2.

[3] *House Committee on Flood Control*, 70th Cong., 1st Sess., 1927, *Comm. Doc.*, no. 13, p. 11.

[4] *Cong. Record*, 70th Cong., 1st Sess., pt. 6, 1928, p. 4568.

[5] *House Committee on Flood Control*, 70th Cong., 1st Sess., 1927, *Comm. Doc.*, no. 18, p. 5.

[6] *House Committee on Flood Control, Hearings 1922*, p. 12.

The direct losses of large firms have frequently run into the hundreds of thousands of dollars per firm in a single great flood.[1]

The single group outside of the delta exercising the most direct economic interest in flood control are those who have money invested in delta enterprises. For the past twenty-five years the people from all parts of the United States and from foreign countries have put a large amount of money into Southern investments. The Investment Bankers Association, which has directed the investment of a large part of the money of this country, at its convention in Seattle in 1927 declared by resolution that floods on the Mississippi " affect and impair the economic welfare of this entire nation ".[2] Levee-board bonds and drainage-district bonds naturally suffered heavy losses from floods.[3] In fact all investors in Southern industry lost something.[4]

A phase of economic welfare frequently creeping into this problem represents a kind of neo-mercantilism. At least, it has an element of the old mercantilistic theory in it. Many have pointed to the great value of cotton and sugar to this country. They conclude that flood protection will enable the United States to hold its favorable position in the production of these crops.[5] This argument received much attention during the fight for the establishment of the Mississippi River Commission, when it was frequently urged that the British Empire threatened our leadership in the production of cotton.[6] The dominant position of this country in

[1] A. S. Caldwell, *Flood Control* (pamphlet), p. 13.

[2] *Commercial and Financial Chronicle*, vol. 125, Oct. 15, 1927, p. 2074.

[3] *House Committee on Flood Control, Hearings 1922*, p. 59.

[4] *House Committee on Flood Control*, 70th Cong., 1st Sess., 1927, *Comm. Doc.*, no. 16, p. 13.

[5] *Cong. Globe*, 42nd Cong., 3rd Sess., pt. 3, 1873, p. 728.

[6] J. M. Wills, *National Importance of Rebuilding and Repairing Levees on Banks of Mississippi River*, p. 7.

world finance and our favorable trade balances have been often ascribed to our great exportation of cotton from the delta area.[1] The production of sugar has received special attention from those who have maintained that a nation should produce what it consumes, which means that the " sugar bowl " in Louisiana, in their opinion, should be saved from inundation.[2]

Closely related to the idea of the general welfare is the theory of internal improvements by the Federal government. A large part of the American people still adhere to the idea that government should use its resources freely to improve the country. This theory fits the position of those who have sponsored control of floods at Federal expense. So, they have been in the front rank in voting appropriations for all types of internal improvements.[3]

The delta, having been made a suitable abode for a large population only by flood-control works and drainage works, now pays a large revenue directly to the United States Treasury. The friends of flood control have often pointed out that increased flood protection would increase revenue, and they have predicted that in the long run the increased revenue would pay the cost of constructing protective works.[4] Doubtless security from floods would lead to increased general prosperity and finally to an increase in population, all of which would swell the revenues paid to the Federal government.[5] The mention of population suggests the fact that some of our citizens see everything in relation to numbers of people. So, they have assured Congress that the delta

[1] *House Committee on Flood Control, Hearings 1916*, p. 28.

[2] *House Report*, no. 300, pt. 2, 63rd Cong., 2nd Sess., 1914, p. 301.

[3] *House Committee on Flood Control, Hearings 1922*, p. 45.

[4] J. M. Wills, *National Importance of Rebuilding and Repairing Levees on Banks of Mississippi River*, p. 8.

[5] *House Committee on Flood Control, Hearings 1922*, p. 108.

lands in the not-far-distant future will become absolutely
necessary to feed, clothe and furnish a place of abode for
our rapidly growing population, a protection which would
indeed pay big returns for any expenditure for security
against floods.[1]

Just how much the feeling of insecurity has retarded the
industrial development of the delta territory would be very
difficult to estimate.   But much testimony has been given
that great anxiety and fear have come from the feeling that
floods will probably inundate the territory every few years.[2]
This state of mind has hindered development and has checked
the " influx of new population ", a condition creating great
economic loss.[3]   The *Magazine of Wall Street* stated that
the flood of 1927 dealt a severe blow to the confidence of the
people of the delta, and that it was highly essential that the
confidence of the people in their ability to earn a living in
that section be restored and sustained.[4]   The conclusion
naturally follows that Federal flood control on an adequate
basis would remove the fear of floods and would restore the
confidence and feeling of safety in the people of the delta.
This would create a general prosperity, based on an economic
margin produced by a continued freedom from floods and
the resulting contentment and absence of fear.[5]

Viewing the problem from the angle of the general welfare has produced some rather strong contentions from many
of our best students of flood control and from many of our

[1] *House Committee on Flood Control, Hearings 1922*, p. 92.

[2] Weather Bureau Bulletin, no. 143, *Floods of Mississippi River*, p. 47.

[3] Walter Parker, *Why Flood Control and River Regulation are Essential to the Economic Welfare of the Mississippi Valley* (pamphlet 1925),
p. 8.

[4] *Magazine of Wall Street*, vol. 40, June 18, 1927, p. 283.

[5] Walter Parker, *Why Flood Control and River Regulation are Essential to the Economic Welfare of the Mississippi Valley*, p. 9.

leading public men. Colonel Robert Ewing, publisher of the *New Orleans States,* asserted that " permanent flood control " would certainly prove " economical at any cost to the government ".[1] General Edgar Jadwin stated that sufficient expenditure to control such a flood as that of 1927 " would be justified even though such a flood occurs but once in 150 years ".[2] Frank O. Lowden enthusiastically declared that the United States could not possibly make a better investment of a half-billion or a billion dollars than to invest it in securing the delta of the Mississippi against floods.[3] Thus, many have given testimony to the effect that the general welfare of our nation makes flood control a national problem.

Those who favor control of floods on the Mississippi by the Federal government have based much argument on the contention that the floods on the lower Mississippi are largely man-made disasters, and that the United States government itself has played a leading part in creating the disasters both by omission and by commission. Gifford Pinchot asserts that a river represents a great natural balance sheet and establishes among its various tributary streams " a vast and beautiful natural equilibrium ".[4] When men destroy the equilibrium they must pay the price. The people of the United States have apparently done almost everything they could to destroy this nice balance. Thus the serious floods have been termed man-made disasters. And the remedy for the situation would be for the United States government to assume complete control and to maintain the integrity of the entire system as a unified whole.

[1] *The New York Times,* April 29, 1928.

[2] *House Committee on Flood Control,* 70th Cong., 1st Sess., 1927, *Comm. Doc.,* no. 13, p. 3.

[3] *Memphis Commercial Appeal,* Oct. 21, 1927.

[4] *The Survey,* vol. 58, July 1, 1927, p. 367.

That contention opens up the whole question of the causes of the floods. Apparently all agree that the causes have many far-flung ramifications. They extend even to the grazing of cattle and sheep far in the interior, when over-grazing of the lands causes rapid run-off and erosion.[1] Even the direction of a furrow in plowing may affect the amount of water that flows from the surface of the field and the amount of sediment it carries.[2] Paved streets and sewage and drainage systems have added an immense amount of water by causing both a heavy and a rapid run-off.[3] Many cities boast of their splendid drainage systems. They do not realize that they have been hastening floods down upon their neighbors to the south. The rapid construction of hard-surfaced and well-drained highways throughout the country has added vast volumes of water to the rapidly draining portion of the rainfall.[4] During recent years, many of these highways have been built under Federal specifications and with the aid of Federal funds. Highways, railways, cities and industrial and commercial enterprises have aided in pil-ing up the flood waters by encroaching upon the natural beds of streams and making their cross sections too small to carry the large bodies of waters. Bridges, embankments, piers, terminals and even building lots have been constructed in the natural highwater beds of the streams.[5] Such encroach-ments upon the navigable streams of the country have been made with the express permission of the Federal govern-ment, which thereby became an agent in creating these en-croachments and, therefore, in causing destructive floods.

[1] Robert Reynolds, *Grazing and Floods*, p. 5.

[2] C. McD. Townsend, Speech at St. Louis, 1913 (pamphlet), *Flood Control of Mississippi River*, p. 5.

[3] *Cassiers Engineering Monthly*, vol. 44, July, 1913, p. 36.

[4] *Ibid.*, p. 35.

[5] *Ibid.*

However, the influence of the above activities on floods must be relatively small in comparison with that of general deforestation, drainage, and development of the vast valley territory.[1] The people of the interior have drained large areas of swamps and lowlands. Ohio, for example, formerly was a very swampy state but now it is well drained by numerous tiles and ditches that hasten the water from lands on which it formerly tarried and from which it drained slowly.[2] The same process has gone on in all states with areas of swamp lands, a movement which has destroyed the great system of natural reservoirs and has forced an exceedingly heavy run-off that could only result in frequent floods.[3] And the people of the hill country have done their part to increase the flood problem. They have cleared away the forests and have used their lands in such a way as to cause much erosion and rapid run-off.[4] The hills pour torrents of turbid waters through millions of man-made gullies into the river and fill its bed with mud and overflow its banks. The aim of landowners has been to drain their lands as rapidly as possible, a practice which naturally caused their neighbors below them to get the full complement of flood waters, because the chances for evaporation or percolation were reduced to a minimum.[5] The process that has developed the up-river areas has indeed greatly injured the down-river areas. The vast losses from recent floods in comparison with past ones certainly can be traced to some extent to paving, road building, erosion, encroachment on stream beds and drainage.[6] The annual report of the Mississippi River

[1] *House Committee on Flood Control, Hearings 1927*, p. 2524.

[2] *Ohio Archeological and Historical Quarterly*, vol. 34, Oct., 1925, p. 475.

[3] *The Survey*, vol. 58, July 1, 1927, p. 367.

[4] *House Committee on Flood Control, Hearings 1922*, p. 104.

[5] *Senate Executive Document*, no. 49, 32nd Cong., 1st Sess., 1852, p. 43.

[6] *Cassier's Engineering Monthly*, vol. 44, July, 1913, p. 35.

Commission in 1883 recognized the truth of this statement when it said "that the annual height of the floods in the rivers is now believed to increase as the country they drain is cleared up ".[1]   The " advance of civilization " over wide areas of the United States has been in a large measure responsible for the great problem of the delta.[2]   The title of the " nation's drainage ditch ", which has frequently been used does not seem to be far wrong.[3]

Two factors that have attracted attention on several occasions but have had little importance should perhaps receive brief mention here. The statement has been made many times that much of the water causing floods fell on and ran off the national domain, which placed the Federal government in the position of contributing directly to the floods.[4]   In some areas the public domain furnishes considerable water.[5] However, the total from that source must be of small consequence. Then, the permission of the Federal government for the construction of the Chicago drainage canal and the consequent diversion of water from Lake Michigan to the Mississippi has been listed as proof that the United States government itself has been a factor in the creation of floods.[6]   Of course, all additional water makes the problem more serious in times of flood crises, but these small additions appear rather insignificant.

By far the most substantial part of the contention that places much of the blame for the production of flood crises on the Federal government has been based on the acts of its

[1] *Mississippi Commission, Annual Report*, 1883, p. 2431.

[2] *House Committee on Flood Control*, 70th Cong., 1st Sess., 1927, *Comm. Doc.*, no. 24, p. 28.

[3] *Senate Sub-Committee on Commerce, Hearings 1914*, p. 3.

[4] *Cong. Record*, 70th Cong., 1st Sess., pt. 5, 1928, p. 3570.

[5] *Document*, no. 262, 59th Cong., 1st Sess., p. 73.

[6] *New York Times*, January 29, 1928, pt. 5, p. 6.

agents and employees in the construction of works for improving navigation and controlling floods. The creation of cut-offs has been severely condemned by many hydrographical engineers. In our early history the Mississippi river was a very different river from the one now under consideration. The distance from Cairo to the mouth was much greater, which meant that the water followed a more sinuous course. The distance from Cairo to the Gulf by river is still almost two times the air-line distance, which shows how crooked the river really is.[1] In many cases the river flows around ox-bow bends only a few hundred yards across the neck and several miles around. Many intelligent men have held the opinion that " by shortening the channel and cutting off the bends of the river " the velocity of the current would be increased so that it would scour out the channel wider and deeper and " convey the floods more quickly to the sea ".[2] The President of the United States told the first President of the Mississippi River Commission, whom he had just appointed, that the first task should be " to take some of the kinks out of the river ".[3] Such a well known authority as Captain Eads wanted to straighten the river.[4] However, expert opinion and past experience point out that the effects of cut-offs is to increase the destruction of floods. The water above the cut-off hastens forward and lowers the height of the flood at that point, but " it will be precipitated more rapidly " into the river below the bend " and will raise the height of the flood there ".[5] The state of Louisiana had such an experience in its very unfortunate experiment, which

[1] *House Committee on Flood Control, Hearings 1916*, p. 252.

[2] *Senate Executive Document*, no. 49, 32nd Cong., 1st Sess., 1852, p. 39

[3] R. S. Taylor, *Mississippi River Improvement*, pt. 5, 1879, p. 10.

[4] *Cong. Record*, 45th Cong., 3rd Sess., pt. 1, p. 508.

[5] *Senate Executive Doc.*, no. 49, 32nd Cong., 1st Sess., 1852, p. 39.

had been ordered by the legislature against all engineering advice, in cutting off the Raccourci bend in 1848. Cut-offs would help if the river could be made straight from Cairo to the Gulf and held in that condition. But the river cannot be maintained in a straight line. Bends are absolutely necessary to establish a regimen that will conduct the river to the Gulf at a rate of speed that its fragile banks can withstand.[1]   The acts of the agents of the Federal government in straightening, or permitting others to straighten, the Mississippi at various points has been listed as a very direct means by which the United States itself has been responsible for serious floods in the delta.[2]   The straightening process simply transferred the problem from upper areas to lower ones.[3]   The Mississippi River Commission has strenuously fought efforts to have the river straightened. In its first annual report in 1880 it stated that the channel should be stabilized as it then was and that no cut-offs should be permitted.[4]   But, powerful pressure from navigation and upstream interests sometimes caused cut-offs to be made in spite of engineering advice to the contrary.

By far the strongest part of the accusation that the United States government has helped to create the flood problem of the delta rests upon the relation of flood-control works in various areas to the causes of floods in other areas. In our early history the Mississippi spread out over an immense territory when it was at flood. The water mostly precipitated from the river by means of creeks and bayous into numerous storage basins, where much of it remained to evaporate or to drain slowly back into the river as it receded.[5]   Those natural

[1] R. S. Taylor, *Mississippi River Improvement*, pt. 5, p. 10.

[2] *Cong. Record*, 47th Cong., 1st Sess., pt. 4, 1882, p. 3091.

[3] *The Scientific Monthly*, vol. 16, April, 1923, p. 352.

[4] *Manufacturers Record*, vol. 91, May 12, 1927, p. 66.

[5] Amos Stoddard, *Sketches of Louisiana*, p. 203.

storage basins consisted of ox-bow lakes, bayous, sloughs, swamps and timbered areas.[1] They extended over a long territory fifty to sixty miles in width.[2] The river at flood simply appropriated as much as it needed of the delta which it had created.[3] The early settlers inhabited the small areas of ground that rose above the flood-line. But the natural growth of population sent men into the lower areas which the river had reserved for its flood waters. Thus, man invaded the river's domain.[4] Then man began to build protective works to shut the river from lands that he desired for cultivation. As the protective works grew the areas left for natural storage basins became less and less.[5] The confinement of a stream formerly fifty miles wide between dykes a mile apart naturally piled up the water and raised the flood heights both in protected and in unprotected areas. *De Bow's Review* in 1850 stated that the extension of the levee system had rendered the levees of lower Louisiana less efficient than they had formerly been, because the water had in the past been discharged into swamps and was then confined to the river.[6] Such a process caused water to rise over land that in the natural state was above the water. One of the finest sections of alluvial land in America in Rapides and Avoyelles parishes, Louisiana needed no levee for protection until the extension of protective works forced up the flood water on its unprotected front and this region finally became

[1] *Annals of the American Academy of Political and Social Science,* Jan., 1928, p. 2.

[2] *Cong. Record*, 45th Cong., 3rd Sess., Appendix, 1879, p. 259.

[3] *The Nation*, vol. 124, May 11, 1927, p. 518.

[4] *House Committee on Flood Control*, 70th Cong., 1st Sess., 1927, *Comm. Doc.*, no. 1, p. 84.

[5] *Annals of the American Academy of Political and Social Science,* Jan., 1928, p. 3.

[6] *De Bow's Review*, vol. viii, Feb., 1850, p. 101.

inundated with every large flood.[1]   The St. Francis basin in
Arkansas formed a gigantic natural reservoir until a great
levee confined the water to the river and raised flood heights
from two to ten feet for one hundred miles.[2]   Many of the
levees have actually been built across great natural outlets.
Bullet's Bayou in Louisiana was the first outlet closed by
governmental orders, in 1836.   Bayou Lake Argent in the
same state was closed in 1838.   The process gained such
headway that practically all of those great outlets had been
crossed by powerful levees by 1844.[3]

The Mississippi River Commission realized that carrying
out its plans would inundate lands that in the natural state
were not affected by floods.[4]   In its annual report in 1884,
the Commission stated that the continued construction of
levees " to aid navigation " would damage property by increased flood heights.   This situation would make it necessary to build more levees.[5]   Then, in its annual report in
1910, the Commission, speaking of several areas that had
suffered from the construction of protective works on other
portions of the river, said " that these people should be condemned to perpetual inundation without possibility of relief
or redress for the sake of an improvement from which their
fellow citizens are enjoying great benefits is intolerable to
any man's sense of justice ".[6]   The courts of the various
states and the Supreme Court of the United States have held

[1] House Committee on Flood Control, Hearings 1922, p. 73.

[2] H. C. Frankenfield, Floods of the Spring of 1903 in the Miss. Water-
Shed, p. 7.

[3] Barbour Lewis, Speech on Levees of Mississippi, House, June 6,
1874, p. 9.

[4] B. E. Moses, The Problem of the Mississippi River, p. 6.

[5] Mississippi River Commission, Annual Report, 1884, p. 20.

[6] House Committee on Flood Control, 70th Cong., 1st Sess., 1927, Comm.
Doc., no. 1, p. 122.

that neither the United States government nor the levee
boards are responsible for damages to one section caused by
improvements in another, so that the people who suffer in
such cases cannot recover damages from any source.[1] But
there have been much public opinion and sentiment favorable
to the sufferers. Many have taken the position that loss of
property through such a process violated the fourteenth
amendment by taking property without due process of law.[2]
Certainly, levees have increased flood heights, and, thereby,
have caused flood damages to unprotected areas and greater
damages from crevasses.[3] The responsibility and obligations of the Federal government because of its activities in
building levees have at times been recognized in Congress.[4]
The Rivers and Harbors Act of 1912 directed the Mississippi
River Commission to purchase small areas of land that could
not profitably be protected by levees and which had been inundated only because of the construction of flood-control
works elsewhere.[5]

" To stand on the banks of the Mississippi is to compre-
hend why primitive man made offering to river gods ".[6]
Mark Twain said that anyone who knew the Mississippi
would aver that " ten thousand river commissions " with all
of the " mints of the world at their backs " could never confine or curb it, nor could they " bar its path with an obstruction " that it would not tear down.[7] The task of holding

[1] House Committee on Flood Control, Hearings 1916, p. 82.

[2] J. P. Kemper, Proposed Plan for Flood Control below the Arkansas,
p. 1.

[3] G. W. Pickels, Drainage and Flood-Control Engineering, p. 312.

[4] Cong. Record, 55th Cong., 1st Sess., pt. 1, 1897, p. 215.

[5] House Committee on Flood Control, 70th Cong., 1st Sess., 1927, Comm.
Doc., no. 1, p. 120.

[6] The Outlook, vol. 146, May 25, 1927, p. 104.

[7] Commerce and Finance, vol. xvi, April 7, 1897, p. 6.

that mighty stream within its banks proved too much for
nature and has so far been too huge a task for man.[1]   " Only
one who has sailed across new lakes twenty miles long over-
lying farms, homesteads and hamlets, who has seen broken
levees drop cataracts on the houses below them " can understand the nature of a mighty flood on that mighty river.[2]
General Edgar Jadwin described a great flood on the Mississippi as " less serious only than war itself ".[3]   Secretary
Hoover and others described the flood of 1927 as the greatest peace-time disaster that has befallen the American
people in all our history.[4]   The immensity of the task of
curbing such a powerful stream has forcibly impressed the
American people and has challenged the skill and resources
of the combined governments of this nation.[5]   The colossal
nature of the problem has caused many to feel that its control
became the duty of the Federal government, because no other
power had a chance to cope with it.   President Harding
said that the problem was " so big that the general basis of
government activities must be broadly conceived " and
studied by men who were thoroughly capable of dealing with
a colossal problem.[6]   Many officials and many more laymen
have made the simple and direct statement that flood control
on the Mississippi cannot be accomplished by states or local
governments.[7]   The stupendous size of the task has been an
important factor in bringing the work all the way from the

[1] *The San Francisco Chronicle*, April 7, 1897, p. 6.

[2] *The Survey*, vol. 58, July 1, 1927, p. 358.

[3] *Manufacturers Record*, vol. 91, June 7, 1927, p. 59.

[4] *House Committee on Flood Control*, 70th Cong., 1st Sess., 1927, *Comm.
Doc.*, no. 7, p. 1.

[5] *U. S. Daily*, June 4, 1927, p. 4.

[6] *New Orleans Times-Picayune*, May 4, 1922.

[7] *The Memphis Commercial Appeal*, May 4, 1897.

individual planters through local and state governments to the Federal government.[1]

James A. Garfield stated in the House in 1879 that the problem was " too vast for any state to handle; too much for any authority less than that of the nation itself to manage ".[2] In 1890, a great river convention at Vicksburg declared that the people and the states of the lower valley could not " cope with the deluges " that from time to time " swept down upon them from the northern and western rivers ".[3]   The Nelson Report of 1897, submitted to the Senate after a very extensive investigation, stated that the burden of flood control had become too much for local and state authorities.[4] Representative Frank R. Reid, Chairman of the House Committee on Flood Control in 1927, concluded " that the United States government alone " could prevent the recurrence of destructive Mississippi floods.[5]   The Flood Committee of the Chamber of Commerce of the United States in 1927 urged the Federal government to assume the financial burden of controlling floods on the Mississippi because the local governments had " reached the end of their resources ".[6] The *St. Louis Globe-Democrat* maintained that the " paramount obligation " to control the floods rested " squarely " upon the Federal government.[7]   The evidence that the great size of the task has been a strong point for those who seek Federal control appears almost limitless.

The great report of Humphreys and Abbott in 1861

[1] *The New York Times*, May 2, 1927.

[2] *Cong. Record*, 46th Cong., 1st Sess., pt. 2, 1879, p. 2283.

[3] Tompkins, *Riparian Lands of Mississippi River*, p. 4.

[4] *House Report*, no. 300, pt. 2, 63rd Cong., 2nd Sess., 1914.

[5] *House Committee on Flood Control*, 70th Cong., 1st Sess., 1927, *Comm. Doc.*, no. 7, p. 1.

[6] *The U. S. Daily*, Oct. 7, 1927, p. 2.

[7] *Literary Digest*, vol. 95, Dec. 24, 1927, p. 8.

pointed out that one of the outstanding faults in the flood-control system was the very inefficient work of the local governments.[1]   This phase of the question has received increasing attention since that time.   A very bad result of levee building by local units has been a kind of competition, through which the financially stronger areas have sought to maintain a margin of safey over neighboring areas whose levees would break first in case of floods.[2]   Yet, the weak districts have continued to build weak levees that have frequently broken and flooded the lands behind strong levees.[3] When poorly located and badly constructed levees have been built they become a serious problem.   The people who pay the taxes want to improve and to maintain them instead of building better and more favorably located ones.[4]   Then, another unfortunate phase of the local boards appears.   They have been affected by much petty political intrigue and endless trivial bickerings due to influences of larger interests in the local districts seeking to dominate the boards for personal gain by protection to their own holdings.[5]   Also, the local interests have frequently been in sharp contrast with the general interests, a situation which has created political fights between adjoining local areas.   Thus, the state of Mississippi prevailed upon Congress to pass a law prohibiting even a survey for a spillway through Lake Pontchartrain because of probable damage to the sea-food industry in the State of Mississippi.[6]   However, the

[1] Humphreys and Abbott, *Physics and Hydraulics of Miss. River*, p. 152.

[2] *House Committee on Flood Control*, 70th Cong., 1st Sess., 1927, *Comm. Doc.*, no. 13, p. 4.

[3] *House Committee on Flood Control*, 70th Cong., 1st Sess., 1927, *Report to Accompany House Bill 8219*, p. 84.

[4] Tompkins, *Riparian Lands of the Mississippi*, p. 67.

[5] *House Executive Document*, no. 127, 43rd Cong., 2nd Sess., 1875, p. 25.

[6] *The Survey*, vol. 58, July 1, 1927, p. 372.

people of the Biloxi area willingly agreed to sacrifice local
interest to the general good after the flood of 1927, and the
law was repealed.[1] Such conflicting interests could not produce an efficient line of defense against floods so long as
each local district raised the funds and carried out the program of construction.

When it is realized that six agencies have been building
levees, the United States, the state, levee boards, parishes
and counties, railways and individuals, and that ten agencies
in the Departments of War, Interior, Commerce and Agriculture have had authority in the development and control of
streams it appears rather remarkable that the task has been
performed as well as it has been.[2] But a satisfactory
public policy could never develop under such conditions.
Each engineer in charge naturally established his own problem and proceeded to work it out with little reference to those
of his neighbors.[3] The various engineers who have made
separate plans for many local districts have freely admitted
that the general good outweighed the local good, and that
their plans frequently conflicted with the general interests.[4]
J. Russell Smith stated that the conflict between local and
general interests represented one of the " inherent troubles
of the situation ".[5] Levee boards organized and operating
under laws of several states and acting independently could
not work with the Mississippi River Commission created by
and functioning under Federal law without reflecting some
evils of divided authority.[6] That situation caused a very

[1] *New Orleans Times-Picayune*, Dec. 9, 1927, p. 1.

[2] *House Committee on Flood Control, Hearings 1916*, p. 191.

[3] *Literary Digest*, vol. 94, July 2, 1927, p. 21.

[4] *Cong. Record*, 70th Cong., 1st Sess., pt. 6, 1928, p. 4254.

[5] *The Survey*, vol. 58, July 1, 1927, p. 371.

[6] *House Committee on Flood Control*, 70th Cong., 1st Sess., 1927, *Report to Accompany House Bill 8219*, p. 21.

widespread demand for a unified control.[1]   The suggestion has often been made that local levee boards should be abolished and that there should be created a " single bureau or agency " to control the construction and maintenance of all levees.[2]

A very widespread opinion has been voiced that the agency having the duty of carrying out the flood-control program should possess very broad powers.[3]   The conclusions of the Pittsburgh Flood Commission maintained that the authority should extend to all phases of the problem from the source to the mouth of the river because these various phases were inseparable from others.[4]   The power of initiative has thus far rested with Congress, but many have insisted that it should be given to the agency in charge of the work in the field.[5]   The people of the delta doubtless would welcome some authoritative body that would abolish levee boards and assume complete control.[6]   They want some power that goes beyond the jurisdiction of any of the states.[7]   Then, the conclusion that the problem must be financed and controlled entirely by one head, and that only the Federal government has the authority and power to do so, appears quite logical.[8]

A very simple and direct argument for Federal control holds that the United States government has already committed itself to the task and that it cannot afford to stop

[1] House Committee on Flood Control, Hearings 1927, p. 681.

[2] Memphis Commercial Appeal, June 20, 1928.

[3] U. S. Daily, Sept. 20, 1927, p. 1.

[4] House Committee on Flood Control, Hearings 1916, p. 24.

[5] National Waterways, vol. i, Francis G. Newlands, p. 321.

[6] Public Opinion, vol. 22, May 20, 1897, p. 614.

[7] House Committee on Flood Control, Hearings 1927, p. 45.

[8] Ibid., p. 2808.

until the work has been finished. In the past, that contention has been used in urging appropriations for further construction.[1] The United States government really pledged itself to the task in 1881 by the appropriation of a million dollars for control floods, even if it was in " the interest of navigation ".[2] The creation of the Mississippi River Commission and subsequent appropriations have demonstrated that the United States has accepted responsibility for flood control.[3] The acts of 1916 and 1923 frankly stated that they were flood-control acts and left the impression that the Federal government expected to finish the job.[4] These acts caused many expressions to the effect that flood control had been definitely established as an obligation of the Federal government.[5]

The commerce clause of the constitution has furnished the basis for one of the strong points in the attack of the proponents of Federal control. They maintain that the constitution places the duty directly upon the Federal government to see that interstate commerce goes on uninterrupted and to take whatever steps that may be necessary to maintain the commerce among the states.[6] Some have gone so far as to assert that the commerce clause and the obligations arising under it furnished the main factor in bringing the Union together under the constitution.[7] Certainly, interstate commerce has demanded much attention throughout our history. Naturally, the commerce on the river itself

[1] *House Committee on Flood Control, Hearings 1916*, p. 36.

[2] B. G. Humphreys, *Floods of the Mississippi River*, p. 2.

[3] *House Committee on Flood Control, Hearings 1927*, p. 43.

[4] *The Outlook*, vol. 146, June 15, 1927, p. 221.

[5] *The New York World*, April 16, 1927.

[6] *The New Orleans Times-Picayune*, Dec. 6, 1927, p. 1.

[7] *Cong. Record*, 70th Cong., 1st Sess., pt. 3, 1927, p. 1889.

would suffer greatly from floods.[1]   But in recent years inter-state transportation by railways and highways has received most attention.   The flood of 1927 interrupted service on three thousand miles of railway, in some cases for as long as four months.[2]   Practically all transportation east and west from St. Louis south stopped.[3]   Telephone and telegraph services received serious injuries and in many cases completely broke down, thereby leaving many communities without communication with others.[4]   The highways in many sections completely disappeared under several feet of water. This inundation not only stopped all travel over the highways but also caused very heavy damages to them.[5]   The flooding of a wide area of country certainly stopped interstate commerce.   The only logical remedy for the situation seems to be flood control by the Federal government, if it is its duty to maintain commerce among the states.

The people of the United States have a strong opposition to anything that delays the mails of this country.   Mississippi floods have been a positive hindrance to the movement of United States mails on many occasions.   It has been estimated that without the levees no deliveries could be made to many sections for at least two months per year.[6] During the flood of 1927, 299 post offices went completely out of business and 1805 miles of railway post office ceased operation.   W. I. Glover, Second Assistant Postmaster General in charge of headquarters " in the field ", reported that in one day 290,000 sacks of mail had been listed as delayed at least forty-eight hours.   Postmaster General

---

[1] *Cong. Record*, 43rd Cong., 1st Sess., pt. 4, 1874, p. 3245.

[2] *House Committee on Flood Control, Hearings 1927*, p. 43.

[3] *Ibid.*, p. 1129.

[4] *Ibid.*, p. 3548.

[5] *Ibid.*, p. 1007.

[6] *Ibid., Hearings 1922*, p. 59.

[7] *Ibid., Hearings 1927*, p. 2771.

Harry S. New stated that the flood of 1927 caused the suspension of many rural routes and star routes, the discontinuance of free delivery in many cities, and the complete isolation of " great areas that were inundated ".[1]   But the mails were not only affected locally, but also generally throughout a large part of the country.   Much interstate and transcontinental mail had to be rerouted for several weeks, thus costing the government a large sum of money and causing serious delay.[2]   The delay of large amounts of mail for several weeks could hardly fail to impress the American people and to serve as an agent in creating public sentiment for flood control.[3]   Protection of the mails has been accepted as a solemn duty of the Federal government.[4]

The relation of floods to the public health has received brief mention.[5]   The attitude of the United States government has been one of active participation in any movement to prevent the spread of disease and to protect the public health.   Floods have frequently been listed as agencies in the spread of various diseases and in the general lowering of the public health in the inundated areas.[6]   The relation of floods to disease and the work of the Federal government in combating disease have led some to assert that obligations toward the public health make flood control a duty of the United States.   The record of the flood of 1927 tends to bear out such a contention.   During that flood the United States Department of Health cooperated with the Red Cross

[1] *House Committee on Flood Control, Hearings 1927*, p. 2767.

[2] *House Committee on Flood Control*, 70th Cong., 1st Sess., 1927, *Comm. Doc.*, no. 18, p. 98.

[3] *National Geographic Magazine*, vol. 52, Sept., 1927, p. 260.

[4] *House Committee on Flood Control*, 70th Cong., 1st Sess., 1927, *Comm. Doc.*, no. 7, p. 2.

[5] *House Committee on Flood Control*, 70th Cong., 1st Sess., 1927, *Report to Accompany House Bill 8219*, p. 229.

[6] *Cong. Record*, 45th Cong., 3rd Sess., pt. 1, 1879, p. 501.

and the Rockefeller Foundation in waging war on disease.[1]
Almost a half-million persons were inoculated against
typhoid fever; 141,229 were vaccinated against smallpox;
and 25,000,000 grains of quinine were distributed as a part
of the gigantic public health program.[2]

The national defense has furnished a two-fold argument
for Federal control.   Military men have pointed out that in
case of war such a flood as that of 1927 would seriously
handicap the United States by dividing it into two parts and
by devasting a wide area of the country.[3]   If the flood of
1927 had occurred in the spring of 1918 when the country
was straining " every sinew for national defense " it would
have affected the government's operations very adversely.[4]
The President of the Mississippi River Commission thought
a great flood would endanger the nation in time of war.[5]   The
Chamber of Commerce of the United States listed the
national defense as a reason for Federal control.[6]   The
other phase of national defense presents an interesting viewpoint.   The theory has frequently been advanced that the
Mississippi river at flood becomes a public enemy as much
as an invading army.   The river has been pictured as invading the delta and destroying the property, homes, and
lives of citizens of this country.[7]   The Federal government
has the duty of repelling invasions.   Therefore, the duty of
controlling the floods rests upon it.

[1] *House Committee on Flood Control,* 70th Cong., 1st Sess., 1927, *Report to Accompany House Bill 8219,* p. 229.

[2] *Ibid.,* p. 233.

[3] *House Committee on Flood Control, Hearings 1916,* p. 51.

[4] *House Committee on Flood Control,* 70th Cong., 1st Sess., 1927, *Comm. Doc.,* no. 24, p. 51.

[5] *House Committee on Flood Control, Hearings 1927,* p. 2017.

[6] *The New Orleans Times-Picayune,* Oct. 18, 1927, p. 1.

[7] *House Committee on Flood Control,* 70th Cong., 1st Sess., 1927, *Comm. Doc.,* no. 1, p. 316.

CHAPTER IV

Arguments Against Federal Control

THE arguments against Federal control of floods on the Mississippi have been neither as numerous nor as long as those for Federal control. This situation naturally followed because the burden of proof for formulating and carrying out a vast program rested upon those who wanted to curb the river. Existing conditions always offered an excuse or a reason for conservative groups to align themselves against proposed measures. The opponents often remained quiet while the proponents worked hard and talked much. But arguments against control by the Federal government have occurred with enough frequency to show the attitude of the opposing groups.

The fact that the construction of protective works cost large sums of money and meant increased taxation was always a serious obstacle in the way of securing desired legislation. Before the establishment of the Mississippi River Commission, Representative L. A. Sheldon of Louisiana anticipated the arguments of his opponents and attempted a rebuttal against them. He listed as the strongest contention against the proposed legislation the claim that the treasury had all it could bear without added expenses for building levees.[1] During the period immediately preceding the creation of the Commission, members of Congress had much to say about the growth of paternalism in the United States government.[2] They deplored the growing practice of placing the

[1] *Cong. Globe*, 42nd Cong., 2nd Sess., pt. 1, 1871, p. 284.
[2] *Cong. Record*, 43rd Cong., 1st Sess., pt. 5, 1874, p. 4653.

expense for everything on the General Government. They also pointed out that the cost of flood control had been greatly under-estimated in proposed legislation, and that it would, in reality, cost several times as much as its proponents claimed.[1]

Granting that the Federal Government had the authority to build levees, the watch-dogs of the treasury have ever been ready with strong arguments against proposed appropriations. Representative N. C. Blanchard, Chairman of the House Committee on Rivers and Harbors in 1904, realized the formidable array of arguments against taxes when he complained that it was difficult to induce Congress to appropriate a large outlay of money for any project.[2] The watch dogs have frequently reflected the position of big business by complaining that it was unwise to place such heavy taxes upon business for purposes " in which capital and industry cannot be enlisted by the promise of profit ".[3] They have frequently shouted the words extravagance and inefficiency when appropriations were being discussed.[4] They have considered most appropriations for flood control as wholesale raids upon the treasury.[5] In 1916, the proposed measure was called by a member of Congress " the most stupendous loot of the Federal Treasury that has ever been submitted to this Congress during the past fifteen years ".[6] The efforts to secure legislation in 1928 received the name of a billion dollar " drive on the Treasury ".[7] The *Cleveland Plain Dealer* complained that " no burden is too great for the

[1] *Cong. Record*, 47th Cong., 1st Sess., pt. 2, 1882, p. 1914.

[2] *Senate Committee on Commerce, Hearings 1904*, p. 69.

[3] *The Chicago Tribune*, April 24, 1882.

[4] *Cong. Record*, 67th Cong., 3rd Sess., pt. 7, p. 5207.

[5] *Cong. Record*, 64th Cong., 1st Sess., pt. 10, p. 8318.

[6] *Ibid.*, pt. 11, p. 8784.

[7] *Cong. Record*, 70th Cong., 1st Sess., pt. 6, p. 7294.

broad back and deep purse of Uncle Sam ", in the minds of
the raiders of the treasury.[1]   And the *New York Sun* concluded that the passage of the Jones-Reid bill in 1928 would
usher in an " orgy of profiteering " at the expense of the
United States, as a result of one of the most daring raids of
all time upon the treasury.[2]

In order to hold appropriations to the lowest possible
figures many have advanced the idea that partial and
reasonable control could be established at a feasible cost but
that complete control would be too expensive to justify it.
The cost of control certainly mounts very rapidly as the
size of protective works increases.   Thus, large areas of
land may become submarginal in relation to productivity and
cost of protection.[3]   The suggestion has been made that
lands that yield less than it costs to protect them should be
abandoned.   " It is a question of land planning to secure the
wisest use of land ".[4]   A member of the legislature of Mississippi in 1913 argued that the cost of protecting much of
the delta land in that state would bankrupt the owners if
they had to pay it.   He concluded, " If so, then, the game is
not worth the candle ".[5]   Such a position logically produces
the conclusion that sparsely populated and frequently submerged areas should be abandoned and that only the more
populous and more prosperous areas ought to be protected.[6]

A great amount of talking and writing has taken place
against Federal flood control on the ground that it constituted
a reclamation project for the benefit of private property.

[1] *Literary Digest*, vol. 97, April 14, 1928, p. 10.

[2] *Ibid.*

[3] *American Review of Reviews*, vol. 76, Nov., 1927, p. 487.

[4] *Ibid.*

[5] *Memphis News Scimitar*, May 12, 1913.

[6] *Annals of the American Academy of Political and Social Science*,
Jan., 1928, p. 14.

That contenion has received most bitter denunciation, but it has considerable foundation on which to stand.   Timothy Flint, in his early account of the Mississippi, told of the great inundated area a hundred miles wide in places.[1]   A well-known observer stated in 1812 that " not more than one twenty-seventh part of the delta " was suitable for culti- vation, and that that portion was located along the river banks.[2]   Hundreds of 'thousands of acres of that land passed to private owners from various states at prices of twelve to fifteen cents per acre.[3]   Those same lands have been made productive and have become valuable largely be- cause floods have been kept in check.   Thus, many have concluded that the major purpose of flood control was the reclamation of swamp lands for the benefit of private owner.[4]   Members of Congress in 1879 proclaimed that the law creating the Mississippi River Commission represented a gigantic reclamation scheme under the guise of protecting navigation.[5]   Senator Benjamin Harrison in 1882 contended that flood control was reclamation for the benefit of private property and that the Federal treasury should not pay for it.[6] Some members of Congress have gone so far as to say that the proponents of flood control knew it was a reclamation scheme, and that they purposely beclouded the issue to hide the real facts.[7]   During the past few years much has been said concerning reclamation of lands owned by large corpora-

[1] Timothy Flint, *History and Geography of the Mississippi Valley*, p. 98.

[2] Amos Stoddard, *Sketches of Louisiana*, 1812, p. 165.

[3] *House Committee on Flood Control, Hearings 1922*, p. 61.

[4] *Journal of the Association of Engineering Societies*, vol. 46, March, 1911, p. 191.

[5] *Cong. Record*, 46th Cong., 1st Sess., pt. 1, 1879, p. 2282.

[6] *Cong. Record*, 47th Cong., 1st Sess., pt. 3, 1882, p. 2983.

[7] *Cong. Record*, 64th Cong., 1st Sess., pt. 9, 1916, p. 6670.

tions, which has furnished considerable argument for the opponents of appropriations.[1] The conclusion has naturally followed that protection and reclamation enhances the value of property of the private owners and that the costs should be borne by those who receive the benefit.[2] Such a conclusion removes flood control from a claim for Federal money and leaves the problem of constructing protective works entirely with the people of the delta.[3]

The argument that the Federal government has no authority under the constitution to control floods occasionally appears. The opponents of Federal control have proved surprisingly slow to advance that argument, which appears to be a rather strong one. The proponents of Federal control have said much more about the constitutionality of it than the opponents have. In fact, the continued efforts to prove that the Federal government had constitutional grounds for the control of floods has furnished the strongest indication that there must have been many who really thought it was unconstitutional.

Representative Barbour Lewis of Tennessee stated in 1874 that only occasionally could one hear a " faint suggestion " of the unconstitutionality of using Federal funds for building levees.[4] *The New York Times* in 1882 said that spending Federal funds on levees looked ridiculous in view of its undoubted unconstitutionality; and called members of Congress severely to task for favoring such a scheme.[5] The strongest point in the argument of unconstitutionality rested on the contention that the lands protected lay solely under

---

[1] *Cong. Record*, 70th Cong., 1st Sess., pt. 8, 1928, p. 6150.

[2] *House Committee on Flood Control, Hearings 1922*, p. 32.

[3] *Review of Reviews*, vol. 75, p. 598.

[4] *Cong. Record*, 43rd Cong., 1st Sess., pt. 5, 1874, p. 4657.

[5] *The New York Times*, April 22, 1882, p. 4.

the jurisdiction of the states in which they were located.[1]
The Chicago Tribune in 1882 wanted to know where Congress could find authority for " confiscating the property "
of the nation's people for the benefit of people on the banks
of the lower Mississippi.[2]   The very little discussion of
state's rights and state sovereignty, which have received only
passing mention in debates over flood control, indeed presents a peculiar phase of the situation.[3]

The opponents of flood control by the Federal government have strenuously denied that either the people or the
government of the United States have caused the floods.
They have, therefore, maintained that the people of the
delta have no claim either under the common law or in
equity against the people or the states of the up-river areas.
They have produced much evidence to support these contentions.[4]   Perhaps the greatest flood in the history of the
Mississippi came before the adoption of our constitution and
the high-water mark at St. Louis was established in 1844.[5]
Serious floods came frequently while the native Indians inhabited the entire valley.   Rains have caused the floods.
Much expert opinion maintains that excessive rains do not
occur more frequently than formerly and that floods have
not become more frequent within our history.[6]   The floods
have simply resulted from heavy rains on the tributaries,
especially the Ohio, which is " pre-eminently one of the turbulent rivers of the United States ".[7]   Since the floods have

[1] *Cong. Record*, 45th Cong., 3rd Sess., 1879, p. 979.

[2] *The Chicago Tribune*, April 24, 1882.

[3] *United States Daily*, Nov. 18, 1927.

[4] *The Indianapolis Star*, May 13, 1927, p. 6.

[5] Water Supply Paper, no. 96, U. S. Weather Bureau, *Destructive Floods in U. S. in 1913*, p. 19.

[6] *United States Monthly Weather Review*, vol. 42, March, 1914, p. 178.

[7] A. J. Henry, *Floods in the Ohio River*, 1870-1913, p. 11.

been caused by nature and not by the people nor the government, the people of the delta have no claim against anyone. When the King of France granted lands in Louisiana the grants contained the expressed condition that the grantee would build levees at his own expense and that whatever property loss he suffered from floods was a servitude incident to his grant.[1] Many think that servitude has ever rested on those who have appropriated the river's natural flood bed. And the United States ceded much of those lands to the states with the idea that they would be reclaimed and the returns used for drainage and protective works.[2] Much of the land that the United States government considered as worthless overflowed land now demands protection at the hands of the government that gave it away.[3]

Much of the opposition to flood control by the Federal government has not really been opposition to flood control but to the particular type that had been proposed. One cannot say how much real opposition lies beneath that type of argument. When levees have been proposed some have fought the bills on the ground that they favored reservoirs or some other type of control. Perhaps they did prefer reservoirs or outlets, but their votes against levee bills have been a constant factor in hindering the development of a program of control.[4] Levees have been severely criticized but they have furnished the basis for all flood-control legislation, a fact which has given the opponents a good opportunity to attract attention by supporting other methods.[5] A favorite means of attack along this line has been the proposal of many amendments embodying other means of control. Although

---

[1] *House Committee on Flood Control, Hearings 1916*, p. 103.

[2] *The Outlook*, vol. 146, June 15, 1927, p. 221.

[3] *Cong. Record*, 70th Cong., 1st Sess., 1928, pt. 8, p. 6160.

[4] *Cong. Globe*, 42nd Cong., 2nd Sess., 1871, pt. 1, p. 283.

[5] *Cong. Record*, 64th Cong., 1st Sess., 1916, pt. 10, p. 8318.

the amendments generally met defeat, they seemed to strengthen the opposition to appropriations for levees.[1]

A type of sectionalism has entered the fight for appropriations and has created serious handicaps in the development of a flood-control policy. A very lengthy discussion and a rather heated debate took place over the very first appropriation for the work of the Mississippi River Commission as to the amount spent in the various states for rivers and harbors. Each section attempted to show that it was unjustly discriminated against.[2] Other sections have often accused the South of receiving more than its fair share, and of being willing to sacrifice almost anything to procure money for flood control.[3] The " arid states " have caused much embarrassment to the proponents of Federal control by demanding money for irrigation when an appropriation for the Mississippi came before Congress.[4] In 1917, several members of Congress from the western states fought the flood-control appropriation because they could not get an amendment adding an appropriation for irrigation.[5] During that debate Senator George W. Norris of Nebraska openly accused Congress of sectionalism. He said that Congress would give two dollars to one dollar from the local interests to build a dam to hold back the flood waters in Louisiana; it would give dollar for dollar to build flood-control works in California, a state " less favored by the powers that be "; but that in the " arid country, where man is striving to reclaim the desert ", it will pay nothing at all.[6] In recent years the statement has frequently been made 'that the lower

[1] Cong. Record, 70th Cong., 1st Sess., 1928, pt. 10, p. 7721.
[2] Cong. Record, 47th Cong., 1st Sess., pt. 3, 1882, p. 2947.
[3] The Hartford Daily Courant, May 30, 1882.
[4] Senate Committee on Commerce, Hearings 1904, p. 93.
[5] Cong. Record, 64th Cong., 2nd Sess., pt. 6, 1917, p. 4775.
[6] Ibid., p. 4776.

Mississippi had received more than its just share of money from the Federal treasury.[1] This form of opposition has meant the loss of a few votes in Congress each time an appropriation for the Mississippi floods has been voted upon.

Pork-barrel politics has been listed as an objection to flood-control appropriations in most debates in Congress on the subject. Two charges against Southern people in their efforts to secure federal funds have received special condemnation. The levee boards of the delta have been accused of dominating delta politics, including their representatives in Congress.[2] They have undoubtedly wielded a wide influence both locally and in Congress. They have been permitted by legislation to spend money in "developing public sentiment".[3] The contractors who have built the levees have stood shoulder to shoulder with the levee boards. They have for years worked through central committees organized and incorporated for that specific purpose. Thus, the levee boards, the levee contractors and the Mississippi River Commission have been accused of dictating the form and content of flood-control legislation. Levee-board politicians have spent much and worked long to "enlighten the country" in behalf of pork-barrel politics to secure appropriations to build levees.[4] They have been able to exert great influence over members of Congress who have used familiar political methods to carry their points. "The log-rolling of past years in Congress" has been, in the opinion of many, the main factor in determining the content of flood-control measures and incidentally in hindering progress in formulating a permanent program.[5] For years friends of

[1] *Cong. Record*, 64th Cong., 1st Sess., pt. 10, 1916, p. 8313.

[2] *Ibid.*, pt. 11, 1916, p. 8639.

[3] *Ibid.*, p. 8638.

[4] B. E. Moses, *The Problem of the Mississippi River*, p. 4.

[5] *Public Opinion*, vol. 22, April 1, 1897, p. 393.

Federal control did not dare to ask for a separate appropriation. The rivers and harbors bill proved to be their favorite vehicle. And the sponsors of rivers and harbors bills welcomed the flood-control people to their ranks, because that meant additional votes. It has long been known that members of Congress have regarded the rivers and harbors bills as splendid instruments for securing appropriations for local purposes.[1] Thus, it appears reasonable that flood-control appropriations should be called pork-barrel when enacted as a part of such bills.[2] It is not surprising that opponents called the flood-control legislation of 1928 the " fattest pork barrel in history ".[3] And it seems natural that the accusation should be made that it was a great victory for " lobbying and log-rolling ".[4]

A rather odd fight, however, not reaching much importance, has been based on the contention that the railways favored flood control because they hoped to benefit from it. It is a fact that the valley railroads have universally supported levees. They have hundreds of millions of dollars in property that suffer heavy losses from every flood. Their losses totaled almost seventeen million dollars in the 1927 flood alone.[5] So, they have had good reason to favor flood control. But whatever railways favor is regarded as prima facie evidence to a class of American people that something is wrong with the proposition. So, the railways have been accused of selfishness and of unduly influencing the Mississippi River Commission.[6] Some have gone so far as to

---

[1] *Cong. Record*, 64th Cong., 1st Sess., pt. 11, 1916, p. 8787.

[2] *Ibid.*, p. 8633.

[3] *Cong. Record*, 70th Cong., 1st Sess., pt. 8, 1928, p. 6162.

[4] *Literary Digest*, vol. 97, April 14, 1928, p. 10.

[5] *Mississippi River Flood Control Association; Losses and Damages Resulting from the Flood of 1927*, p. 5.

[6] *Senate Committee on Improvement of Mississippi River, Hearings 1888*, p. 35.

state that the railways knew that levees would finally destroy the navigability of the river and that they favored levees for that very purpose.[1] The most damaging evidence against the railways came in 1914 when testimony before Congressional Committees showed that eight of the leading lines of the lower valley had contributed one thousand dollars each per year for five years to the Mississippi River Levee and Improvement Association for the purpose of carrying on a public educational campaign in behalf of control by the Federal government.[2] The railways have frankly favored Federal control and have been powerful influences in bringing it about, but they have aroused some opposition.

In the discussion during the seventieth Congress, Presidential booms received mention as a cause for the support of flood-control legislation by several members of Congress. The fact that several of the valley states looked doubtful in the approaching Presidential campaign makes these declarations significant. *The St. Paul Dispatch* concluded that " the Republicans are not eager to alienate affections in a region so important ".[3] The complaint came from the floor of the House that several Presidential booms had forced the Jones bill through the Senate " beyond the speed limit ".[4] Even strong supporters of the bill admitted that Presidential politics had become somewhat mixed up with it.[5] Thus, some concluded that the legislation of 1928 represented a " piece of politics without justification ".[6] However, opposition for that reason certainly amounted to very little when the measure came to a vote.

[1] *The Memphis News Scimitar*, Jan. 12, 1914.

[2] *Cong. Record*, 63rd Cong., 2nd Sess., pt. 19, p. 16784.

[3] *Literary Digest*, vol. 97, April 14, 1928, p. 10.

[4] *Cong. Record*, 70th Cong., 1st Sess., pt. 10, 1928, p. 7295.

[5] *Ibid.*, p. 7298.

[6] *Literary Digest*, vol. 97, April 14, 1928, p. 10.

CHAPTER V

CONSTITUTIONAL BASIS FOR FEDERAL FLOOD CONTROL

THE proponents of flood control by the Federal government have furnished by far the largest part of discussion concerning the constitutional phases of the question. They have ever been ready to submit proof to substantiate their contentions at the slightest suggestion of the unconstitutionality of the project. The large amount of discussion along that line in the consideration of past flood-control legislation suggests that there has existed considerable feeling in Congress that the constitution did not permit the expenditure of Federal funds for such a purpose. Yet, it may also suggest that the friends of Federal control have been confident that they could defend its constitutionality against all attacks. At least they have made many bold statements that flood control was a proper function of the Federal government for which there existed undoubted constitutional warrant.[1]

Representative James R. Chalmers of Mississippi in discussing the bill that created the Mississippi River Commission declared that flood control could be held constitutional according to court decisions and " precedents of practice " under more clauses than any other work of internal improvement ever undertaken by the Federal government.[2] President Arthur in urging an appropriation for levees contended that " the constitutionality of a law making appropriations

[1] *House Committee on Flood Control,* 70th Cong., 1st Sess., 1927, *Report to Accompany House Bill,* no. 8219, p. 110.

[2] *Cong. Record,* 45th Cong., 3rd Sess., pt. 1, 1879, p. 503.

in aid of these objects cannot be questioned ".[1]   That remark called forth the suggestion from the editor of the Chicago Tribune that the President " ought to point out to Congress the clause in the constitution, which eminent lawyers of that body have overlooked " that justified his bold statement.[2] Yet, the claim of constitutionality seems to have been generally accepted.   The people of the country have frequently shown that they have considered the problem of flood control a proper one for the Federal government to solve.[3]

Although the proponents of Federal control have generally appeared fully satisfied that they could convince both the public and Congress of the constitutionality of their measures, occasionally some one has suggested an amendment. Colonel H. M. Chittenden, a famous student of floods and flood control, said that the improvement of the river for protection against inundation under the guise of benefit to navigation was "scarcely creditable to a great nation ", and that if the power did not exist for the Federal government to control floods the " constitution should be amended ".[4]   Others who have wanted an amendment have recently concluded that we have really been in the process of amending by a gradual accumulation of precedent.[5]

Several strong points for the constitutionality of flood control by the Federal government have been advanced, but the one that has furnished the bulwark for most of the arguments along that line has been based on the jurisdiction of the Federal government over interstate commerce.   The early participation of the United States in flood control was based

---

[1] *Cong. Record*, 47th Cong., 1st Sess., pt. 4, 1882, p. 3041.

[2] *The Chicago Tribune*, April 22, 1882, p. 4.

[3] *Century Magazine*, n. s., vol. 9, Sept., 1927, p. 639.

[4] *House Document*, no. 2, 64th Cong., 1st Sess., p. 27.

[5] *American Academy of Political and Social Science*, vol. 135, Jan., 1928, p. 55.

entirely on the proposition of improving navigation for the facilitation of commerce on the Mississippi. Congress and the public paid particular attention to the provision in the early appropriation acts that no part of the money should be spent for levees to prevent injury to lands by overflow.[1] The discussion of the first appropriation for levees showed that many members of Congress who supported it were very particular to tell the public that they did so for the sole purpose of improving navigation. Senator Wade Hampton of South Carolina made a long statement to the effect that he seriously doubted the constitutional right of the Federal government to control floods, but that he had no doubt of its rights to control navigation. If engineers in charge of the work decided that levees would improve navigation, and then those levees incidentally protected against floods, the jurisdiction of the United States and the right of the Federal government to construct the levees could not be doubted. Therefore, he supported the appropriation.[2] Concerning this appropriation the *New York Times* stated that the most liberal construction of the constitution could not find a right of the Federal government to protect lands against floods but that there existed undisputed right for the " improvement of the navigation of the stream for the general benefit of commerce ".[3] Members of Congress from the delta gladly accepted the proviso in the measures that forbade the use of any of the funds for flood control because they knew that the Mississippi River Commission was committed to a policy that would protect the lands against floods, as this protection was as effective in the guise of improving navigation as it would be in their openly favoring the measure for flood control. They had no doubt about the constitutionality of spending

[1] *The Chicago Tribune*, April 12, 1882, p. 2.

[2] *Cong. Record*, 47th Cong., 1st Sess., pt. 4, 1882, p. 3214.

[3] *New York Times*, April 21, 1882, p. 4.

Federal funds for protective works, but they did little until 1890 to prevent the proviso that all funds had to be spent for the improvement of navigation, when the proviso finally disappeared.[1] But the idea of spending money only to improve navigation prevailed after this date. Many argued that the bills which provided funds " for the general improvement of the Mississippi " permitted expenditure of money for levees for the unconstitutional purpose of flood control. They thought the same levees would be all right to improve navigation.[2] Many members of Congress continued to vote money for the improvement of navigation long after it became wholly apparent that the Mississippi River Commission spent practically all of its funds for flood control.[3] As late as 1928, Gifford Pinchot emphasized the importance of navigation in relation to flood control when he said, in speaking of the levee system, " Whenever its use affects navigation, albeit indirectly, the authority of the Federal government is supreme ".[4]

In the meantime, the people of the lower valley and their representatives in Congress sought to establish the right to control the river under the commerce clause on a wider basis than that of merely improving navigation. They became bold enough in 1917 to present a bill that frankly stated that it was a flood-control measure.[5] They took the position that legislation for the improvement of navigation had been " predicated upon the power of Congress to regulate commerce " for the word " navigation " did not appear in the constitution

[1] *Miss. River Commission, Report of 1913*, p. 3352.

[2] *Cong. Record*, 52nd Cong., 1st Sess., pt. 3, 1892, p. 2312.

[3] *American Society of Civil Engineers, Proceedings*, vol. 34, Nov., 1908, p. 1250.

[4] *Annals of the American Academy of Political and Social Science*, vol. 135, Jan., 1928, p. 57.

[5] *Annals of the American Academy of Political and Social Science*, vol. 135, Jan., 1928, p. 31.

but had been written in as a part of the interpretation of the commerce clause.[1]   They turned their attention to statements of legal authorities and to court decisions apparently with satisfactory results.   Representative B. G. Humphreys of Mississippi, who must be rated as one of the outstanding students of flood control, quoted the *American Law Register* No. 16, page 154: " The commerce of the river and the commerce across the river are both among the states, and may be regulated by Congress, and should be regulated by that body when any regulation is necessary ".[2]   The United States Supreme Court held in the Debs Case (158 United States 564) that the Congress of the United States by " express statute assumed jurisdiction " over commerce among the states when carried on by railways.   " It is charged, therefore, with the duty of keeping those highways of interstate commerce free from obstruction ", because it has always been a duty of the government to remove obstructions from the " highways under its control ".[3]   Storey considered that commerce was more than traffic and that included intercourse.   The regulation of commerce, therefore, included " prescribing rules for carrying on that intercourse ".[4]   The United States Supreme Court held in the Minnesota Rate Case (230 United States 495) " that the authority of Congress extends over every part of interstate commerce and to every instrumentality by which it is carried on ".   The paramount jurisdiction of Congress enabled it to " intervene at its discretion " and to substitute laws of its own for local laws.[5]

[1] *House Committee on Flood Control*, 70th Cong., 1st Sess., 1927, *Report to Accompany House Bill 8219*, p. 110.

[2] B. G. Humphreys, *Floods and Levees of the Mississippi River*, p. 128.

[3] B. G. Humphreys, *Floods and Levees of the Mississippi River*, p. 118.

[4] *Ibid.*, p. 128.

[5] *House Committee on Flood Control*, 70th Cong., 1st Sess., 1927, *Report to Accompany House Bill 8219*, p. 111.

Several of the great trunk-line railways cross the delta. The Missouri Pacific alone in 1927 had more than six hundred miles of road bed under water. A total of three thousand miles of railways suspended operation for periods from ten days to four months during this flood.[1] The result of the inundation was the " total suspension with the activities " of large areas.[2] Thus, the proponents of flood control by the Federal government have sought to place their contention of its constitutionality under the commerce clause on a much broader basis than the mere improvement of navigation. They have included all intercourse under commerce and have urged the Federal government's duty to remove all obstructions from highways, railways and all other agencies. Floods have certainly constituted a very serious obstruction to all intercourse among the states and, therefore, should be controlled by the Federal government.

The general welfare has naturally furnished a strong point for those who sought to prove the constitutionality of flood control by the United States. It has been suggested that the constitution has been expanded by usage and by interpretation to include many things under the general welfare. To many the government had as much right to make land suitable for habitation by protecting it against floods as it did to give away the public domain.[3] President Arthur placed flood control in the class of the general welfare when he asked for an appropriation for levees because of " the immense losses and widespread suffering of the people ".[4] Congress has made very large grants of lands to railways. That fact has caused members of Congress to say frequently that flood

---

[1] *House Committee on Flood Control*, 70th Cong., 1st Sess., 1927, *Report to Accompany House Bill 8219*, p. 44.

[2] *Cong. Record*, 70th Cong., 1st Sess., 1928, p. 2767.

[3] *Cong. Globe*, 42nd Cong., 2nd Sess., pt. 1, 1871, p. 286.

[4] J. D. Richardson, *Messages and Papers of the Presidents*, vol. 6, p. 4682.

control certainly had a better constitutional basis than the
granting of lands and subsidies to railways.[1]   Also, Congress has been very liberal in voting money to relieve suffering among the victims of floods.   Very little question as to
the constitutionality of aiding victims of flood disasters has
ever been raised.   It has been urged with apparent logic that
appropriations for flood protection mean as much for the
general welfare as appropriations for the relief of flood
sufferers and that they are, therefore, just as constitutional.[2]
Storey maintained that if the benefit were general, whether
it was of " large or small extent ", or whether it was located
in " one state or several ", Congress could appropriate money
for it because it was for the general welfare.[3]   The United
States Supreme Court held in Hunter *v.* Martin, 1 Wheaton
304, that the constitutional powers had been expressed in
general terms and left to Congress to exercise them from
time to time as " its own wisdom and the public interests
should require ".[4]   The flood of 1927 drove 700,000 people
from their homes and " paralyzed industry and commerce "
over a wide area.[5]   It has been said that this flood " touched
the heart and affected the daily life of every individual in the
country ".[6]   It certainly had such a wide affect as to react
on the general welfare.

Congress has the power under the constitution to control
the property of the United States.[7]   It has been contended
by the proponents of Federal control that the Mississippi

---

[1] *Cong. Record*, 47th Cong., 1st Sess., pt. 4, 1882, p. 3134.

[2] *Ibid.*, p. 3040.

[3] B. G. Humphreys, *Floods and Levees of the Mississippi River*, p. 134.

[4] *Ibid.*, p. 136.

[5] *House Committee on Flood Control*, 70th Cong., 1st Sess., 1927, *Report to Accompany House Bill 8219*, p. 3.

[6] *Ibid.*, p. 121.

[7] B. G. Humphreys, *Floods and Levees of the Mississippi River*, p. 122.

river is the property of the nation. Senator Benjamin Harrison, of Indiana, in discussing the first appropriation for the use of the Mississippi River Commission took the position that Congress had the right to regulate and control the river because it belonged to the nation.[1] Some have considered that the Louisiana Purchase gave the United States ownership of the river, a right which has never been alienated.[2] The Supreme Court of the United States has declared that all interstate navigable streams are " the public property of the nation, and subject to all requisite regulation of Congress ".[3] Then, the Federal government has invested large sums in highways and bridges throughout the delta, which was done under undoubted constitutional authority. Thus, the constitutional right of the Federal government to protect its property both in the river itself and in the highways and bridges in the overflowed area has frequently been maintained.

Many have urged that the provisions in the constitution for the common defense gave Congress sufficient warrant for controlling the river. Certainly, Congress has very wide powers in regard to the common defense that really seem to offer ample reasons for including flood control.[4] The importance of transportation across the lower valley in time of war can hardly be overestimated. Such a flood as that of 1927 completely cuts off all communication for hundreds of miles and seriously affects the transportation system of the whole nation. In view of this condition, the Flood Committee of the Chamber of Commerce of the United States in

[1] *Cong. Record*, 47th Cong., 1st Sess., pt. 4, 1882, p. 3139.

[2] *Cong. Record*, 45th Cong., 3rd Sess., pt. 1, 1879, p. 503.

[3] B. G. Humphreys, *Floods and Levees of the Mississippi River*, p. 124.

[4] *House Committee on Flood Control, Hearings 1916*, p. 9.

1927 declared that the national defense required a system of permanent flood control.[1]

A memorial from the legislature of the state of Mississippi to Congress in 1927 stated that the jurisdiction of the United States on the Mississippi river was paramount to that of the states bordering thereon.[2]   That paramount jurisdiction has caused the conclusion that the duty of flood control rested on the Federal government.   The act of Congress that permitted Louisiana to make a constitution provided for a clause that the river should remain under the jurisdiction of the nation.[3]   The United States Supreme Court held in Van Brocklin v. Tennessee (117 United States 154) that the United States had the right to acquire all property necessary for the construction of flood-control works without concurrent acts by the states.[4]   But the right of eminent domain could be relied upon if local areas proved unwilling to furnish the necessary property.   This right is " incident to sovereignty and requires no constitutional recognition ", the fifth and fourteenth amendments merely being limitations upon the exercise thereof.[5]   The right of eminent domain may be exercised when the public good requires it.   Thus, the Federal government has paramount jurisdiction over the river and power to construct protective works.   Also, the fact that states cannot enter into contracts among themselves makes it rather necessary for a higher power than state governments to supervise the work.[6]   The states most concerned with flood control have sought to remove all doubt about the

[1] Annals of the American Academy of Political and Social Science, vol. 135, Jan., 1928, p. 31.

[2] Cong. Record, 70th Cong., 1st Sess., pt. 4, 1927, p. 2355.

[3] B. G. Humphreys, Floods and Levees of the Mississippi River, p. 123.

[4] Cong. Record, 70th Cong., 1st Sess., pt. 6, 1928, p. 4253.

[5] Memphis, The Commercial Appeal, November 22, 1927.

[6] Cong. Record, 43rd Cong., 1st Sess., pt. 4, 1874, p. 3246.

power of Congress by placing clauses in their constitutions declaring the jurisdiction of the Federal government paramount to their own.[1]

The public health has ever been a topic of grave concern to the Federal government. The floods on the Mississippi river have been great enemies to the health of the people of the valley. Flood control may be justified under the constitution because it is a preventive of disease and a benefit to the public health, a phase of public welfare which certainly is a duty of the Federal government.[2]

The right and duty of Congress to provide for the safe conduct of the United States mails has received considerable attention.[3] Section 3964 of the Revised Statutes declares that the waters of the United States, while the mails are being carried on them, are post roads.[4] The Supreme Court of the United States has declared that Congress had the right and the duty to remove any " obstruction to the carrying of the mails ".[5] The floods by inundating post offices and post roads have certainly seriously affected the service. It seems that the proponents of Federal control have a point here that should have received more attention from them than it has in the past.

A discussion of the constitutional phases of this question would hardly be complete without presenting a brief rejoinder to the one outstanding argument of those who contend that Federal flood control is unconstitutional. The friends of Federal control appear to have felt the responsibility of refuting the claim that it was reclamation of lands of private interests. They have spent much time and effort

[1] *Cong. Record*, 70th Cong., 1st Sess., 1927, p. 4247.

[2] *Century Magazine*, n. s., vol. 92, Sept., 1927, p. 639.

[3] *Engineering and Contracting*, vol. 41, March 18, 1914, p. 341.

[4] B. G. Humphreys, *Floods and Levees of the Mississippi River*, p. 116.

[5] *Ibid.*, p. 118.

in showing that reclamation has not been involved. They
have maintained that the lands had already been reclaimed
when they sought protection.[1]   Much of the land seeking
protection has been highly developed for generations.[2]   Reclamation has for its purpose the creation of utility in lands,
while flood control has for its purpose the restraint of floods
and the benefit of developed areas.[3]   Of course the people on
the lands adjoining the levees would reap special benefits, but
the unearned increment has always accrued to those who held
property near public improvements.[4]   But the probaility of
an unearned increment should not restrain Congress from
protecting a thriving country, much of which has been settled
and reclaimed since our very early history.[5]   The Supreme
Court of the United States held in Cubbins *v.* the Mississippi
River Commission that the construction of levees for control
of floods and the improvement of navigation was not for the
purpose of reclamation.[6]   Thus, the proponents of Federal
control have sought to establish the difference between reclamation and the protection of a developed area against floods.

[1] *House Report*, no. 300, 63rd Cong., 2nd Sess., 1914, p. 48.
[2] *The Literary Digest*, vol. 95, Dec. 24, 1927, p. 9.
[3] *Cong. Record*, 70th Cong., 1st Sess., pt. 3, 1928, p. 1792.
[4] *House Report*, no. 300, 63rd Cong., 2nd Sess., 1914, p. 51.
[5] *Cong. Record*, 70th Cong., 1st Sess., pt. 6, 1928, p. 4247.
[6] *Ibid.*, p. 5850.

CHAPTER VI

THE American people for many years have shown a widespread interest in the prevention of the dreadful calamities produced by the floods. Their interest is greatest during the years in which floods are the severest.[1] This is evidenced by the fact that every flood of any considerable magnitude in recent years has brought forth volumes of discussion and multitudes of plans. Several of the plans have had large numbers of protagonists who have presented them as certain remedies.[2] The people of the United States have wasted an enormous amount of " ingenuity ", usually unsupported by technical knowledge, in seeking a way to control the floods of the Mississippi. The public sees it as an unsolved problem badly needing a solution that " Yankee ingenuity " ought to provide.[3]

People generally have never realized the absolute necessity for much deep study of the problem by experts in hydraulic engineering. Thus, many ridiculous and laughable plans have been proposed by men from all walks of life. Various Congressional Committees, and even Presidents, have shown great patience in listening to many highly preposterous propositions from apparent cranks.[4] One man proposed a great

[1] *Scientific Monthly*, vol. 16, April, 1923, p. 344.

[2] *Journal of the Association of Engineers*, vol. 49, Sept., 1912, p. 54.

[3] *Engineering News-Record*, vol. 94, April 2, 1925, p. 559.

[4] *House Committee on Flood Control*, 70th Cong., 1st Sess., 1927, *Committee Doc.*, no. 1, p. 128.

canal to carry the flood waters straight from the Ohio river above Cairo to Mobile Bay.[1]   Another would have built gigantic boilers to convert the flood waters into steam.[2] Some have proposed enormous pipes at the bottom of the river to carry away the sediment and hasten the flow, and others have wanted to filter the water.[3]   These are only a few of the dozens of very preposterous suggestions that have been presented.   They show the wide ramifications of the theories of the people on flood control.   Many went hundreds of miles at their own expense to present these comical plans which often had been prepared in elaborate detail at great expense and much effort.

In the meantime, technical experts both in civil life and in the Corps of Engineers of the United States Army have given profound and prolonged study to the problem.[4]   Such a vast problem could hardly fail to create a wide difference of opinion even among hydraulic engineers as to the best method of solving it.   The technical men who have applied much knowledge and study to the problem have proposed methods, which, for the purpose of discussion in this chapter, have been designated as follows: to strengthen the river by cutting across the numerous bends so as to hasten the discharge of the water; to construct reservoirs either on the headwaters of the various tributaries or along the main stream to impound and hold back the water; to reforest and afforest large areas to increase the sink-in and percolation; to construct outlets or spillways to divert the water through them to the Gulf of Mexico; to build levees sufficiently high and strong to confine the water to the main stream; and to combine

---

[1] *House Committee on Flood Control*, 70th Cong., 1st Sess., 1927, *Committee Doc.*, no. 1, p. 128.

[2] *The Scientific Monthly*, vol. 16, April, 1923, p. 344.

[3] *Engineering News-Record*, vol. 94, April 2, 1925, p. 559.

[4] *Ibid.*

several or all of the above methods into one comprehensive scheme that would include the whole river system.

Not one of those methods is new or peculiar to this country. All had been proposed and tried in European, African and Asiatic countries before the Mississippi problem received serious attention.[1] If one wonders why experts disagree over methods that have been tried many times, he has only to consider the nature of the river that they seek to control. The colossal fluvial mastodon has been regarded by many as a river that defies all " acknowledged laws of hydronomics " and frequently " disappoints calculations based on recognized principles ".[2] This means that the Mississippi must be studied as a distinct problem with much allowance for its own peculiarities. " No similar problem of similar size has ever been mastered by man " stated A. E. Morgan, who perhaps knows as much about flood control as any one.[3] No one can afford ever to consider the Mississippi by the law of averages. The treatment of this mighty stream must be considered from the standpoint of its peculiar and sometimes almost mysterious vagaries.[4]

This chapter will discuss some of the outstanding peculiarities of the father of waters only far enough to give a limited idea of the difficulties involved as a reason for the differences of opinion as to the proper method of control. The first fact that impresses itself upon us is the vast amount of water this river carries to the Gulf and the remarkable variability of its discharge. The low-water discharge reaches the very small amount of about 70,000 second-feet, or 70,000 cubic feet

[1] B. G. Humphreys, *Floods and Levees of the Mississippi River*, p. 32.

[2] *Senate Executive Document*, no. 49, 32nd Cong., 1st Sess., 1852, p. 30.

[3] *Annals of the American Academy of Political and Social Science*, vol. 135, Jan., 1928, p. 56.

[4] Jacksonville *Times-Union*, April 4, 1897.

per second.[1]   On the other hand, the Mississippi River Commission estimated the maximum discharge of the flood of 1927 at 2,800,000 second-feet, which represents a greater volume of water than man has previously attempted to control.[2]   The volume alone must be awe-inspiring to those who seek the solution.   The difference in gauge readings between high water and low water varies at different points but reaches as much as fifty feet at points about the middle of the length of the delta.[3]

The next important group of facts grows out of the geological formation of the lower basin.   The delta formerly was a shallow arm of the ocean extending far into the continent.   This shallow area of water became filled with sediment brought down by the great river.[4]   Thus the entire delta has been built up through the ages to its present form by its present great enemy.   The bed of the lower Mississippi lies wholly within the alluvium deposited by it.   Borings made by the Mississippi River Commission in 1908-9 established the mean depth of the " undoubtedly alluvial " deposits beneath the bed of the river between Cairo and New Orleans at 131 feet.[5]   Logs have been found in many places at depths ranging from 100 feet to 300 feet.[6]   As the river rose and flowed out over the surrounding country its velocity became less and it deposited much of its sediment.   The coarsest sediment was deposited nearest the river, building up the

---

[1] *Annals of the American Academy of Political and Social Science,* vol. 135, Jan., 1928, p. 11.

[2] *House Committee on Flood Control,* 70th Cong., 1st Sess., 1927-8, *Comm., Doc.,* no. 24, p. 103.

[3] *House Document,* no. 35, 17th Cong., 2nd Sess., p. 13.

[4] *Mississippi River Commission Report,* 1882, p. 2315.

[5] *House Committee on Flood Control,* 70th Cong., 1st Sess., 1927, *Committee Doc.,* no. 1, p. 6.

[6] Herman Haupt, *The Problem of the Mississippi,* p. 11.

banks of new coarse materials until they became higher than the surrounding territory.[1] This process continued until the plane of the delta adjacent to the river slopes off at right angles to the river " into the interior for five or six miles at the rate of three or four feet per mile ".[2] The slope of the delta toward the Gulf is only eight inches per mile. Thus, the river banks occupy the highest part of the delta and the land falls away from the stream far more rapidly than it slopes toward the Gulf. This peculiar situation accounts for the fact that the first settlers generally occupied the banks; while land further from the river remained unoccupied.[3] It also explains why the front riparian proprietors have suffered less from floods than those who lived several miles from the river.[4]

The territory through which the Mississippi flows from Cairo to the Gulf forms one of the flattest surfaces in America. The great fan-shaped, gently-sloping plane has been formed by the river and in turn makes a bed for the river to flow through. This alluvial plane is naturally an extremely flat area.[5] The actual distance from the mouth of the Ohio to the Gulf coast may be stated in round numbers at about 500 miles. The length of the river from Cairo to the Gulf totals more than two times the air-line distance.[6] This added distance has been created by the numerous ox-bow bends which the river has made in an effort to establish

---

[1] *Cong. Record*, 70th Cong., 1st Sess., pt. 11, 1927-8, p. 11008.

[2] *House Committee on Flood Control*, 70th Cong., 1st Sess., 1927-8, *Committee Doc.*, no. 17, p. 30.

[3] *Annals of the American Academy of Political and Social Science*, Jan., 1928, p. 12.

[4] *House Report*, no. 44, 42nd Cong., 2nd Sess., 1872, p. 6.

[5] *Senate Executive Document*, no. 49, 32nd Cong., 1st Sess., 1852, p. 29.

[6] *House Committee on Flood Control*, 70th Cong., 1st Sess., 1927, *Committee Doc.*, no. 17, p. 29.

a regimen that its fragile banks could maintain. The banks have been built from loose and unconsolidated materials which erode very easily.[1] The enormous pressure of the water has naturally cut away the earth and sought a gradient that could be maintained. The river finally established a fairly permanent course of a very sinuous nature with a fall of only 3¼ inches per mile.[2] Many of the ox-bow bends are only a few hundred feet across the necks; while they are several miles around.[3] The river constantly works on these bends and often cuts across the narrow necks. Because the water continuously cuts away the soil, the river is said to " eat " its banks. This is one of the most serious difficulties to be combated on the Mississippi.[4] " Eating " its banks has produced most of the vast amount of sediment that has furnished a major problem for hydraulic engineers.

The river at flood has a greatly increased velocity, giving the vast flood waters a force of about 60,000,000 horsepower, a force which is " consumed in eating away the banks of the river, stirring up the bed and getting the water into the Gulf ".[5] The eroded materials from the banks, most of which goes into the stream at flood time, has been determined by the Mississippi River Commission at approximately 1,000,000 cubic yards per mile per year.[6] This vast amount of sediment receives great additions from its various tribu-

[1] *Annals of the American Academy of Political and Social Science,* vol. 135, Jan., 1928, p. 12.

[2] *House Committee on Flood Control,* 70th Cong., 1st Sess., 1927, *Committee Doc.,* no. 17, p. 29.

[3] *Senate Executive Document,* no. 49, 32nd Cong., 1st Sess., 1852, p. 90.

[4] Barbour Lewis, *Speech on Levees of Mississippi,* House, June 6, 1874, p. 8.

[5] *House Committee on Flood Control,* 70th Cong., 1st Sess., 1927, *Committee Doc.,* no. 24, p. 102.

[6] *Mississippi River Commission, Report 1892,* p. 3110.

taries, especially from the Missouri river. The total amount of soil that the Mississippi has to transport and dispose of annually has been authoritatively placed at more than a billion cubic yards.[1] The sediment moves down the river for indefinite distances, most of it rolling along the bottom of the river.[2] This material rolling along the bottom and the currents of the river produce scouring at some places and depositing at others, so that the bed of the river is composed of alternating bars and pools which move down the river in " waves ", creating a condition whereby the shallow places of one week may be the deep ones of the next and vice versa.[3]

The large number of channels leading from the Mississippi, some to lakes or swamps and others to the Gulf, is a peculiarity that has caused much consideration by both experts and laymen.[4] The apparent ease with which the water of the Mississippi could be diverted through some of those channels has caused many to oppose plans that would confine the floods to the river. They believe that the flood heights could be lowered by diverting the water with much less effort and at much less cost.

The vast and varied area drained by the Mississippi and the complicated causes of floods have created a wide difference of opinions as to the proper methods of control.[5] Topography, precipitation, climate and other phases of the wide drainage areas have certainly furnished much reason for study and for disagreement.[6] The floods on the Mississippi

[1] *House Committee on Flood Control*, 70th Cong., 1st Sess., 1927, *Committee Doc.*, no. 6, p. 19.

[2] *Ibid.*, p. 24.

[3] *Engineering and Contracting*, vol. 53, Jan. 14, 1920, p. 37.

[4] *Senate Executive Document*, no. 49, 32nd Cong., 1st Sess., 1852, p. 60.

[5] *House Committee on Flood Control, Hearings 1927*, p. 1139.

[6] Alvord and Burdick, *Relief from Floods*, p. 11.

have also been complicated by various combinations of concentration of waters from the many tributaries.[1] The Ohio has always been an important factor in all great floods, but the other tributaries have varied greatly in their contributions.[2]

Although some have held that the river should be straightened in order to hasten the discharge into the Gulf, the official reports made by United States Engineers have universally condemned cut-offs.[3] Expert opinion seems of one accord that cut-offs only pile up the flood waters below them.[4] If the river could once be straightened and so held, it might be of some benefit to straighten it.   But all agree that the river flows by what may be designated as the law of " uniform descent ".[5]   If a cut-off occurs, the river establishes a maintainable regimen by immediately creating other curves to take the place of the one it lost.   Cut-offs have been tried by various countries in Europe as a means of reducing floods but have been universally abandoned. They have not only failed to work, but have made conditions worse.[6]   They now receive little attention as a means of flood control.   In this respect, the interests of navigation and those of flood control have been in sharp conflict, for the navigation interests have been very active in reducing the length of the channel.

The damage from floods is " felt down stream but the responsibility is up-stream " according to the *Chicago*

---

[1] *Engineering News-Record*, vol. 96, April 29, 1926.

[2] *United States Weather Review*, vol. 27, Sept., 1899, p. 406.

[3] *House Executive Document*, no. 127, 43rd Cong., 2nd Sess., 1875, p. 31.

[4] *House Committee on Flood Control*, 70th Cong., 1st Sess., 1927-8, *Committee Doc.*, no. 17, p. 55.

[5] *Ibid.*

[6] *Times-Picayune*, New Orleans, May 19, 1913.

Tribune. Thus, the only sensible way to control floods in the lower valley is to construct reservoirs on the tributaries that will enable the people to control the waters before they reach the main river.[1] " Minor floods from the smaller flood areas " create all of the great floods by combining their waters by a concentration in the lower river.[2] The Report of the Inland Waterways Commission in 1908 stated that the only "logical way to control a river " was to control the head waters of its tributaries, and that the only way to prevent floods was " to use these reservoirs to catch and temporarily hold the flood waters " to prevent them from descending upon the lower valley in such large volumes.[3] Undoubtedly, the floods of any stream could be controlled by the construction of an adequate number of reservoirs of sufficient size and favorable location.[4] Whether such control could be secured at any reasonable cost by comparison with other systems has long been a question of controversy between large groups of students of drainage and flood control.

Reservoirs have been built for the purpose of flood control and stream regulation in the United States, but it appears that they have not been of sufficient size or number to furnish conclusive data on either side of the question. The Miami Conservancy District has five reservoirs to prevent destructive floods on the Miami River.[5] They were designed to affect only the larger floods, and to remain empty at other times. " These works appear to have been very successful

---

[1] *Chicago Tribune*, April 18, 1927, p. 10.

[2] *Cong. Record*, 70th Cong., 1st Sess., pt. 11, 1927-8, p. 11008.

[3] *Senate Document*, no. 325, 60th Cong., 1st Sess., 1908, p. 451 (Inland Waterways Comm., Report 1908).

[4] G. W. Pickles, *Drainage and Flood-Control Engineering*, p. 340.

[5] *House Committee on Flood Control*, 70th Cong., 1st Sess., 1927-8, Committee Doc., no. 2, p. 4.

in affording the designed protection to the Miami valley ".[1]
This plan has apparently been accepted by all competent to
pass judgment.   It has caused friends of reservoirs to maintain that the Miami Conservancy District has established the
fact that floods on the Mississippi could also be controlled by
reservoirs.   The United States constructed six large reservoirs in the state of Minnesota for the purpose of aiding low
water navigation on the upper Mississippi.[2]   The reclamation service has built a number of large reservoirs on the
headwaters of the western tributaries.[3]   The Pittsburg
Flood Commission decided that the flood problems of that
city could be very largely remedied by reservoirs.[4]   These
examples of actual going flood-works, of reservoirs for control of navigation and irrigation together with the exhaus-
tive study by a highly competent commission have formed the
basis for most of the support of reservoirs as a means of controlling floods.   But the opponents of reservoirs have used
the same examples in condemning them.

Lyman E. Cooley has been generally regarded as one of
our most competent authorities on all phases of flood control.
He enthusiastically supported reservoirs, which he believed
could be built at a reasonable cost.[2]   He did not contend
that reservoirs would be able to hold back all of the flood
waters, but that they would be able to hold back enough to
take several feet off the crest.   An authority from the United
States Geological Survey in 1908 maintained that enough of
the flood waters of the Ohio could be controlled feasibly to

[1] *House Committee on Flood Control*, 70th Cong., 1st Sess., 1927-8,
Committee Doc., no. 2, p. 4.

[2] *Ibid.*, p. 7.

[3] *Ibid.*, p. 6.

[4] *Journal of the Association of Engineers*, vol. 49, Sept., 1912, p. 57.

[5] *Journal of the Western Society of Engineers*, vol. 5, Aug., 1900, p. 292.

reduce flood heights on the Mississippi seven feet at Memphis and eight feet at Vicksburg.[1] If such a statement is true, the serious danger could be removed from floods by reservoirs on our leading tributaries, for such a reduction would enable present control works to conduct almost any imaginable flood safely to the Gulf. In 1927 the Chief of Engineers appointed a special board to study the control of floods by reservoirs. The report of that board was published for the use of the House Flood Control Committee as a committee document. It was estimated that enough reservoirs could be constructed on the headwaters of the tributaries of the Mississippi to reduce flood heights 5.7 feet at Cairo and 5.4 feet at the mouth of the Red river at a cost of $1,292,000,000.[2] Such an estimate of course made the project utterly impracticable. However, the reservoir proponents could gain some comfort from another section of the report, which estimated that reservoirs could be built for $242,000,000 on the Arkansas and White rivers that would reduce the stage at Arkansas City 8 feet and at Red river 5 feet.[3] Whether this part of the report suggested anything practical remains open to question.

We should note in passing that most of those who have urged reservoirs have not urged them as the means by which floods could be controlled but rather as an aid to flood control. They have demanded reservoirs as an "additional safeguard" instead of a substitute for levees.[4] They have argued with much logic that a few feet taken from the crest of floods would reduce the serious danger so that present works would be sufficient. Viewed in this light, the sup-

[1] *Engineering News*, vol. 59, June 11, 1908, p. 632.

[2] *House Committee on Flood Control*, 70th Cong., 1st Sess., 1927-8, Committee Doc., no. 2, p. 1.

[3] *Ibid.*

[4] *Journal of the Association of Engineers*, vol. 49, Oct., 1912, p. 107.

porters of reservoirs appear to have a very firm basis for much of their contention.

The prospect of selling electricity that could be generated by the water held by the reservoirs has had much consideration. That possibility has been rejected by the best engineering talent. Yet Gifford Pinchot in 1927 restated the old idea that the government could make much money in this way.[1] Reservoirs have the possibility of combining both functions to a limited extent only, for the two purposes are opposite by nature.[2] For flood control the reservoirs would need to be empty, and for power generation they would need to be full.[3] Obviously, as they were used more for one purpose they would reduce their utility for the other.

The opponents of reservoirs have rejected the whole proposition with the statement that reservoirs possibly could control floods, but that they are utterly impracticable because of the prohibitive cost in comparison with other flood-control works. The Mississippi River Commission has been a severe critic of this system, and is still to a large extent.[4] Col. C. McD. Townsend, an active speech-making member of the Commission, severely criticized the plan in a speech at St. Louis in 1913, and on many other occasions. He asserted that a reservoir at the junction of the Mississippi and Ohio large enough to have held the flood waters of 1912 would have been 7,000 square miles in area and fifteen feet deep, requiring excavation that would furnish dirt for 7,000 miles of levee 150 feet high.[5] While Col. C. L. Potter was serv-

---

[1] *The Survey*, vol. 58, July 1, 1927, p. 367.

[2] *House Committee on Flood Control*, 70th Cong., 1st Sess., 1927-8, *Committee Doc.*, no. 2, p. 18.

[3] *Engineering and Contracting*, vol. 41, March 18, 1914, p. 340.

[4] *U. S. Daily*, Sept. 28, 1927, p. 1.

[5] C. McD. Townsend, *Flood Control of Mississippi River*, St. Louis, 1913, p. 8.

ing as President of the Mississippi River Commission he stated that flood control for the Ohio valley alone at the same rate of cost as for the Miami valley, which was the only real example of flood control in the United States by reservoirs, would cost $1,718,000,000.[1] The Pittsburgh Flood Commission found that by building seventeen dams at the estimated cost of $21,672,100, a flood of 35.5 feet on the Pittsburgh gauge would be lowered to 27 feet, and that further protection would cost much more in proportion.[2] To show how little this proposed system would affect the main flood, engineers have frequently stated that to cut the Ohio absolutely off at Pittsburgh and the Mississippi at St. Paul would have no appreciable effect on the river at Cairo; only 35,000 second feet in 1913 out of a total of about 2,000,000 second-feet.[3] The Mississippi above St. Paul has the largest system of reservoirs in the world with 93,000,000,000 cubic feet capacity.[4] The board of United States Engineers in 1927 estimated that this system reduced flood heights 1/5 of an inch in 1912 and slightly increased the height of the 1913 flood at Cairo.[5] Although there has been much talk about reservoirs, and such talk has a strong appeal for the man in the street, their supporters have not convinced the engineers of the United States Army and the Mississippi River Commission that they are practical. These engineers have gone even further and have suggested that the danger from probable breaks among scores of gigantic dams would be as much as the danger from present flood conditions.[6] Thus, a lead-

[1] *Engineering News-Record*, vol. 94, April 2, 1925, p. 557.

[2] *Journal of the Association of Engineers*, vol. 49, Sept., 1912, p. 57.

[3] *Engineering and Contracting*, vol. 41, March 18, 1914, p. 340.

[4] *Ibid.*, p. 339.

[5] *House Committee on Flood Control*, 70th Cong., 1st Sess., 1927-8, *Committee Doc.*, no. 2, p. 7.

[6] *Journal of the Association of Engineers*, vol. 49, Sept., 1912, p. 59.

ing paper of the lower valley called the proposed reservoir system a wild and extravagant dream and urged support of levees as the one feasible system of control.[1]

The relation of forestation and deforestation to floods and stream control has been a live topic during recent years. The idea that devastating floods of late years have been caused by the destruction of forests has gained wide distribution.[2] Forested areas certainly hold back a portion of the water that falls upon them.[3]   Therefore, forests must receive consideration in any plan that includes the whole stream from source to mouth.[4]   They would have a definite place in any plan of permanent control that included the upper reaches of the tributaries.   No system of "rational water management" could disregard them as an important factor.[5]

The opponents of flood control by reforestation contend that deforestation has not caused floods and that forests could not aid materially in controlling them.   They have pointed out that a most remarkable series of floods came in the decade from 1857 to 1867.[6]   And certainly, no one could even hope to restore the forests to the conditions of that period.   Gen. Harry Taylor, a well-known engineer member of the Mississippi River Commission, estimated that it would take 533,000 square miles of forest reserve to reduce as much as a foot a great flood at Memphis.[7]   He further maintained that deforestation had not increased the frequency of floods.   He has much expert testimony to support him in

[1] *Times-Picayune*, New Orleans, April 25, 1913.

[2] New Orleans, *Times-Picayune*, April 30, 1913.

[3] *American Forests and Forest Life*, vol. 33, July, 1927, p. 409.

[4] *The Journal of Forestry*, May, 1927, p. 508.

[5] *American Forests and Forest Life*, vol. 33, July, 1927, p. 391.

[6] *Scientific Monthly*, vol. 16, April, 1923, p. 34.

[7] *The Scientific Monthly*, vol. 16, April, 1923, p. 346.

this statement. Both army and civil engineers and meteorologists generally believe that cultivated soil offers as good conservation of rainfall as forest areas.[1] Prof. D. W. Meade of the University of Wisconsin made a thorough study of the rivers of that state and concluded that forests had little influence on stream flow.[2] A careful study of the Merrimac river in New Hampshire and Massachusetts has been made by Col. Edward Burr of the Corps of Engineers of the United States Army. That basin offered a splendid experimental case because complete records were available for the period of deforestation and then of reforestration. The study showed little or no relation of deforestation to stream flow.[3] Forests can store a quantity of water equal to .16 of an inch, and in very favorable conditions .24 of an inch, but this amount represents only an insignificant fraction of the great quantities of precipitation that cause floods.[4] Another argument against forests is that it would simply be impossible to take the time and to find area enough to grow forests to control floods. Foresters claim that an extensive program of reforestation could be felt in five years, and maximum results could be obtained in twenty years.[5]

It should be borne in mind that of the technical foresters not one of any authority has even suggested that forests would control floods.[6] They have only maintained that in stream control the " upper watersheds tributary to the river " form an important factor. They have contended for forests

[1] *Engineering News*, vol. 63, April 14, 1910, p. 428.

[2] *National Waterways Commission, Final Report*, 1912, p. 29.

[3] *Ibid.*

[4] *American Forests and Forest Life*, vol. 33, July, 1927, p. 387 (Raphael Zon).

[5] Lamar T. Beman, The Reference Shelf, vol. v, no. 7, *Flood Control*, p. 65.

[6] *The Journal of Forestry*, May, 1927, p. 508.

only as a supplement to engineering works.   Neither have
the foresters wanted to plant agricultural lands in trees.   It
is the vast areas of waste lands that they want to put in
forests.   The Mississippi River Commission did not study
that type of areas.[1]

On one point there seems to be almost unanimous agreement, namely that forests aid in flood control.   The Mississippi River Commission itself has suggested the value of
forests in preventing erosion.[2]   The sediment in the Mississippi at flood time has been a serious problem.   The prevention of erosion has, therefore, been listed as perhaps the
most important benefit of forests to stream control.[3]   Forests
would certainly prevent much erosion that takes place on wide
areas of waste lands at present.

In its natural state, the Mississippi flowed to the Gulf at
flood time through many mouths.   Long bayous, natural
outlets, took the water from the main channel.   Du Pratz in
his history of Louisiana in 1774 spoke of the water being
conveyed through several lakes to the sea.[4]   He added the
comment that it appeared strange that a river that overflowed
its banks should not recover its waters.   The construction of
levees has closed these former outlets.[5]   On the lower Mississippi the pressing problem has not been to let out the surplus waters but to keep the river from breaking through at
its old outlets.[6]   The apparent ease with which the flood
waters could be taken away by diversion channels or waste

[1] Lamar T. Beman, *Flood Control*, Reference Shelf, vol. v, no. 7, p. 66.

[2] *Mississippi River Commission, Report 1881*, p. 125.

[3] *National Waterways Commission, Final Report, 1912*, p. 35.

[4] Du Pratz, *History of Louisiana*, 1774, p. 127.

[5] Charles Ellet, *Plans for the Protection of the Delta from Inundation,*
p. 97.

[6] *House Committee on Flood Control*, 70th Cong., 1st Sess., 1927-8,
Committee Doc., no. 17, p. 80.

weirs has caused this method of flood control for the part of the river below the mouth of the Arkansas to receive almost universal recommendation among laymen. The advocates of the outlet theory have, throughout the history of flood-control legislation, been highly energetic in presenting their plans. As early as 1816 Darby made the statement that levees were inferior " in efficacy to artificial sluices ", which would conduct the flood waters to the Gulf by other routes than the main river.[1] In 1850 De Bow's Review published a plan to take the floods to the Gulf through a vast diversion channel from the Arkansas over very much the same route that was accepted as a part of the 1927 plan.[2] The Ellet report of 1852 gave arguments both for and against diversion channels but concluded that the advantages outweighed the disadvantages.[3] James A. Cowden for years appeared before all possible Congressional Committees with elaborate plans for constructing spillways and diversion channels and with severe criticisms against the supporters of levees. The presiding officer at the great River Improvement and Levee meeting at New Orleans in 1903, whose delegates represented the whole valley, said that he was aware of the fact that the " outletters " were abroad in the land and that they would be " to the end ".[4]

The place of residence has had much influence upon people's attitude toward flood-control methods. Upper-river men have favored reservoirs, middle-river men have wanted levees, and lower-river men have demanded diversion channels in large numbers of cases.[5] So, the most active agent

[1] Darby, *Geographical Description of Louisiana*, p. 59.

[2] *De Bow's Review*, vol. viii, Feb., 1850, p. 284.

[3] Charles Ellet, *Plans for the Protection of the Delta from Inundation*, p. 18.

[4] *Senate Committee on Commerce, Hearings 1904*, p. 44.

[5] *Cassier's Engineering Monthly*, vol. 44, July, 1913, p. 33.

working for diversion of the flood waters since 1922 has been the Safe River Committee of 100 of New Orleans, a committee of leading persons whose avowed purpose was to secure safety from flood for their city.[1]   The committee has labored ceaselessly since its organization to present the case of New Orleans.   It sent an abundance of well prepared and convincing literature to governors, cabinet members, congressmen and even presidents.[2]   It furnished much evidence and made strong fights before Congressional Committees and argued the case of New Orleans throughout the country, especially before organizations of engineers.[3]

The stock argument of the " outletters " is simple, and it appears well-founded.   The flood water can admittedly be taken away very easily by diversion channels below the mouth of the Arkansas to such an extent as to remove serious floods below that point.   The direct conclusion is that diversion channels should be constructed without delay.[4]   The river has naturally sought its former outlets that have been closed by levees.   Many crevasses in past floods have poured water into these outlets.   New Orleans has been frequently benefited by the crevasses that ruined the people of nearby communities. The wealth of that city has enabled it to maintain a margin of safety over its less wealthy neighbors by a competitive system of levee building.[5]   The influence of a crevasse was clearly shown by the one at Poydras in 1922.   It gave New Orleans 2.7 feet relief; and it had some influence for a distance of 160 miles up and down the river.[6]   A crevasse that sends the

[1] *House Committee on Flood Control, Hearings 1922*, p. 161.

[2] John Klorer, *Report of Engineers Committee of the Safe River Committee of 100*, 1922, p. 1.

[3] *Engineering News-Record*, vol. 90, Jan. 4, 1923, p. 21.

[4] *The New Orleans States*, April 18, 1897.

[5] *House Committee on Flood Control, Hearings 1916*, p. 105.

[6] *Ibid., Hearings 1922*, p. 159.

water to the Gulf by a route other than the Mississsippi simply serves as an uncontrolled diversion channel that was accidentally made, and it has the same effect as the withdrawal of an equal amount of water by a controlled diversion. The supporters of the outlet theory have pointed out the fact that levees have been built higher and higher after each great flood with apparently no way of telling what the ultimate height will be; and that withdrawal of water from the river offered the only real hope for control.[1]

The city of New Orleans has made an especial plea for a definite control height because of its port facilities. These facilities have been built on the levees. They must be kept above flood heights.[2] It will cost many millions to raise the wharves and other facilities which New Orleans has built with public funds. Thus, citizens cannot be blamed for wanting absolute protection if such can be obtained. They have for several years earnestly urged that levees have not and cannot give such protection.[3] This has been especially true since the remarkable series of floods from 1912 to 1922 seriously shook the faith of the people of the lower part of the delta in the levee system and demonstrated to them the value of crevasses in reducing flood heights.[4]

As aggressive and determined as the " outletters " have been, they have been met with just as determined and stubborn resistance from the supporters of the policy of levees only. Practically every report by an United States official board of engineers prior to 1927 severely condemned the outlet theory of control.[5] The Senate Committee on Commerce

---

[1] *Chicago Tribune*, April 25, 1897, p. 32.

[2] *House Committee on Flood Control, Hearings 1916*, p. 107.

[3] *Ibid.*, p. 113.

[4] *House Committee on Flood Control*, 70th Cong., 1st Sess., 1927-8, *Committee Doc.*, no. 10, p. 7.

[5] *House Executive Document*, no. 127, 43rd Cong., 2nd Sess., 1875, p. 31.

in 1882 expressed the viewpoint of the committees that preceded and followed it when it expressed a " firm opposition " to any plan to reduce flood heights by " so-called outlets ".[1] The state legislature of Louisiana expressed the views of southern states' officials in 1890 by a concurrent resolution severely condemning the " outlet theory as impracticable and as destructive of the property interests of this state and people ".[2]   The Inter-State Mississippi River Improvement and Levee Convention, which was the recognized organization of those responsible for improvement of the river, in a great convention at Vicksburg in 1890, resolved that it was the judgment of that convention that the " outlet theory was impractical and dangerous ".[3]   Practically all of the commercial bodies and all of the leading newspapers opposed diversion until a comparatively recent date.[4]

The Mississippi River Commission, which has dominated the flood-control policy since its creation in 1879, has until very recently been opposed to anything but levees.   The Commission has frequently been accused of prejudice against diversion.[5]   However, its attitude became less certain as the flood heights increased.   Col. C. McD. Townsend stated in 1923 that the majority of the Commission had endorsed favorably located spillways since 1912.[6]   During this period it was felt that the plea of New Orleans sprang from a desire to protect her wharves, which had been built, upon advice of the city's own engineers, on levees below standards set by

[1] *Senate Document*, no. 245, 58th Cong., 2nd Sess., 1904, p. 3.

[2] *Cong. Record*, 51st Cong., 1st Sess., pt. 6, 1890, p. 5271.

[3] *Inter-State Mississippi River Improvement and Levee Convention, Resolutions*, 1890, p. 1.

[4] New Orleans, *Times-Democrat*, April 10, 1882, p. 4.

[5] *House Committee on Flood Control, Hearings 1922*, p. 164.

[6] *Engineering News-Record*, vol. 90, Jan. 4, 1923, p. 24.

the Commission.[1] As far back as 1893, three members of
the Commission filed a minority report, which agreed with
the majority report, that a diversion channel that took off
water at all stages of the river would be inadvisable, but suggested that a waste weir that would only take off the tops of
floods might be beneficial.[2] Members of the Commission
have frequently admitted that flood heights would certainly
be reduced by spillways.[3] The Commission has, in fact until
the present, maintained one very important outlet. When
the water in the Mississippi is higher than the water in the
Red river it flows through Old river, which connects the
Mississippi and the Red, into the Red and the Atchafalaya.
Then, it flows through the Atchafalaya to the Gulf.[4] This
outlet was the subject of a very detailed official study in
1914 by a special board of engineers. This board favored
keeping open the Atchafalaya outlet in spite of strong pressure
in favor of closing it.[5] However, until the 1927 flood the
Mississippi River Commission can only be considered as
hostile to diversion because it always clung to the policy of
levees only and rejected all efforts to get construction of
diversion channels.

The main argument of the Commission against diverting
flood waters has been based on the supposed effects of
diversion on the main stream of the river. The first part
of the contention holds that outlets decrease the cross section
below them. This phase of the question was stressed in
1879 by Professor Caleb G. Forshey, one of the best students

[1] *House Committee on Flood Control*, 70th Cong., 1st Sess., 1927-8,
Committee Doc., no. 1, p. 50.

[2] *House Committee on Flood Control, Hearings 1922*, p. 164.

[3] *Senate Committee on Commerce, Hearings 1904*, p. 88.

[4] *Engineering News-Record*, vol. 90, Jan. 4, 1923, p. 24.

[5] *House Document*, no. 841, 63rd Cong., 2nd Sess., p. 2.

of flood control in his time.[1]   The action of the outlet means increased velocity above it, and decreased velocity below it. That condition would cause large deposits of sediment in the bed of the main stream below, which would in turn cause a piling up of water and give only temporary relief.[2]   The opponents of outlets have never failed to stress this point. They have cited the records of such methods in European countries where diversions were tried and abandoned years ago.[3]   Silt-bearing streams certainly have complex engineering problems in handling the silt as well as in handling the flood waters.   However, the opinion that sediment would deposit below outlets and, therefore, in the long run, so disturb and limit the capacity of the main stream as to seriously impair its carrying capacity has not been universally held, although this theory has received the sanction of many engineers.   Ellet doubted that diversion would seriously affect the channel of the main stream.[4]   The engineers of the Safe River Committee of 100 maintained that sediment would not deposit in the main channel because the river did not carry the maximum of sediment at its greatest height, but after it had receded a few feet.[5]   However, this conclusion did not have sufficient support, since it had been drawn wholly from a series of tests by the New Orleans water-purification plant.

The danger that the flood water might break through to the Gulf and cause the river to leave its present channel has been the cause of much opposition to diversion.   The soil of the lower delta erodes very easily.   The distance to the Gulf

[1] *Cong. Record*, 45th Cong., 3rd Sess., pt. 1, 1879.

[2] *Engineering News-Record*, vol. 94, April 2, 1925, p. 556.

[3] *Journal of the Association of Engineers*, vol. 49, Oct., 1912, p. 126.

[4] *House Committee on Flood Control*, 70th Cong., 1st Sess., 1927-8, *Commitee Doc.*, no. 17, p. 82.

[5] John Klorer, *Report of Engineering Comm. to Safe River Committee of 100*, 1922, p. 9.

by some of the natural channels is only half as far as it is by the main river. The total difference in elevation being the same, the velocity of the currents would be much greater than that of the main stream.[1] That situation becomes more alarming when the slope of the territory adjacent to the river is taken into consideration. The natural fall of the Mississippi in the vicinity of New Orleans is about one-tenth of a foot per mile. The slope of the land from the river to Lake Borgne two miles away totals eight feet.[2] The fear that the river might make itself a new mouth has frightened most hydraulic engineers and most of the people of the lower part of the delta. Major Dabney, perhaps the outstanding personality in the history of levee building, feared the consequences of diversions and outlets.[3] The record of the Atchafalaya river furnishes a good basis for this contention. In our early history it was only an insignificant little stream. Flood waters from the Mississippi enlarged it until at flood it approached the size of the main stream. Government engineers became alarmed over the prospect of the river turning entirely through it and built engineering works to stop the enlargement. It is the opinion of the engineering profession that without these works the Mississippi would have gone through the Atchafalaya.

Another strong point in the opposition's arguments against the outlet theory has been that it would prove expensive and impracticable in comparison with the cost and practicability of control by levees. If diversion channels are used they must either be controlled by levees or permitted to run wild and perhaps flood large areas. The levees used to control diversion channels would not lessen the cost of control, but would increase it in the opinion of the Mississippi River

[1] *Journal of the Association of Engineers*, vol. 46, March, 1911, p. 188.
[2] *Engineering News-Record*, vol. 90, Jan. 4, 1923, p. 25.
[3] *Times-Picayune*, New Orleans, July 10, 1927, p. 14.

Commission.[1]   If waste weirs should be constructed proper foundations and regulation of flow would certainly be difficult and expensive to obtain.[2]   If a diversion channel protected by levees should be used the channel would have to be maintained.   Also, the flow would have to be carefully regulated.   Too great a velocity would be disastrous and too slow a one would cause it to fill with sediment.[3]   In 1923 the Chief of Engineers said at New Orleans that it would be cheaper to blow up the country levee when the city was menaced than it would be to pay the interest on the big investment of five or six million dollars to build a spillway.[4] That remark becomes exceedingly interesting in the light of developments during the 1927 flood.   The Mississippi River Commission in 1922 concluded that a spillway with a capacity of 230,000 second feet would be very hazardous and too expensive, and that both the hazard and the expense would increase rapidly as the danger of floods on the main stream was reduced.[5]

So, the people of New Orleans, represented by the Safe River Committee of 100, and the Mississippi River Commission could not agree on the method of control.   The President of the Commission said in 1925, " They will not be satisfied short of actual construction and demonstration, and the Commission will not recommend it ".[6]   Each side gathered many supporters and many critics both among those directly interested and among those technically qualified to speak.

[1] Col. C. McD. Townsend, *Speech at Memphis*, 1912, p. 7 (Pamphlet).

[2] *Engineering News-Record*, vol. 90, Jan. 4, 1913, p. 25.

[3] *House Committee on Flood Control*, 70th Cong., 1st Sess., 1927-8, *Committee Doc.*, no. 17, p. 30.

[4] *Ibid.*, no. 10, p. 7.

[5] New Orleans, *Times-Picayune*, May 23, 1922.

[6] *Engineering News-Record*, vol. 94, April 2, 1925, p. 556.

So far as any actual results have been concerned, the policy of the Federal government through 1926 adhered strictly to the theory of control by confining the water to the main stream by levees. The first official report of engineers to Congress in 1822 stated that the construction of levees was the only way to control the Mississippi.[1] Since that time Congress and army engineers have ordered many surveys and investigations of the river by engineers, committees, and commissions. Every report resulting from such surveys and investigations has practically recommended levees only.[2] A large majority of the members of Congress over a long period of years seemingly have had little doubt about the advantages of levees above all systems of control. Representative L. A. Sheldon of Louisiana in 1871 remarked that there was no question whatever at that late date but that levees were the only " proper means to be employed to prevent overflow ".[3] One Congressional Committee after another almost unanimously affirmed the " most absolute confidence in the sufficiency of levees ".[4] The Mississippi River Commission, which has since its creation been dominated by the Corps of Engineers of the United States army, never has varied its program of levees only; and that Commission had almost absolute control of the formulating and carrying out of the plans for federal participation in all flood-control works. The Commissioners from the beginning and through nearly fifty years almost unanimously agreed that confinement was the only practicable way.[5] The Commission's argument may be summed up by its own statement in it's official report for 1884 that " it is assumed that no argument " is necessary

[1] *House Committee on Flood Control, Hearings 1922*, p. 197.

[2] *Ibid., Hearings 1916*, p. 26.

[3] *Cong. Globe*, 42nd Cong., 2nd Sess., pt. 1, 1871, p. 284.

[4] *Senate Document*, no. 245, 58th Cong., 2nd Sess., 1904, p. 1.

[5] B. G. Humphreys, *Floods and Levees of the Mississippi River*, p. 45.

to prove the practicability of the levee system, which has been thoroughly " established by a large experience ".[1]   Civilian engineers likewise have almost unanimously urged embankments only.   The official report of the Committee of Engineers to the Convention at Vicksburg in 1890, which represented the organized flood-control element of the whole valley, stated that the " testimony of all engineers familiar with the subject " was that there was " no engineering difficulty " in controlling the river by levees and that the levee system was the " only agency " by which control could be accomplished.[2]   In 1912 the Louisiana Engineering Society, three hundred strong, and the Louisiana State Board of Engineers almost to a man urged levees only.[3]

The legislatures of delta states contributed their support to levees by resolutions and memorials that asserted unhesitatingly their " entire confidence " in the system as proposed by the Mississippi River Commission.[4]   Scores of towns and hundreds of various types of organizations deluged not only all committees but each Congress that dealt with flood control with resolutions and memorials, advocating control by a system of levees.[5]   Until the formation of the Safe River Committee of 100 the commercial interests of New Orleans stood squarely behind levees, being a real active interest in the early years of the Mississippi River Commission in fighting the " foolish and mischievous vagaries of Captain Cowden " and his followers who wanted diversion.[6]   The Asso-

[1] *Mississippi River Commission, Report of 1884*, p. 17.

[2] *Report of Committee of Engineers to Convention at Vicksburg in 1890*, p. 3.

[3] *House Committee on Flood Control*, 70th Cong., 1st Sess., 1927-8, *Committee Doc.*, no. 10, p. 6.

[4] *Cong. Record*, 51st Cong., 1st Sess., pt. 6, 1890, p. 5271.

[5] *Ibid.*, p. 5468.

[6] New Orleans, *Times-Democrat*, April 5, 1882, p. 4.

ciations of the valley which had as their purpose the securing of flood control could see no other method of control but levees. The great convention of the Mississippi River Improvement and Levee Association, which consisted of over one thousand delegates from twenty-seven states and 166 cities, at New Orleans in 1903, expressed absolute confidence in levees and condemned all methods for reducing flood heights.[1] This convention claimed to have presented the " unalterable sentiment of millions of American citizens ".[2] The press of the nation, especially the press of the delta area, in an almost united front praised levees. As late as 1922 the New Orleans *Times-Picayune* editorially urged levees and advised the people not to scatter or divide on the question.[3] Therefore, the oft-repeated statement that the people of the delta favored levees and that they had great confidence in them certainly was based upon good evidence.[4]

The reasoning of the " levees only " people was simple and direct. They asserted openly that confinement presented not only the best way to control floods on the Mississippi, but absolutely the only practicable way.[5] They maintained that all other plans had been tried in Europe and had failed. No workable plan of flood control could be devised, in their opinion, but to build levees " sufficiently high " and strong enough to hold.[6] They pointed with pride to the decreasing number of crevasses and the decreasing amount of lands inundated by each great flood.[7] The crevasses occurred not

[1] B. G. Humphreys, *Floods and Levees of Mississippi River*, p. 305.

[2] *Senate Committee on Commerce, Hearings 1904*, p. 44.

[3] New Orleans, *Times-Picayune*, May 8, 1922.

[4] *Senate Committee on Commerce, Hearings 1904*, p. 85.

[5] *Scientific American*, Feb. 15, 1913, p. 13.

[6] *House Committee on Flood Control, Hearings 1916*, p. 354.

[7] *House Committee on Flood Control*, 70th Cong., 1st Sess., 1927-8, Committee Doc., no. 2, p. 4.

because of any fault of the plan but because the plan had not been completed.[1]

The construction of a levee system necessarily called for the determination of standard heights and dimensions. The Mississippi River Commission early undertook to determine specifications on the basis of information about past floods, so that the levees would afford a margin of safety of three feet above the highest known water. Flood after flood broke past records. Each time the Commission changed its standards of grade and section to meet the new conditions.[2] Thus, much of the levee has never caught up with the ever-increasing standards. The weaker levees naturally broke first. So, before the flood of 1927, the supporters of levees always steadfastly maintained that no standard levee had ever failed to offer protection, and that a complete system of standard levees would offer ample protection for the whole delta. Representative B. G. Humphreys of Mississippi in 1917 asserted that the Mississippi River Commission had at last been able to ascertain very definitely just how strong to make the levees to withstand the highest flood that in all probability would ever come down the river. The vast majority of people seemed to take it for granted that levees offered the only feasible plan of control.[3]

However, from the beginning a militant, though often submerged, minority insisted either that levees would not protect or that levees needed supplemental agencies to help them. At the time of the formation of the Mississippi River Commission two schools of engineers in the United States held opposite views on the effect of levees on the river. One held that levees would increase the velocity and scour out the

[1] *Scientific American*, Feb. 15, 1913, vol. 108, p. 155.

[2] *House Committee on Flood Control*, 70th Cong., 1st Sess., 1927, *Committee Doc.*, no. 1, p. 25.

[3] *Senate Committee on Commerce, Hearings 1917*, p. 221.

channel so that no increase in flood heights would occur. The other group contended that levees would not enlarge the river section and that greatly increased heights would occur.[1] The Mississippi River Commission in its report of 1881 held that floods confined between embankments would scour out the bed and lower-flood heights.[2] Public opinion apparently agreed with the Mississippi River Commission that flood heights would not increase with the building of levees. The people apparently expected to see levees go up and flood heights go down or remain stationary.[3]

The first real shock seemingly came when the public discovered the fact that levees actually caused the floods to go higher.[4] They caused floods at Memphis to rise more than eight feet above their former levels.[5] At several other points increases were still greater. In 1914 an official board of engineers estimated that the flood of 1912 would have been increased four feet at most lower river points if the levees had been completed and had held. However, the same report contended that the increase would have been temporary because the waters would have finally enlarged the channel.[6]

From the beginning there has been some opposition to levees only, but it was only after they had been tried for a number of years that any considerable opposition developed. The real fight in an organized way began in 1912.[7] Many engineers and many laymen who " formerly ardently " sup-

---

[1] Col. C. McD. Townsend, *Speech at Memphis*, 1912, p. 9.

[2] *Mississippi River Commission Report*, 1881, p. 123.

[3] *House Committee on Flood Control*, 70th Cong., 1st Sess., 1927, *Committee Doc.*, no. 24, p. 102.

[4] *Journal of the Western Society of Engineers*, vol. 5, Aug., 1900, p. 312.

[5] *Nature Magazine*, vol. v, April, 1925, p. 231.

[6] *House Document*, no. 841, 63rd Cong., 2nd Sess., p. 3.

[7] *The Nation*, vol. 124, May 11, 1927, p. 521.

ported " levees only " became convinced that some supplemental aids had to be adopted.[1] Congressional Committees began to hear much testimony from all parts of the country and from many classes of people that " levees only " would not protect entirely against floods.[2] The complaint developed into the firmly established belief that levees represented only a makeshift remedy and that they made " no permanent improvement ".[3] The opponents of the system proclaimed loudly that the policy of confinement had "gone bankrupt".[4] Gifford Pinchot characterized the levees-only policy of the Mississippi River Commission as the " most colossal blunder in engineering history ".[5]

The major contention of the opponents grew out of the increasing height of floods from year to year and the corresponding increasing height of levees. The Mississippi River Commission itself has furnished plenty of evidence as to the greatly increased heights of floods caused by carrying out the confinement policy. A perusal of gauge readings at any station on the lower river will confirm that fact.[6] As the floods rose higher and higher from time to time the Mississippi River Commission simply raised the grade and increased the section of the standard levee. This greatly complicated the whole problem. The very nature of the delta soil suggests that it forms a very poor foundation for any structure of great weight. Recent years have brought numerous levee breaks from collapse due to poor founda-

[1] John Klorer, *Report of Engineering Committee to Safe River Committee of 100*, 1922, p. 6.

[2] *House Committee on Flood Control, Hearings 1922*, p. 36.

[3] *Review of Reviews*, vol. 47, June, 1913, p. 697.

[4] *The Nation*, vol. 124, May 11, 1927, p. 521.

[5] *Manufacturers Record*, vol. 91, June 9, 1927, p. 55.

[6] *House Committee on Flood Control*, 70th Cong., 1st Sess., 1927-8, *Committee Doc.*, no. 10, p. 49.

tions.[1] Outlets for swamps to drain into the Mississippi and the mouths of small tributary streams form particularly poor foundations. And just at those places the levees must be highest. So, engineers have begun to fear that levees of greater grade and section cannot be supported. The worst feature of weak foundations is that they sometimes do not show until the flood reaches great heights and exerts great pressure. And the contractors could not be blamed for they had secured the best possible foundation. The Ferriday levee in 1922 showed no weakness at 53.5 feet on the Natchez gauge, but it failed completely at 55 feet. Hymelia levee appeared secure at 20.3 feet on the Canal Street gauge but went out at 21.5 feet.[2] And, of course, many weaknesses show from the very beginning. Sinking levees offer no novelty to contractors, which means that they simply pile up more earth until the sinking stops and the embankments reach the required standards. The problem becomes more serious when levees cave into the river with the ever-caving banks, because the land nearest the river offers the best side for levees.[3] The land there is not only higher, but also has a thicker deposit of alluvium of more substantial materials over the quicksand foundation. In many places levees have been moved back several times, each time being rebuilt on a poorer foundation.[4] Undoubtedly this is a most serious defect of the system. Crevasses cannot be eliminated under such conditions. And crevasses become much more dangerous as the size of the levees increases and as the population behind them grows.[5] Then, the conclusion that levees offer only temporary relief apparently has a reasonable basis.

[1] B. E. Moses, *The Problem of the Mississippi River*, p. 7.

[2] John Klorer, *Report of Engineering Committee to Safe River Committee of 100, 1922*, p. 7.

[3] *House Committee on Flood Control, Hearings 1916*, p. 63.

[4] *Ibid.*, p. 69.

[5] John Klorer, *Report of Engineering Committee to Safe River Committee of 100, 1922*, p. 8.

The opponents of levees have weakened their position and made themselves ridiculous and laughable by frequent assertions that the bed of the Mississippi was rising and getting higher than the surrounding territory. One feels like dismissing the idea with the assertion of Hon. R. S. Taylor, a well-known member of the Mississippi River Commission, when he said, " I often wonder how so many people get hold of that idea who have so few others ".[1] However, that cannot be done, for this simple statement has not always come from simple people. This was one of the strongest arguments presented against levees to Congressional Committees in their various hearings that preceded the creation of the Mississippi River Commission.[2] Some of our leading men in fields much interested in and rather closely related to flood control as late as 1927 still maintained that silt constantly raised the bed of the river.[3] And some of our leading magazines and newspapers in the same year still clung to that out-of-date theory.[4] The fact that the banks of the river rise higher than the adjoining lands may be responsible for that erroneous belief. And the Yellow river in China, which has a dreadful history of floods, seems to have impressed many. But this is a very flat shallow river practically without banks; while the Mississippi is a very deep river with very high banks, which makes them entirely different problems for the hydraulic engineer.[5] The Mississippi River Commission early established a very scientific system of bench marks and soundings so that as long as the bench marks remained the cross sections of the river could be reproduced scientifically.[6]

---

[1] B. G. Humphreys, *Floods and Levees of the Mississippi River*, p. 48.

[2] *House Report*, no. 44, 42nd Cong., 2nd Sess., 1872, p. 7.

[3] *American Review of Reviews*, vol. 76, Nov., 1927, p. 487.
   The Outlook, vol. 146, May 11, 1927, p. 42.

[5] *House Committee on Flood Control, Hearings 1916*, p. 53.

[6] *Senate Committee on Commerce, Hearings 1904.*

Minute surveys in 1882, 1894, and 1904 showed conclusively that the bed had not risen, but that the cross section had increased very slightly, which variation might have been due to probable error.[1]   There has been no evidence of any material change at all in the river's regimen.   Then, this idea must be listed as perhaps the greatest fallacy concerning the Mississippi river.[2]   The evidence seems indisputable that the bed has not risen.[3]   In the words of a well known writer, that theory appears to be " entirely and literally without foundation ".[4]

But the opposition to levees only has grown stronger with each flood.   And the Mississippi River Commission, until the flood of 1927, remained firm in its contention that levees offered the only hope of relief.   After each flood the Mississippi River Commission's report would assert that the results had shown more clearly than ever that a system of standard levees would control floods, that they represented the only practicable way, and that the failure of the system had been entirely due to the fact that it had not been completed.[5]   As floods grew higher, as damages grew heavier, and as the Mississippi River Commission continued to cling tenaciously to levees only, severe criticism of the Mississippi River Commission naturally developed.   It was accused of clinging to old engineering theories that had long since been disproved.[6]   Competent engineers have said that the Mississippi River Commission put the cart before the horse in

[1] *Engineering and Contracting*, vol. 53, Jan. 14, 1920, p. 37.

[2] *House Committee on Flood Control*, 70th Cong., 1st Sess., 1927-8, *Committee Doc.*, no. 1, p. 244.

[3] *Engineering News-Record*, vol. 92, Feb. 14, 1924, p. 280.

[4] *Current History*, vol. 26, June, 1927, p. 459.

[5] B. G. Humphreys, *Floods and Levees of the Mississippi River*, p. 55.

[6] *House Committee on Flood Control*, 70th Cong., 1st Sess., 1927-8, *Committee Doc.*, no. 10, p. 3.

that it drew its conclusions first and then tried to find evidence to justify the conclusions.[1]   The members of the Commission have been dominated by the Corps of Engineers of the United States army, which has long drawn the fire of many. The army engineers have been called " old fogies and men of routine ".[2]   Their methods have been termed rule-of-thumb methods.[3]   Gifford Pinchot stated that it was a cardinal principle of the engineers that the Corps must never be wrong.[4]   Therefore, the Mississippi River Commission has felt that its duty was to uphold the policy of levees only because many years ago the Corps said that was the only way.   Thus, all contrary facts, even the flood of 1922, had failed to cause any change until the great calamity of 1927. Pinchot quotes Theodore Roosevelt as saying that it was the army engineers who kept the plan of the Inland Waterways Commission from being adopted.   They still insisted on levees only.[5]   In such a situation the people of the country knew that the levees would win.   If they held the result would be a tremendous and overwhelming argument for levees; and, if they broke, the result would also be a convincing argument for the levees.[6]   It is little wonder, then, that the Commission received much severe criticism.   But its supporters were legion, and they did not fail to rush to the aid of the beleaguered Commission.

The final method that has been proposed, strictly speaking, could hardly be called a method, although it has been labeled the comprehensive plan for flood control.   The plan, as the word comprehensive suggests, proposes a combination of all

[1] *House Committee on Flood Control, Hearings 1922*, p. 180.

[2] *Cong. Record*, 43rd Cong., 2nd Sess., pt. 2, 1875, p. 1447.

[3] *Annals of the American Academy of Political and Social Science*, vol. 135, Jan., 1928, p. 54.

[4] *The Survey*, vol. 58, July 1, 1927, p. 367.

[5] *Ibid.*, p. 368.

[6] Memphis, *The Commercial Appeal*, April 4, 1913.

the plans already discussed. Doubtless many of our people have viewed the Mississippi problem in the light of a choice between levees and other methods of control. The people who favor the comprehensive plan insist that the ultimate correct way will be a coordinated combination of all methods.[1] They admit that levees will go far toward solving the flood problem, but maintain that other aids must be added to insure success.[2] The idea that the flood problem would finally have to be considered in a very large and inclusive way has constantly grown.[3] The group composing the comprehensive plan supporters has in it practically all who favor forests, reservoirs, or any other plan for flood control besides levees.[4]

Prior to 1927, only one important official United States engineering report had suggested any idea of a comprehensive plan. That was the Ellet report of 1852, which suggested levees, spillways and reservoirs.[5] But many outside the official circles early began the fight. A writer in *De-Bow's Review* in 1851 stated that the " prevailing sentiment " seemed to be that levees alone could not be depended upon.[6] However, the present century was about a decade old before much headway had been made in the movement for a more comprehensive plan of control. President Roosevelt, by appointing the Inland Waterways Commission, which urged a scientific study of all rivers as units from their sources to their mouths, gave great impetus to the movement.[7] The

[1] *Annals of the American Academy of Political and Social Science,* vol. 135, Jan., 1928, p. 55.

[2] Barbour Lewis, *Speech on Levees of the Mississippi*, House, June 6, 1874.

[3] *American Review of Reviews*, vol. 75, p. 566.

[4] *Journal of Forestry*, May, 1927, p. 508.

[5] Charles Ellet, *Mississippi and Ohio Rivers, Plans for the Protection of the Delta from Inundation*, p. 18.

[6] *De Bow's Review*, vol. x, Feb., 1851, p. 224.

[7] *Senate Committee on Commerce, Hearings 1917*, p. 8.

National Waterways Commission, which Congress created in 1909, served to some extent to further the idea.[1] The Pittsburgh Flood Commission was organized in 1906 by public-spirited citizens as a civic organization devoted solely to the regulation of rivers and the utilization of water resources. It soon spent large sums studying the flood problem.[2] The work, the attitude and the reports by that Commission have been strong influences for an elaborate plan of control.[3]

Senator Francis G. Newlands emerged in Congress as the leader of those who wanted a comprehensive plan. For several years he introduced at every session of Congress a flood-control bill that provided for large expenditures to control rivers from their sources to their mouths.[4] He also introduced several bills for the co-ordination of the several Executive Departments interested in water regulation and control for the purpose of regulating rivers through a single board.[5] In 1917 Senator Broussard of Louisiana joined him in introducing the Newlands-Broussard bill that provided an elaborate plan of co-ordination of agencies and a comprehensive plan of control.[6] He never succeeded, but his long fights and his presentation of so much data did much to advance the idea that he fought for and made him a thorn in the side of the Mississippi River Commission. He perhaps made a serious mistake in frankly including lots of projects to get votes in Congress.[7] The death of Senator Newlands in 1919 relieved the Mississippi River Commission of his

[1] *Senate Document*, no. 301, 1910, p. 3.

[2] *House Committee on Flood Control, Hearings 1922*, p. 171.

[3] *United States Daily*, May 6, 1927, p. 1.

[4] *Journal of the Association of Engineers*, vol. 49, Oct., 1912, p. 115.

[5] Francis G. Newlands, *National Waterways*, vol. i, p. 316.

[6] *Senate Committee on Commerce, Hearings 1917*, p. 15.

[7] *Journal of the Association of Engineers*, vol. 49, p. 115.

powerful opposition.[1]   The only tangible result of his long
and determined fight was section 18 of the Rivers and
Harbors bill of 1917, by which the levees-only people were
compelled to accept a compromise that allotted $250,000 for
investigations and reports concerning various plans of stream
regulation.[2]   But Newlands' death did not end the fight.
Gifford Pinchot and many others have continuously argued
that no one point of view ought to control, but that plans
should be co-ordinated into a unified single plan.[3]   They
hold that prevention is better than cure.   George H. Max-
well, Executive Director of the National Reclamation Association, in 1922 spoke prophetically when he prophesied that
a " cataclysm " for the lower valley was eminent unless a
broad-minded plan was soon adopted.[4]   J. Russell Smith has
recommended a most comprehensive scheme that ranges all
the way from a new type of hill-farming to a utilization of
the silt of the Mississippi as fertilizer.[5]   Of course he would
retain levees but he would supplement them with forests, reservoirs, spillways and other methods.   Judged in this light,
the economic idea that flood control may be regarded as a by-
product of the effective use of land does not seem at all far
fetched.[6]   The people who have supported the comprehensive plan have had splendid arguments for their main contentions.   But they have not been able to get Congress nor the
general public to accept such a complex and far-sighted plan.

[1] Walter Parker, *Why Flood Control and River Regulation Are Essential to the Economic Welfare of the Mississippi Valley*, p. 7.

[2] *The Nation*, vol. 124, May 11, 1927, p. 521.

[3] *The Survey*, vol. 58, July 1, 1927, p. 369.

[4] *Manufacturers Record*, vol. 91, June 2, 1927, p. 79.

[5] *The Survey*, vol. 58, July 1, 1927, p. 372.

[6] *American Forests and Forest Life*, vol. 33, July, 1927, p. 447.

CHAPTER VII

Progress under the Mississippi River Commission, 1879-1926

The strong agitation that had been carried on in behalf of the control of floods on the Mississippi resulted in the creation of the Mississippi River Commission in 1879. Congress officially recognized, for the first time, that it had a share in the control of floods on the Mississippi.[1] Thus, 1879 marked the beginning of systematic efforts to control floods both on the part of the nation and on the part of the local governments.[2] The people of the delta about 1875 had made renewed efforts to rebuild their dilapidated levees, but they still worked in the old independent and disorganized way.[3] From the Civil War to 1879 they had spent approximately five million dollars in their unrelated efforts.[4] They had little to show for their efforts and expenditures.

In the meantime, the United States government had been spending considerable money on the improvement of the Mississippi, but that had nothing to do with flood control. Before the creation of the Mississippi River Commission all Federal funds for the Mississippi had been under river and harbor control and had been spent wholly for channel and harbor improvement.[5] These two jurisdictions had control of the Mississippi, each going its own way with little regard

[1] *Senate Committee on Commerce, Hearings 1904*, p. 68.

[2] *House Committee on Flood Control, Hearings 1922*, p. 105.

[3] *Rand-McNally Banker's Monthly*, vol. 32, Feb., 1915, p. 14.

[4] *Cong. Record*, 47th Cong., 1st Sess., pt. 4, 1882, p. 3215.

[5] *Journal of the Association of Engineers*, vol. 49, Sept., 1912, p. 92.

to the other.[1] The states responded to the Federal legislation creating the Mississippi River Commission by the creation of levee boards that could more easily co-operate with the new Commission.[2] The Mississippi River Commission and the levee boards thus inherited the work of a century of levee building of the most disorganized manner.[3] The levees then existing had been built by crude methods; they had been neglected and even destroyed wilfully during the Civil War; and a remarkable series of floods had finally almost annihilated them.[4] The new organizations really had very little with which to start work. But the fact that the United States was coming to the rescue loomed highly important.[5] The Mississippi River Commission had to establish standards for its work without any accurate data.[6] Its original work was done under an appropriation act of 1881. The first projects were confined to two small reaches of river totaling seventy-two miles in length, and were designed to aid navigation.[7] For the first three years the Commission limited its work to repairing and closing gaps in levees. But that afforded plenty of work, for practically all of the levees needed repairs, and many miles had been destroyed leaving extensive gaps. In 1884 the Commission revised its policy somewhat and decided to strengthen levees to "prevent further breaks".[8] Then, in 1895, the Commission again

[1] *House Committee on Flood Control*, 70th Cong., 1st Sess., 1927-8, *Report to Accompany House Bill*, no. 8219, p. 6.

[2] *House Report*, no. 300, pt. 2, 63rd Cong., 2nd Sess., 1914, p. 31.

[3] *World's Work*, vol. 54, Aug., 1927, p. 409.

[4] *Mississippi River Commission, Report 1923*, p. 1887.

[5] R. S. Taylor, *Mississippi River Improvement*, p. 30.

[6] Col. C. McD. Townsend, *Speech at Memphis*, 1912, p. 9.

[7] *House Committee on Flood Control*, 70th Cong., 1st Sess., 1927, *Committee Document*, no. 1, p. 22.

[8] *Mississippi River Commission, Report 1884*, p. 287.

changed its policy, much to the pleasure of the people of the delta, and decided to aid in the construction of new levees. The first Federal aid in the construction of new flood-control works under the Mississippi River Commission was in the St. Francis basin.[1]   This change in the policy of the Federal government was very significant.

The Mississippi River Commission consists of seven members, of whom three are appointed from the Corps of Engineers of the United States army, three from civil life and one from the United States Coast and Geodetic Survey.[2] It has the power to initiate plans.   The law creating the Commission provided for surveys and plans, but it did not make any provision for actual construction.   The first meeting was held on August 19, 1879 for the purpose of organizing to carry out the provisions of the act of that year.[3]   But actual construction had to await appropriations from Congress.[4] For the construction of works, the jurisdiction of the Commission originally was limited to the main river from the mouth of the Ohio to the Head of the Passes, but for surveys and investigation it had jurisdiction to the headwaters.[5] Jurisdiction has been extended from time to time until by 1926 the Mississippi River Commission had control over construction on the main river from Rock Island, Illinois to the Head of the Passes, and on tributaries in so far as they influenced floods on the Mississippi river.[6]   The Commission holds three or four meetings annually.   Two of the meetings usually consist of inspection trips of about ten days each.

[1] *Engineering and Contracting*, vol. 53, Jan. 14, 1929, p. 36.

[2] *House Committee on Flood Control*, 70th Cong., 1st Sess., 1927, *Committee Document*, no. 7, p. 5.

[3] *Cong. Record*, 47th Cong., 1st Sess., pt. 3, 1882, p. 2942.

[4] *House Committee on Levees and Improvements, Hearings 1906*, p. 2.

[5] *Ibid.*

[6] *Mississippi River Commission Report*, 1923, p. 1869.

For purposes of administration committees have been created, such as the levee committee or the dredging committee.[1] Then, the river itself has been divided into districts as administrative units. However, the Commission does not do the actual construction. The Secretary of War details any required number of army engineers to supervise the work of contractors.[2]

In the matter of building levees, the Commission's jurisdiction has been divided with, or in a large part superseded by, that of the State. The jurisdictions of the Federal government and state governments have from the beginning been peculiarly mixed in the regulation of the Mississippi. However, levee building at first was purely a local function with Federal authority confined strictly to matters concerning navigation.[3] When the Federal government succeeded in actually aiding in construction the people of the delta saw that some agency having wide powers must represent the jurisdiction of the state. The levee boards provided the answer. The various states created levee districts, which were governed by commissioners in varying numbers from three to twenty-four, generally appointed by the governors.[4] The states gave those districts very wide powers, almost unlimited, within their spheres of action. They could levy taxes and issue bonds against the property of the districts.[5] They could condemn property under the power of eminent domain.[6] The titles to levees in the districts passed to the

[1] *House Committee on Flood Control, Hearings 1916*, p. 241.

[2] *Mississippi River Commission Report*, 1923, p. 1873.

[3] *House Committee on Flood Control*, 70th Cong., 1st Sess., 1927-8, *Report to Accompany House Bill*, no. 8219, p. 6.

[4] *House Committee on Flood Control, Hearings 1916*, p. 255.

[5] *Ibid.*, p. 48.

[6] *Ibid.*, p. 66.

levee boards and have remained there.[1]   The Mississippi
River Commission then worked through the local levee
boards.   The local boards in some states have a loose supervision by a state board of engineers, which has only a limited
veto power, and in some cases the power to locate levees.[2]
Whether the Mississippi River Commission has dealt with
local boards or with state engineers its advice has generally
been willingly followed, both in the location and in the construction of levees, although the local authorities theoretically
have broad powers.[3]   Those who have maintained that the
Mississippi River Commission had become merely an agency
for distributing funds to the state levee boards have overlooked the very general manner in which the advice of the
Commission has prevailed.[4]

The Mississippi River Commission and the local boards
have apparently worked well together.   The Commission
after much study established a standard grade and section for
levees.   Although standards have been changed from time
to time to meet new conditions all seem to have striven enthusiastically to raise levees to the existing standards.[5] Naturally,
they have not always had the funds they desired or needed.
Often one had the money and the other did not, a condition
which caused the work to lag considerably.[6]   The Commission had to depend on appropriations by Congress and the
local boards had to raise funds by taxation and by floating
loans.   The levee boards generally went the legal limit in
bonds.   They then resorted to almost every type of tax

[1] *Cong. Record*, 64th Cong., 1st Sess., pt. 11, 1916, p. 8792.

[2] *American Railway Engineering Association*, vol. 29, July, 1927, p. 11.

[3] *House Committee on Flood Control, Hearings 1916*, p. 240.

[4] B. E. Moses, *The Problem of the Mississippi River*, p. 3.

[5] *House Committee on Flood Control*, 70th Cong., 1st Sess., 1927-8,
Report to Accompany House Bill, no. 8219, p. 10.

[6] *Ibid.*, p. 11.

possible in their districts, namely, general property, acreage, mileage tax on railways, commodity tax on crops grown, and others.[1] Generally, the Commission has had more funds than the local boards, but some time the reverse has been true. After the Flood Control Act of 1917 most levee boards obtained special permission from the legislatures to exceed the legal bonded indebtedness. At the same time creditors became very liberal with them. So, the local boards had large amounts of funds available that the Commission could not meet.[2]

The conflict of jurisdiction becomes most noticeable in times of danger from floods. Fighting floods requires military discipline and military precision. Men work twenty-four hours per day, if necessary, and levee boards spend money freely.[3] Some strong centralized power has frequently been greatly needed. But the Commission has generally assumed rather full authority. For example, during the flood of 1913, the Mississippi River Commission wired all local levee boards, United States employees, and contractors, giving very explicit and detailed instructions concerning the impending fight; instructions which were enforced.[4] The work of fighting floods under the Commission has progressed so smoothly that the vast majority of the leaders and of the people of the delta have seemed rather well satisfied with it.[5]

Yet, there has been much criticism of the Commission. Federal incorporation of levee boards has been urged as a means of co-ordinating the work.[6] Bills have been intro-

[1] *House Committee on Flood Control, Hearings 1916*, p. 48.

[2] *House Committee on Flood Control*, 70th Cong., 1st Sess., 1927-8, *Report to Accompany House Bill*, no. 8219, p. 11.

[3] *House Committee on Flood Control, Hearings 1922*, p. 87.

[4] *Mississippi River Commission, Report 1913*, p. 3575.

[5] *House Committee on Flood Control, Hearings 1916*, p. 65.

[6] *Ibid.*, p. 45.

duced to place the powers of the Mississippi River Commission in another commission of a more inclusive nature and with more authority,[1] or directly under the President.[2] Francis G. Newlands went so far as to accuse Congress of avoiding co-ordination efforts at the request of the army engineers, who desired to " maintain absolute isolation ".[3]

A very peculiar feature of the flood-control efforts of the Federal government has been the determination of Congress to carry it on in the name of navigation, although all knew that channel improvement had very little or nothing to do with the problem. Prior to 1890 the United States government spent all funds for levees strictly for the purpose of improving the navigation of the river.[4] Its policy has been stated by the Rivers and Harbors bill of 1881, which adopted the project of the Mississippi River Commission with the proviso that absolutely no part of the funds provided should be used for building levees to protect lands against overflow, and that all funds must be spent for channel improvement.[5] Thus, Congress began the construction of levees, which have protected against floods, solely in the aid of navigation. Senators and Representatives from the delta states from the beginning wanted appropriations for the avowed purpose of controlling floods, and for that purpose they frequently offered bills and amendments which they withdrew as soon as they saw that their contentions might endanger the passage of appropriation acts. Senator Garland of Arkansas said in 1882, in discussing this phase of the question, that he had no doubt but that " this work will be done directly in a few years " but at that time it was best to build levees only to improve

[1] Francis G. Newlands, *National Waterways*, vol. i, p. 321.

[2] B. E. Moses, *The Problem of the Mississippi River*, p. 5.

[3] Francis G. Newlands, *National Waterways*, vol. i, p. 321.

[4] *House Committee on Flood Control, Hearings 1916*, p. 17.

[5] B. G. Humphreys, *Floods and Levees of the Mississippi River*, p. 42.

" navigation ".[1] The plans of the Mississippi River Commission always provided extensive levee repair, replacement and construction on the lower river. The Congressional committees knew that these plans meant flood control, but they had the evidence of practically all official reports that they meant the improvement of navigation.[2] Of course the fear of the unconstitutionality of flood control was the great force behind the determination to keep navigation to the front, because none expressed a doubt about the constitutionality of Federal expenditures to improve navigation. Senator Benjamin Harrison of Indiana exhibited a typical position in 1882.[3] He made a lengthy argument for levees to aid navigation, but frankly admitted in his speech that he well knew that they would be largely for the purpose of preventing overflows. He firmly believed any expenditure for protection against floods was contrary to the constitution. Yet, he voted for the appropriation, because he could hide behind channel improvement. The first idea of navigation improvement was that it applied only to low-water navigation. In the appropriation bill of 1892, admitted flood control advanced a step when its supporters obtained the statement that the money could be expended for " the general improvement of the river " and for the " building of levees . . . . in such a manner as in their opinion shall best improve navigation and promote the interests of commerce at all stages of the river ".[4] The addition of highwater improvement of navigation proved important in advancing toward avowed flood-control expenditures, but the idea of navigation improvement hung on. The appropriation act of 1906 offered an illustration. The money was made available for the improvement

[1] *Cong. Record*, 47th Cong., 1st Sess., pt. 4, 1882, p. 3260.

[2] *Ibid.*, pt. 3, 1882, p. 2941.

[3] *Ibid.*, 1882, pt. 4, p. 3136.

[4] B. G. Humphreys, *Floods and Levees of the Mississippi River*, p. 52.

of the river with the proviso that " such expenditure shall only be made for improvements which shall be useful for the purposes of navigation ".[1]   The appropriation of 1916 was made " to improve navigation and promote the interests of commerce ".[2]

The various Congressional Committees that have held hearings and have made reports on flood control and river improvement have appeared very anxious to keep navigation before Congress.   For that purpose they have frequently asked members of the Mississippi River Commission and other witnesses whether they would build levees if the control of floods were entirely left out of the question and only the improvement of navigation were considered.[3]   The witnesses have well understood the purpose of that hypothetical question and have almost invariably replied with a knowing affirmative.   Early commissioners frequently stated that they would most assuredly build levees to deepen and improve the channel if flood considerations were entirely left out.[4]   Lieut.-Col. C. R. Suter, a member of the Mississippi River Commission, in 1890 testified before the Senate Committee that he would carry out the Mississippi River Commission plans if the people of the valley were entirely disregarded.[5]   The annual reports of the Commission, especially those of 1893 and 1896, contain full and well-developed expositions of the effects of levees on navigation.   Then Senate Committee on Commerce in 1904 showed its feelings when it reported that in addition to providing for the prevention of floods " the mind of the nation should be constantly advised of the commercial importance of the Mississippi river as a highway of

[1] *Cong. Record*, 59th Cong., 1st Sess., pt. 10, 1906, p. 9281.
[2] *Cong. Record*, 64th Cong., 1st Sess., pt. 9, 1916, p. 6673.
[3] *House Report*, no. 300, pt. 2, 63rd Cong., 2nd Sess., 1914, p. 57.
[4] B. G. Humphreys, *Floods and Levees of the Mississippi River*, p. 78.
[5] *Ibid.*, p. 247.

commerce ".[1] Even under the most liberal construction of
the term navigation improvement, one can hardly see how in
some cases the members of Congress could connect navigation
with some of its acts and with the acts of the Commission.
In March, 1897, an act of Congress provided $250,000 to
relieve flood sufferers and took that amount out of the appropriation made June 3, 1896, for river improvement.[2] Since
1882, the Commission has met funds of local boards for levee
building with no consideration of aid to navigation.[3]

Slowly but surely events moved toward building levees for
the avowed purpose of flood control by the Federal government. The Mississippi River Commission Report of 1912
stated what practically everyone knew when it said that " the
main purpose " of levees was " to protect the alluvial lands
and their owners " against overflow.[4] The plea became
stronger and stronger both in Congress and among the
people at large to remove the mask and to quit spending
money for flood control under the pretext of improving navigation.[5] Thus, in 1917 the Federal government for the first
time went into levee building frankly as a measure of flood
control.[6] The Flood-Control Act of that year stated that
the Federal government would spend money to control floods.

When the Mississippi River Commission organized itself
into an agency for the control of floods, even though the control had to be done in the name of navigation, its first task
was to determine what its objective in building levees would
be. The Commission gave much thought to the problem of

[1] *Senate Document*, no. 245, 58th Cong., 2nd Sess., 1904, p. 5.

[2] *Cong. Record*, 55th Cong., 1st Sess., pt. 1, 1897, p. 457.

[3] R. S. Taylor, *Mississippi River Improvements*, p. 7.

[4] *Mississippi River Commission, Report 1912*, p. 3724.

[5] *Cong. Record*, 64th Cong., 1st Sess., pt. 11, 1916, p. 8784.

[6] *House Committee on Flood Control*, 70th Cong., 1st Sess., 1927-8, p. 2017.

a proper standard for levees and went to work on the basis of protection against the highest known water.   Following the great flood of 1897, it decided to base its standard levee on the data secured from that flood.[1]   In the meantime, it had been decided that there should be three feet of levee above the water to furnish a proper margin of safety.[2]   So the standard levee was determined as three feet above the estimated confined heights of the highest flood on record.   Soon thereafter the standard section was determined.   It should have an eight-foot crown; a front slope of one on three; a rear slope of one on four with a banquette on land side twenty feet wide with a slope of one in ten.[3]   These standards were objected to by some as neither high nor strong enough; by others because they were higher and stronger than needed. They were regarded generally as only temporary standards which would be changed from time to time in the light of new experiences and new observations until the ultimate standard had been reached.[4]   The Commission took a moderate position on the data at hand, which naturally placed it between two groups of disputants.

Although the Commission has called all of its standards provisional and has refused to estimate the ultimate height of floods, it frequently has expressed great confidence in its program of levees only.   In 1895 Hon. R. S. Taylor, speaking for the Commission at Vicksburg, declared that he believed that the grade then standard was high enough and strong enough to confine any flood.[5]   After the flood of 1897 the Commission said that flood furnished proof that levees of sufficient height and strength to control floods could

[1] *Senate Document*, no. 600, 62nd Cong., 2nd Sess., p. 7.

[2] *House Committee on Levees and Improvements, Hearings 1906*, p. 9.

[3] *Journal of the Association of Engineers*, vol. 49, Sept., 1912, p. 63.

[4] Col. C. McD. Townsend, *Speech at Memphis*, 1912, p. 9.

[5] R. S. Taylor, *Mississippi River Improvement*, p. 11.

be built at reasonable cost and without any considerable difficulty.[1]   Before the flood of 1912, the Commission stated
that it had always been its purpose to require the most
possible from the riparian owners with the idea of ultimately
turning over the entire burden to them, and that the time
was very near for " the realization of that expectation ".[2]
Then in 1912 and 1913 came two of the worst floods in history.   Congress asked for an investigation and a report.
The entire membership of the Commission frankly admitted that the floods called for a revision of standards.
But they staunchly contended that levees offered the only
means of restraining such floods.   It was estimated that the
yardage in the levee line would have to be about doubled.[3]
The Commission further claimed that those floods had given
it sufficient data so that it could " resume operations with a
definite knowledge of the problem " before it.[4]   Meantime,
civilian engineers had frequently defended levees and expressed confidence in them.   After the 1912 flood it was
maintained that reason suggested that the ultimate high
water would hardly exceed the records of that year.[5]   The
Chief Engineer of Louisiana in the same year heartily condemned all propositions that were " tangible only in speech
and print " because the solution of the problem had come
" easily within our grasp " through the levee system.[6]   So,
the Commission revised its standards to meet conditions
shown by the results of the floods of 1912 and 1913, and continued confidently on its course of building levees only.   By

[1] *Mississippi River Commission, Report 1897*, p. 3721.

[2] *Ibid., Report 1911*, p. 12.

[3] B. G. Humphreys, *Floods and Levees of the Mississippi River*, p. 60.

[4] Col. C. McD. Townsend, *Speech at Memphis*, 1912, p. 11.

[5] *Journal of the Association of Engineers*, vol. 49, Sept., 1912, p. 63.

[6] *Ibid.*, p. 93.

1920 the Commission held the opinion that the levee line had become powerful enough to offer reasonable security against all but the greatest floods and to offer a good fighting chance of success against such floods as those of 1912 and 1913.[1] In 1923 members of the Commission showed confidence in their standards by declaring a five-foot margin above the flood line to be an expensive luxury except in front of large cities.[2]   Then, in 1926 the Mississippi River Commission took the position that the levees had reached a stage of construction that offered full protection to the delta.[3]

A perusal of the records of the work of the Commission during this period affords much reason for the confidence of both the people and the Commission in the levee system and in the ability of the Commission to cope with the problem. However, few could agree with a committee of New Orleans business men who declared after the flood of 1912 that New Orleans was as safe from Mississippi river floods as Boston.[4] In 1882 the levees contained about 33,000,000 cubic yards of earth and in 1913 about 251,000,000 cubic yards.[5]   By 1926 the amount of earth in the system reached the enormous total of 472,000,000 cubic yards.   To give a comparison, the levees in the Yazoo Basin in 1882 averaged eight feet in height and contained 31,500 cubic yards per mile, and in 1926 the levees of the same basin averaged twenty-two feet in height and contained 421,000 cubic yards per mile.[6]   In 1926, the system contained a total of 1815 miles of levee on

[1] Engineering and Contracting, vol. 53, Jan. 14, 1920, p. 37.

[2] Engineering News-Record, vol. 90, Jan. 4, 1923, p. 27.

[3] Annals of the American Academy of Political and Social Science, vol. 135, Jan., 1928, p. 45.

[4] Engineering News-Record, vol. 90, Jan. 4, 1923, p. 27.

[5] Engineering and Contracting, vol. 53, Jan. 14, 1920, p. 36.

[6] House Committee on Flood Control, 70th Cong., 1st Sess., 1927-8, Committee Doc., no. 1, p. 25.

the main river averaging eighteen feet high, although some remained below standard grade and section.[1]

The number of crevasses offer a fair estimate of the success of a levee system, a count of which shows great advance in flood control during the period. In 1882 the number of breaks in the levees reached the total of 284 with a combined length of more than fifty-six miles. One year later there occurred 224 crevasses totaling thirty-four miles.[2] In 1912 and 1913 two of the worst floods in history caused only twelve and eight crevasses respectively, totaling only a few thousand feet.[3] A great flood passed down the river in 1916 and left in its wake only one crevasse along the main levee line, although for about three hundred fifty miles in the heart of the delta the river reached record heights.[4] The flood of 1922, which broke many records in the lower valley, created only two breaks, one of which occurred below New Orleans.[5] And the Mississippi River Commission could proudly proclaim that no break had ever occurred in a levee that had been built up to the Commission's standard grade and section.[6]

Such a record could well impart confidence, even though the Mississippi River Commission had utterly miscalculated the cost of the system in its early estimates. The report of 1883 maintained that $11,450,000 would furnish protection enough.[7] By 1926 more than twenty times that amount had been expended and the system had not been completed.[8] But

[1] *American Railway Engineering Association Bulletin*, vol. 29, July, 1927, p. 95.

[2] Tompkins, *Riparian Lands of the Mississippi River*, p. 22.

[3] J. M. Cline, *Floods in the Lower Mississippi Valley*, p. 17.

[4] *Engineering and Contracting*, vol. 53, Jan. 14, 1920, p. 37.

[5] *The Outlook*, vol. 146, June 8, 1927, p. 182.

[6] *House Committee on Flood Control, Hearings 1922*, p. 34.

[7] *Mississippi River Commission, Report 1883*, p. 28.

[8] *House Committee on Flood Control*, 70th Cong., 1st Sess., 1927-8, *Committee Doc.*, no. 1, p. 28.

the people had confidence in the ability of the levees to keep
the water off their lands if they were up to the standards.

The matter of securing adequate funds forms a most important part in carrying out any program of public improvement.   The Mississippi River Commission has depended entirely on funds appropriated from time to time by Congress.
However, the appropriations came to be mere routine under
provisions of acts previously passed by Congress to carry out
plans of the Commission.[1]   The first appropriation for the
Commission provided $175,000 in 1879 for surveys and
formulating plans.   An act in 1881 appropriated $1,000,000,
which represented the first fund of any considerable size for
the Commission, for the improvement of the channel.   Until
1892, the amounts provided varied considerably, totaling
about $13,500,000.   However, only $4,000,000 went for
work on levees.[2]   From 1892 to 1910, the appropriations
averaged about $2,000,000 annually.[3]   Including the Rivers
and Harbors Act of 1916, the aggregate appropriations
reached almost $83,000,000.[4]   However, the Commission
had often complained that it had never had ample funds.
The opinion had been frequently expressed that adequate
flood control did not present so much of an engineering problem as it did a problem of getting Congress to vote sufficient
funds, which placed Congress in the position of being criticized for the failure to protect the delta.[5]   Senator W. E.
Chandler of New Hampshire made precisely that charge
against Congress in 1892.[6]

[1] *Cong. Record,* 55th Cong., 1st Sess., pt. 1, 1897, p. 351.

[2] *Cong. Record,* 52nd Cong., 1st Sess., pt. 3, 1892, p. 2315.

[3] *Mississippi River Commission, Report 1923,* p. 1896.

[4] *House Committee on Flood Control,* 70th Cong., 1st Sess., 1927, *Committee Doc.,* no. 1, p. 27.

[5] New Orleans, *Times-Picayune,* Oct. 18, 1927, p. 1.

[6] *Cong. Record,* 52nd Cong., 1st Sess., pt. 3, 1892, p. 2315.

The most general complaint by the Mississippi River Commission has been that under the prevailing system before 1917 it did not know just how much it would have to spend from year to year. The uncertainty had often caused wasteful methods because the Commission could only let contracts up to the limit of available funds. Senator W. P. Frye of Maine urged Congress in 1892 to make appropriations covering several years so that a continuous program could be developed.[1] Judge R. S. Taylor told the Senate Commerce Committee in 1910 that the Commission had been compelled to do its work piecemeal because Congress had not granted funds enough to carry out its program, and because it worked all the time in the face of " tremendous possible disasters ".[2] Much money has been lost because the physical plant could not expand rapidly enough to enable it to get much ahead of the destructive agents at work, floods and caving banks. Incomplete levees offered an easy mark for floods, a weakness which means that a levee-building program should be rapidly carried out.[3] Levee construction calls for special machines and specialists to operate them. Idleness means serious loss because no other industry could employ them for a few months. In 1921 and 1922 seven Bucyrus Tower machines, costing $150,000 each, suspended operation for seven months and simply stood idle by a non-standard levee that could easily have been built up to standard in the meantime. While those great machines remained idle the levee by which they stood was overtopped by a flood, and only a heroic fight and the expenditure of $400,000, which was completely wasted, prevented a serious crevasse.[4] The vast waste in such a situation is evident. Yet the Commission could hardly be blamed

---

[1] *Cong., Record*, 52nd Cong., 1st Sess., pt. 3, 1892, p. 2313.

[2] B. G. Humphreys, *Floods and Levees of the Mississippi River*, p. 169.

[3] *House Committee on Flood Control, Hearings 1922*, p. 38.

[4] *Ibid.*, p. 87.

for doing makeshift and temporary work to meet pressing conditions.[1] In that case Congress must accept much of the responsibility for the vast amount of money that has been wasted through idleness of physical plant, through increased prices paid to contractors because of part-time work and because of the general increase in price levels, through the vast amount lost by the destruction of incomplete and non-standard levee, through the expenditure of money to protect such levees in floods, and through the huge amounts that have been lost in floods that might have been prevented if the levees had been complete. However, it must be admitted that the ability of both the Commission and the physical plant had limits that made it necessary to carry on the work over a long period of years, even though Congress had provided ample funds at all times. A well-known engineer estimated in 1922 that it would cost one-half as much to complete the levees in five years as it would cost to complete them in fifteen years, but he doubted the wisdom of attempting to do the work in less than five years.[2]

The nature of the problem has caused the Mississippi River Commission to urge a policy of continuing contracts which would permit it to extend the work from year to year. Contractors have been slow to invest in equipment unless they could have assurance that Congress would make sufficient appropriations. And the Commission has been definitely committed to the policy of contracting for the work.[3] Prior to 1917 Congress had generally disregarded the plea for a continuous program. However, on two occasions in Congress the idea of continuous contracts had been adopted. In 1892 the appropriation act provided $2,000,000 and gave the Mississippi River Commission authority to contract for works

[1] *Senate Sub-Committee on Commerce, Hearings 1914*, p. 15.

[2] *House Committee on Flood Control, Hearings 1922*, p. 61.

[3] *House Report*, no. 300, 63rd Cong., 2nd Sess., 1914, pt. 2, p. 6.

and materials not to exceed $2,665,000 per annum for the next three years.[1] The act of 1907 provided for another three-year program totaling nine million dollars.[2] Another phase of appropriations that has produced criticism is that Congress has sometimes provided that money should be spent at certain specified places. The Commission engineers have always contended that appropriations should be made in lump sums to be used at the discretion of the Commission as the needs of the various districts might suggest.[3]

The economy of a continuing program afforded one of the strongest points of argument for the flood-control acts of 1917 and 1923.[4] They were the only real flood-control acts prior to 1927.[5] The act of 1917, for the first time, provided money openly for flood control, and the act of 1923 used the same language in setting forth its purpose " for controlling the floods of the Mississippi River and continuing its improvements ".[6] These acts embodied practically all of the suggestions of the Commission and put the Federal government definitely and apparently determinedly on record as an agency for flood control.

The flood-control act of 1917 introduced a new principle of sharing Federal and local contributions. Before 1917 Congressional appropriations had not required any local contribution, although it had been the practice of the Commission to meet the funds of levee boards very much on a fifty-

[1] R. S. Taylor, *Mississippi River Improvement*, p. 5.

[2] *Mississippi River Commission, Report 1907*, p. 2607.

[3] *Senate Committee on Commerce, Hearings 1910*, p. 32.

[4] *Cong. Record*, 64th Cong., 2nd Sess., pt. 6, 1917, p. 4760.

[5] *House Committee on Flood Control*, 70th Cong., 1st Sess., 1927-8, *Committee Doc.*, no. 18, p. 5.

[6] *House Committee on Flood Control, Report to Accompany House Bill*, no. 8219, p. 7.

fifty basis.[1]   The law of 1917 provided that the United
States would pay two dollars to one dollar from the local
boards for levee construction, but the levee boards had to
furnish rights of way and pay maintenance charges in addition to their one-third of the cost of construction, thus
making almost a dollar-for-dollar proposition.[2] This arrange-
ment suited the Commission because it felt that the local
boards should know definitely how much they would have to
pay when they came to the Commission for aid in construction, in order to keep boards with insufficient funds or selfish
aim from asking for aid.   The people of the delta also expressed satisfaction and the belief that the two-to-one ratio,
with local boards furnishing rights of way and maintenance,
was a fair division.[3]   The definite division of funds made a
policy of continuing contracts all the more desirable because it
became very necessary for the Commission and the levee
boards to have funds at the same time.   And the evidence
shows that the construction of works has lagged several times
since 1917 because one party did not have funds when the
other did.[4]

The flood-control act of 1917 was by far the most liberal
act up to that time for the purpose of controlling the Mississippi.   It provided for $45,000,000 in five years, $30,-
000,000 of which was to be spent together with $15,000,000
from the local levee boards in building and repairing levees.[5]
It proved very unfortunate that the act came the very year the
United States entered the World War.   Under war conditions Congress reduced the amount of annual appropria-

[1] *House Committee on Flood Control, Hearings 1916*, p. 4.

[2] *Ibid., Hearings 1922*, p. 60.

[3] *Cong. Record*, 64th Cong., 2nd Sess., pt. 6, 1917, p. 4765.

[4] *House Committee on Flood Control*, 70th Cong., 1st Sess., 1927-8,
Report to Accompany House Bill, no. 8219, p. 11.

[5] *House Committee on Flood Control, Hearings 1922*, p. 216.

tions by extending the period of time to seven years instead of five. Then, the works had to be constructed at inflated prices so that the same amount of money did not go nearly so far as it did under pre-war conditions. The large number of extraordinary expenses during the war period and during the flood of 1923 reduced the percentage spent on levees, so that actually only about $17,000,000 went for levee construction.[1] The flood-control act of 1923 provided still more liberal amounts for the protection of the delta. It provided for $60,000,000 in ten years.[2] In 1923 Congress appropriated $10,000,000 as the first annual installment under the new law, which was the most liberal appropriation by far up to that time.[3]

So far in this discussion, the policy of the Mississippi River Commission has been considered as a levees-only policy. However, in one very important sense the flood-control policy went beyond the levees-only idea. Bank stabilization by means of revetment has been developed as a natural supplement to levees. Disintegration of the banks of the river proved a most serious problem that simply demanded attention.[4] The caving banks ate into the levees and carried them into the river. Near Point Pleasant, Missouri, from 1898 to 1922 the levee had to be rebuilt four times, due to caving banks. The last location was three miles back of the first one.[5] The Lower Yazoo District in 1922 had 184 miles of levee. From 1882 to 1922 it had lost 212 miles in a strategic retreat from caving banks.[6] It has been estimated that

[1] *Cong. Record*, 70th Cong., 1st Sess., pt. 6, 1927–28, **p. 4251.**

[2] *Ibid.*, 1928, p. 4251.

[3] *Mississippi River Commission, Report 1923*, p. 1892.

[4] *House Document*, no. 2, 64th Cong., 1st Sess., p. 34.

[5] *House Committee on Flood Control, Hearings 1922*, p. 69.

[6] *Ibid.*, p. 29.

$100,000,000 spent on construction since 1822 has been lost because of the levees falling into the river.[1] The wastefulness of building levees and permitting them to cave into the river is evident. The Mississippi River Commission has been strongly in favor of bank stabilization as a matter of economy and prevention.[2] In its early years, however, the Commission favored channel improvement and bank stabilization by the construction of permeable dikes for the purpose of contraction of the water. In 1885 Congress provided that no part of the appropriation of that year should be spent for revetments until it was " found that permeable contraction works would not secure the desired stability of the river banks ".[3]

Revetment costs much money. And that part of control by common consent apparently has been consigned unanimously to the Federal government, because the works actually belong under the water.[4] However, the local boards have spent considerable money for revetment, for which they received no credit in allocation of funds. Up to 1927 the Federal government had spent $58,000,000 for revetment, and the work had not been more than one-fourth completed.[5] The loss of levee has been so heavy from caving banks, and the cost of revetment has been so high that the people of the delta have sometimes felt that they would be able to build the levees if the Federal government would complete the work of revetment.[6] In 1922 revetment cost $240,000 on the

[1] *Cong. Record*, 70th Cong., 1st Sess., pt. 6, 1928, p. 4252.

[2] *House Report*, no. 300, 63rd Cong., 2nd Sess., pt. 2, 1914, p. 60.

[3] *Congressional Digest*, Feb., 1928, p. 45.

[4] *Cong. Record*, 70th Cong., 1st Sess., pt. 6, 1928, p. 4252.

[5] *House Committee on Flood Control*, 70th Cong., 1st Sess., 1927-8, *Committee Doc.*, no. 1, p. 29.

[6] *Senate Committee on Commerce, Hearings 1910*, p. 9.

average per mile, whereas the average mile of levee cost only $150,000.[1]

Perhaps a brief description of revetment would enable the reader to better understand the situation. The whole problem, of course, is to prevent the disintegration of the banks and to stabilize them. Above the water, the caving banks are often paved, but ordinarily a good coat of grass will suffice.[2] Below the water line, another method must provide the remedy. The revetments are in reality huge willow mattresses twelve to eighteen inches thick, 250 to 300 feet wide, and sometimes a thousand feet long. They are woven from bank willow three to six inches in diameter and forty to fifty feet long, which are held together by wire cables. They are made on the surface of the stream on large flat barges. Then, at low water, they are fastened in the desired place by the outer edge and are sunken into the river by means of placing many huge stones on them.[3] The willow does not decay under water. This type of revetment has proved strong enough to prevent " scouring and sloughing " and flexible enough to conform itself to the hidden irrigularities of the banks.[4]

No really satisfactory substitute for that costly type of revetment has been found thus far, although several experiments have been tried. The St. Francis District of Missouri has had fair success with the Woodbury system. That system uses what are known as " retards ". They are simply large trees strung along very powerful cables and anchored at the head of the " retard " to concrete on the bottom of the river. When the river attempts to undermine the trees they

[1] *House Committee on Flood Control, Hearings 1922*, p. 65.

[2] *Ibid.*, p. 66.

[3] *Ibid.*, p. 65.

[4] *House Committee on Flood Control*, 70th Cong., 1st Sess., 1927-8, *Committee Doc.*, no. 1, p. 24.

sink deeper and protect the banks.[1]   But that system has not offered the same degree of protection as has been provided by the revetments.   The policy of the Commission still provides for bank revetment as a very necessary part of the flood-control program.

[1] *House Committee on Flood Control, Hearings 1922*, p. 70.

CHAPTER VIII

Forces that Have Created Sentiment for Federal Control

THE transition of flood control on the Mississippi from a purely local function to an almost wholly Federal one has taken place slowly. The movement toward Federal control had its inception very soon after the United States obtained control of the river, but it took a long time for it to grow into a well-defined organization that brought about the creation of the Mississippi River Commission as an agency of Federal control of the mighty Mississippi.[1] After the Commission was formed the movement for Federal control on a larger scale grew rapidly, but another half century was required to reach the present program.

Powerful influences are required to carry forward the spread of an idea from local to national scope and the creation of a Federal program for the expenditure of hundreds of millions of dollars. The major forces in creating the public demand for the present program are easy to ascertain. The people of the delta certainly have been a powerful influence for Federal control. Under whatever conditions of political, economic, or social nature, the residents of the section have stood shoulder to shoulder at all times to secure the greatest amount possible of Federal participation in the control of the Mississippi. For many years no other political consideration has been permitted to stand in the way of a united effort and a solid vote of all members of Congress from the delta area in behalf of flood-control legislation.[2] The repre-

[1] *House Committee on Flood Control, Hearings 1922*, p. 29.
[2] *New York Times*, Sept. 18, 1927, sec. ii, p. 3.

157

sentatives from this section have gone much further. They have been willing to enter into many political trades, to do much bargaining and compromising, and to sacrifice their opinions on many questions in order to secure votes from fellow members for the flood-control bills.[1] The local communities of the delta have stood staunchly back of their Senators and Representatives who voted for flood-control legislation both in the elections and during sessions of Congress. Most of the communities have developed special organizations or local leaders to represent them in advancing the interests of Federal control. Thus, in 1927, the Memphis Commercial Appeal strongly urged every community of the delta to get ready to use " the full weight of its influence " in behalf of the impending legislation.[2] The influence of this strongly united and militant group of people and members of Congress, representing large areas of seven states and controlling politically in most instances the entire delegation, must have been powerful.

The efforts of the people of the delta and their representatives at Washington, however united and determined they may have been, evidently could never have brought about Federal control without help. Outside assistance has developed slowly. The evidence seems quite clear that the most powerful influence in creating a national movement for Federal flood control has been the growing industrial importance of the South and the investments of outsiders in the delta area. Such a condition simply means that the hard-headed business people of the country had to be convinced that flood-control would be profitable to them before they would urge their representatives to support protective legislation.[3] Delta

[1] *House Committee on Flood Control, Hearings 1922*, p. 29.

[2] Memphis, *Commercial Appeal*, Nov. 7, 1927.

[3] *House Committee on Flood Control*, 70th Cong., 1st Sess., 1927-8, *Committee Doc.*, no. 18, p. 12.

people have not failed to understand this fact and they have, therefore, emphasized the national economic aspects of flood control.[1] They have kept before the nation the great economic value of the delta as a source of raw materials, as a place for investment, and as a market for manufactured products.[2] They have also stressed the great need of maintaining the confidence of the business world in the soundness of business conditions in the section, in order that credit might be available for its development. Of course, flood control would be a necessary part of any forward-looking program.[3]

Bradstreet's reviews of business conditions have frequently been quoted on the effects of floods on general business conditions. At times this agency has gone on to suggest the desirability of Federal control.[4] After the flood-control legislation of 1928, the Memphis Commercial Appeal gave a headline notice to Bradstreet's report of improved business conditions, saying that the control of floods assured good business for the Mid-South.[5] The keen interest of bankers in the problem definitely reflects a general business interest. The *Guaranty Survey,* published by the Guaranty Trust Co. of New York, gave recognition to the flood of 1927 as an " important adverse influence " to the general prosperity of the country.[6] In 1913 a booklet of letters of prominent bankers from all parts of the United States was presented to Congress.[7] Letters came from Boston, New York, Phila-

[1] *Cong. Record,* 67th Cong., 4th Sess., pt. 7, 1923, p. 5208.

[2] *House Committee on Flood Control,* 70th Cong., 1st Sess., 1927-8, *Committee Doc.,* no. 18, p. 18.

[3] *Commerce and Finance,* vol. 16, June 1, 1927, p. 1102.

[4] *House Committee on Flood Control,* 70th Cong., 1st Sess., 1927-8, *Committee Doc.,* no. 16, p. 9.

[5] Memphis, *Commercial Appeal,* May 23, 1928.

[6] *Literary Digest,* vol. 93, June 18, 1927, p. 8.

[7] *Mississippi River Levee Association, Letters from Prominent Bankers favoring Legislation by Congress to Prevent Floods.*

delphia, Chicago, Salt Lake City, San Francisco and every city of any importance in the country. From whatever section they came, their authors expressed the belief that flood control assuredly constituted a national problem.[1] The leading banks of delta cities have paid salaries and expenses of employees to go to Washington and to work in behalf of flood-control legislation. The American Bankers Association spoke for 20,000 of the country's banks when its Exeecutive Council said that it was of the " profound conviction " that flood control on the Mississippi was a national problem, and that it should be solved promptly at the expense of the Federal government.[2]

Manufacturers of almost all types of commodities for sale in the delta have become interested in the project. The interest of this large group has its foundation in the desire for more purchasing power in the delta, a section maintaining few factories. Thus, the National Association of Manufacturers has made known by resolutions its decided conviction that the Federal government should undoubtedly use its resources to prevent the recurring disasters in the delta.[3] In due turn, practically all associations of specific branches of manufacturers have added their support by resolutions to Federal control. Thus, the Infant Children's and Junior Wear League of America pledged the support of its membership for Federal control.[4] One might make a list of manufacturers from automobiles to xylophones, and apparently all of their national associations have first and last expressed a strong desire for Federal control. Of course their main allies in trade, the credit men, have been of the same opinion.

[1] *Mississippi River Levee Association, Letters from Prominent Bankers favoring Legislation by Congress to Prevent Floods.*

[2] *New York Times,* April 19, 1928.

[3] *New York Times,* May 19, 1927, p. 19.

[4] *New York Times,* Feb. 26, 1928, pt. 2, p. 19.

The National Association of Credit Men has been a strong supporter of flood control as a great benefit to the general welfare, and especially to those who had products to sell on credit to people living in the delta.[1]

Those who have bought bonds and those who hold mortgages against delta property represent a small army of investors scattered through the nation. The protection of investments has long been recognized as an important function of our Federal government. Then, the conclusion that the United States should protect outside investors in delta securities seems logical, notwithstanding the fact that the high interest rates offer evidence that the investments could not have been considered as absolutely safe when they were made.[2] Outside loans have been secured by various types of bonds; levee board, drainage district, industrial, municipal, county, real estate and others and by mortgages against real estate. The aggregate totals many hundreds of millions of dollars. Naturally any additional margin of safety would accrue to the benefit of those who made the loans. The people of the delta have frequently argued that investors demanded flood control in their pleas for additional protection.[3] One argument advanced seems somewhat amusing. They have maintained that the assurance in 1917 that the Federal government would control floods caused private interests to invest hundreds of millions in the delta. Thus, the duty of the Federal government to protect such investments rested upon the fact that it induced private interests to invest.[4] One must appreciate the need for action on the part of investors when large numbers of the bond issues were in default and

---

[1] *Mississippi River Levee Association, Public Sentiment as Expressed by Mayors of Cities and Commercial Organizations*, p. 46.

[2] *Commerce and Finance*, vol. 16, June 1, 1927, p. 1102.

[3] *Manufacturers Record*, vol. 91, May 19, 1927, p. 62.

[4] *House Committee on Flood Control, Hearings 1922*, p. 35.

when several classes of bonds of the delta could hardly be sold at all, due to the effect of a mighty flood.[1] Such a condition furnished ample reason for the powerful Investment Bankers Association of America to act. The Association's members have directed the investment of most of this nation's money. The convention at Seattle in 1927 resolved that " said association hereby recognizes and declares that the control of the flood waters of the Mississippi River and its tributaries is a national duty " and that the loss of property from floods " seriously affects and impairs the economic welfare of this entire nation ".[2]

Also, the entrepreneural interests of the delta and of industries depending on the delta have exerted great influence on Congress. In this list perhaps the owners of railways stand first. Among the leading railways in the delta are the Illinois Central; the Missouri Pacific; the Southern Pacific; the Chicago, Rock Island and Pacific; the Texas and Pacific; the St. Louis and San Francisco; the Southern; the St. Louis and Southwestern; the Mobile and Ohio; the Yazoo and Mississippi Valley; and the Louisville and Nashville.[3] These roads represent some of the nation's outstanding systems. Their earnings depend, to a large extent, on the general prosperity of the delta. Floods have frequently showed results in lowered earnings for the following year.[4] Then, one should consider the actual loss to railways from the floods. Thousands of miles of road have been inundated, much of the road bed and much rolling stock have been destroyed, and traffic has been paralyzed in many sections for periods of time varying from a few days to two or three months. The

[1] *House Committee on Flood Control*, 70th Cong., 1st Sess., 1927-8, *Committee Doc.*, no. 18, p. 38.

[2] *Commercial and Financial Chronicle*, vol. 125, Oct. 15, 1927, p. 2074.

[3] *House Committee on Flood Control, Hearings 1927*, p. 127.

[4] St. Louis, *The Globe Democrat*, April 7, 1897, p. 6.

losses of the delta railways in the flood of 1927 have been authoritatively estimated at almost $17,000,000.[1] The Illinois Central alone lost $2,000,000.[2] Such a state of affairs could not fail to impress lastingly the owners of stock in the railways, who number hundreds of thousands of influential people in every part of the country.

The result has been that officials of the railway lines of the delta have frequently appeared before Congressional Committees and have almost universally urged federal control. C. H. Markham of the Illinois Central had no hesitancy in proclaiming that those who understood the problem unanimously declared that it " ought to be handled by the National Government ".[3] In the 70th Congress the Chief Engineers of the various lines presented to the House Flood Control Committee a joint report against certain features of the Jadwin plan with the obvious intention of securing the adoption of a more liberal one.[4] When one considers the definite interests of the owners of railways in flood control, because the railway's earnings in the delta section depend largely upon keeping the Mississippi river in its banks, the reason that they have been among the front rank of those wanting Federal control becomes clear enough. The question has been reduced to a matter of dollars and cents in the pockets of hundreds of thousands of people who own the stock of the railways in all parts of the nation.

Owners of real estate in the delta have furnished much agitation for Federal control. Many large companies and many wealthy individuals, both resident and non-resident,

[1] *Mississippi River Flood Control Association, Losses and Damages Resulting from the Flood of 1927,* p. 5.

[2] *New York Times,* July 13, 1927, pt. 3, p. 29.

[3] *Cong. Record,* 70th Cong., 1st Sess., pt. 5, 1928, p. 3573.

[4] *House Committee on Flood Control,* 70th Cong., 1st Sess., 1927-8, Committee Doc., no. 23.

own large acreages along the lower river. They have proved
influential in producing favorable action by Congress.[1] Hon.
Oscar Johnston of Memphis, an officer in a very large and
powerful delta land company, played a very prominent part
in the activities in behalf of the legislation of 1928. He
represented the Memphis Chamber of Commerce. He presented a strong brief to the Flood Control Committee of the
House.[2] Former Senator William Lorimer of Illinois, who
had large holdings in the delta as one of the owners of William Lorimer Lumber Company, presented a very powerful
and lengthy statement of more than thirty pages urging
Federal control.[3] Although each of the above gentlemen
claimed to appear in behalf of the people of the delta rather
than in behalf of their respective companies—and a perusal
of their statements lends strength to that position—they must
have exerted some influence on account of the large land holdings they represented. And many other cases similar to
theirs increased the influence of the large land owners.
Closely related in their activities to these groups are the real
estate companies who deal in delta lands. They have frequently and enthusiastically proclaimed that flood control
would add " greatly to the value of the alluvial lands along
the lower Mississippi ". The delta real-estate men have
unanimously supported the idea of Federal control.[4] The
National Association of Real Estate Boards took up the
fight of the local boards by unanimously adopting a resolution urging Congress to proceed at once to plan to control
floods at the sole cost of the Federal government.[5]

[1] *Cong. Record*, 64th Cong., 1st Sess., pt. 11, 1916, p. 8633.

[2] *Flood Control Committee, House*, 70th Cong., 1st Sess., 1927-8, *Committee Doc.*, no. 22.

[3] *House Committee on Flood Control*, 70th Cong., 1st Sess., 1927-8,
Committee Doc., no. 26.

[4] Memphis, *Commercial Appeal*, May 22, 1928.

[5] New Orleans, *Times-Picayune*, Jan. 26, 1928, p. 2.

The lumber industry of the South has been a staunch supporter of Federal control. This industry in recent years has grown to an immense size in the delta area. The loss from the flood of 1927 alone to the lumber interests has been estimated at almost $5,000,000.[1] Any industry that has lost millions from floods would likely favor the most promising plan of flood control that presented itself. The lumber interests have not only mustered their forces in the delta but they have secured allies from their industry in other parts of the country.[2] Lumbermen from all sections of the nation have urged their representatives to vote for Federal control. They have used their National Association to voice their sentiment by strong resolutions placing the responsibility on the United States.[3] Many other industrial groups with interests in the valley have added their strength to the movement to preserve the alluvial lands from floods by having the Federal government do the work of controlling the Father of Waters.[4]

The engineering profession has been, perhaps unwittingly, a power in securing flood control by the Federal government. The frequent references in this thesis to engineering journals show that the subject has often been fully discussed by many of the nation's leading engineers. The problem must be regarded fundamentally as one of engineering, and one of the biggest in the world. The engineers of this country have proclaimed the controlling of floods of the Mississippi as one of our most important problems.[5] They

[1] *Mississippi River Flood Control Association, Losses and Damages Resulting from the Flood of 1927*, p. 5.

[2] *House Committee on Flood Control*, 70th Cong., 1st Sess., 1927-8, Committee Doc., no. 18, p. 46.

[3] *Mississippi River Levee Association, Public Sentiment as Expressed by Mayors of Cities and Commercial Organizations*, p. 46.

[4] New Orleans, *Times-Picayune*, Oct. 16, 1927.

[5] *American Society of Civil Engineers, Proceedings*, August, 1923, p. 413.

have been witnesses before Congressional Committees. They have often passed resolutions in state and national conventions demanding federal control. No other group of financially disinterested persons has more generally urged complete control of Mississippi floods. They have given serious thought to plans and methods of control that has resulted in much worthwhile discussion and activity.[1] In their plans and discussions the best engineers of the country have urged the immensity of the task and the necessity of federal control. Consequently, a large number of professional men have furnished many sound arguments that have been siezed upon and advanced by the proponents of federal control.

All great public works should have the approval of a majority of the people. Since such approval generally means that the people must get information on any given public work, a period of education seems indispensable.[2] The public refuses to educate itself to the needs and problems of any group or any section, a fact which makes it necessary that some individuals or groups become propagandists or educators. In the case of flood control engineers have done quite a bit to educate the public but their writings and speeches have frequently contained so many technicalities that they failed to interest the general public.[3] The layman has been able to use engineering data in educating the public to a greater advantage than the engineer himself has.

The task of informing the public on any problem as vast as the control of the Mississippi could not be performed through the activities of disassociated individuals. Therefore, the united effort of a group or groups became necessary. The flood problem has not lacked for associated activity seeking its solution. Since 1845 great conventions under various

[1] *United States Daily*, Oct. 14, 1927, p. 1.

[2] Alvord and Burdick, *Relief from Floods*, p. 45.

[3] *Ibid.*, p. 47.

titles have met to consider the problems of the Mississippi valley.[1] The conventions met many times in various cities of the valley. The one meeting in 1881 at St. Louis was typical. The call was issued by the St. Louis Merchants Exchange for the purpose of deliberating upon the improvement of the Mississippi and its tributaries. Delegates came from boards of trade, from cotton exchanges, and from towns where no such organizations existed. The meeting took place under the title of the Mississippi River Improvement Convention.[2] The Memphis Convention of 1845, organized under the same title, was attended by 500 delegates from twelve states and was presided over by John C. Calhoun. The one of 1847 at Chicago was called the River and Harbor Convention. Abraham Lincoln and Horace Greeley attended. Other early conventions met at Dubuque in 1866, St. Louis in 1867 and Vicksburg in 1875.[3]

One of the most important of all of the conventions met at Vicksburg in 1890 while a flood was in progress. By that date the name had become the Inter-state Mississippi Improvement and Levee Convention, which suggested the trend of developments, and the avowed purpose of the Association was to secure flood control by levees at the expense as far as possible of the United States.[4] This was the first strong levee association organized in this country. Charles Scott of Rosedale, Mississippi and W. A. Everman of Greenville, Mississippi were elected president and secretary respectively. One of the most important acts of the convention was the establishing of a Bureau of Correspondence at Washington,

---

[1] *Proceedings Mississippi River Improvement Convention*, St. Louis, 1881, p. 12.

[2] *Ibid.*, p. 5.

[3] *Ibid.*, p. 13.

[4] *Inter-state Mississippi River Improvement and Levee Association, Resolutions*, Vicksburg, 1890, p. 1.

D. C., for the avowed purpose of lobbying and for carrying on a general propaganda for federal funds for flood control.[1] The same association, with Charles Scott still president, held a large and enthusiastic convention at New Orleans in 1903. The gathering was really a gala meeting of the most influential interests from all parts of the valley. It took the position that flood control in the minds of millions of Americans was a national duty and that levees offered the only means of control.[2]   The proceedings of the convention showed what opinion the delegates held by stating that " the campaign of education will go on in Congressional halls and wherever influential bodies of men " may be found or reached.[3] Thus, the association again announced the avowed purpose of " educating " the members of Congress and influential men in all parts of the nation.

Another great convention met at Memphis in 1912. Theodore Roosevelt attended and pleased the meeting with a strong speech in behalf of flood control.   The delegates apparently thought that the work of " educating " the public, and especially Congress, had not proceeded as well as it should have, for in the meeting was born the Mississippi River Levee Association, organized as a corporation in 1913.[4]   During the years when the real work of federal control was having its beginnings in securing the passage of the Flood-Control Act of 1917, the Mississippi River Levee Association proved the most powerful influence in the fight before Congress. A. S. Caldwell was President and John A. Fox was Secretary-Manager. The executive committee of 21 and the board of directors of 60 were made up of lead-

---

[1] Tompkins, *Riparian Lands of Mississippi River*, p. 4.

[2] *Senate Committee on Commerce, Hearings 1904*, p. 44.

[3] *Ibid.*, p. 25.

[4] *House Committee on Flood Control, Hearings 1916*, p. 369.

ing bankers, wholesalers, railway officials, editors, planters, lawyers and manufacturers.[1]   Reaction and relaxation have been the greatest problems of the proponents of Federal control.   People showed much enthusiasm during and immediately after floods but they soon forgot.[2]   This phase of the problem the Mississippi River Levee Association proposed to meet by gathering data and statistics on the flood problem, informing the people of the United States concerning it, and carrying on a great campaign of educational publicity.[3]   Thousands of business men from all parts of the valley furnished the money by voluntary subscription to finance the campaign.   It appears that contributions must have been rather liberal for the size and source of some of them caused much criticism.   Among those who contributed one thousand dollars per year for several years were eight of the leading railways of the section and some of the leading business firms doing business in the delta, including the International Harvester Company.[4]

The sole paid employee of the association was the Secretary-Manager, Mr. John A. Fox.   It became his task to spend the funds in educating the public of the entire United States to the vast problem of controlling Mississippi floods and to the absolute necessity and positive duty of the Federal government in controlling them.[5]   The energetic and systematic way Mr. Fox went about his business indicated that he knew how to bring pressure to bear upon Congress.   He wrote many thousands of letters, circular and personal; published hundreds of pamphlets and several books; delivered

---

[1] John A. Fox, *Mississippi River Flood Problem*, p. 6.

[2] *Manufacturers Record*, vol. 91, June 9, 1927, p. 57.

[3] John A. Fox, *Mississippi River Flood Problem*, p. 6.

[4] *Cong. Record*, 63rd Cong., 2nd Sess., pt. 19, 1914, p. 16784.

[5] *House Committee on Flood Control, Hearings 1916*, p. 369.

and had others to deliver thousands of lectures; distributed information widely by pictures, motion pictures, maps, charts, and all types of publicity devices.[1]   For about five years he travelled to all parts of the country and talked and lectured wherever he could muster an audience to listen to him, addressing business men's clubs, chambers of commerce, various civic clubs, schools and any other type of organization that had people of influence, or seemed to offer fertile soil for propaganda.   He started early to enlist the aid of prominent bankers by sending letters to them explaining the problem. The replies came from every state in the Union.[2]   A book of selected letters from many of the bankers urging federal control was published and given wide distribution.[3]   The commercial and civic organizations of the country offered a fertile field for propaganda.   So in 1913, a full and convincing circular letter went to all such organizations whose names and addresses could be acquired.   Enclosed with each letter were two sets of strong and well-prepared resolutions with a request that each organization adopt and return one set to the Mississippi River Levee Association.   One set called for the passage of the Ransdell-Humphreys bill, then pending before Congress, and the other simply asked for the enactment of legislation that would afford ample protection. Mayors of cities and other public leaders received requests for an expression of opinion.   Then, another book was issued giving selected replies under the title, " Public Sentiment as Expressed by Mayors of Cities and Commercial Organizations ".[4]   The conventions and associations of bank-

[1] *Cong. Record*, 64th Cong., 1st Sess., pt. 10, 1916, p. 8319.

[2] *Rand-McNally Banker's Monthly*, vol. 32, Feb., 1915, p. 16.

[3] *Mississippi River Levee Association, Letters from Prominent Bankers Favoring Legislation by Congress to Prevent Floods.*

[4] *Mississippi River Levee Association, Public Sentiment as Expressed by Mayors of Cities and Commercial Organizations.*

ers, merchants, manufacturers, farmers, lumbermen, credit men, and many others felt Mr. Fox's presence and influence. The same book contained many resolutions from state and national conventions of such associations.

Of course, Congress could not be overlooked, for after all it was to " educate " Congress that all of that militant and far-flung propaganda had been carried on. So Mr. Fox marshaled his forces to send to Washington. Scores of the best business men of the South spent long periods in the Capitol. An associated press dispatch on December 2, 1914, from Washington said: " The white ribbons of the Mississippi River Levee Association are more frequent than stars and stripes here today ". " Three special trains from Memphis and neighboring cities arrived here this morning, and the remainder of the representation will arrive on another special tomorrow ".[1] There is little wonder that the Mississippi River Levee Association drew fire as an agency for lobbying. The flood-control bill of 1917, which fulfilled the wishes of the association, can be charged to a large extent to the activities of Mr. Fox and his associates. Apparently the Mississippi River Levee Association thought its work had been completed in securing the passage of the act of 1917, for in that year it disbanded.

In 1922 two organizations that have since that date played highly important roles in creating sentiment for federal control came into existence. The Mississippi Flood Control Association is a co-operative enterprise composed of the various levee boards of the delta with headquarters at Memphis.[2] The Safe River Committee of 100 is a committee of citizens of New Orleans, organized as a result of a mass meeting to discuss remedies for conditions that had

[1] *Memphis News Scimitar*, December 2, 1914.
[2] *House Committee on Flood Control, Hearings 1922*, p. 33.

arisen during the flood of 1922.[1]   The task of educating the
public was not so great as it had been ten years before, nor
was the burden of proof that flood control was a duty of the
Federal government so strongly on the shoulders of the later
associations.   But the act of 1917, which had been framed
with the idea of completing the job, was soon to expire and
the flood of 1922 had produced sufficient evidence to show
that the problem remained far from solution.   The major
task, therefore, for the two organizations was to secure another flood-control act that would finish the job.

The Mississippi River Flood Control Association received
its support from the various levee boards, assessed according
to their funds.   For example the St. Francis Levee Board of
Arkansas was assessed $1,500 per year.[2]   The Association
had no paid employees except the secretary and office force.[3]
But it had little trouble in securing employees of various
business and industrial firms of the delta to do its work and to
carry on its propaganda.   The new association used very
much the same methods as its predecessor had used, except
that it did not employ a travelling agent to spread propaganda.   This organization has indeed been a " wonderful
assistance " in securing suitable flood-control legislation.[4]

The change in name with the re-establishment of the
organization appears significant.   Though the new one was
of a different type from the old one, it nevertheless represented the same interests.   The delta people who wanted
flood control by the Federal government dominated and formulated the policies of both.   The Mississippi River Levee
Association wanted flood control by the Federal government

[1] *Manufacturer's Record*, vol. 91, May 19, 1927, p. 61.

[2] *St. Francis Levee District of Arkansas, Report of Officers*, 1924-5, p. 7.

[3] *House Committee on Flood Control, Hearings 1922*, p. 33.

[4] *St. Francis Levee District of Arkansas, Report of Officers*, 1924-5,
p. 7.

by means of levees only.   The Mississippi River Flood Control Association, although its membership is composed wholly of levee boards, has fought for ample control with less emphasis on the levees, showing the strong position of the proponents of other methods of control in recent years.

The Safe River Committee of 100 has had a two-fold purpose.   One has been to secure Federal flood control and the other to secure a part of that control by means of diversion channels on the lower part of the river.   This is wholly a New Orleans organization, composed of 100 of the leading men of various trades and professions of the city and supported entirely by voluntary contributions.[1]   It has been the most powerful agency in the country giving a major portion of its energies to fighting for outlets.   It has taken the position that New Orleans should know the ultimate height of floods in order to protect herself and to build adequate port facilities.   With flood heights and levee standards ever increasing, the conclusion was reached that diversion of the waters of the Mississippi offered the only safe and logical protection.[2]   The committee employed splendid engineering and publicity talent to show the world the value of lowering flood heights by diversion.   The intense campaign won " converts " from the beginning.   In 1926 the committee secured permission from the War Department to remove a stretch of levee below Pointe-a-la-Hache, sixty miles below New Orleans, a venture costing the state of Louisiana $1,000,000. It also secured the passage of the Wilson bill providing for a survey and a study of the possibility of spillways.[3]   The influence, the engineering studies and the propaganda of this committee undoubtedly had much to do with securing the Poydras Cut in 1927.

[1] *Manufacturers Record*, vol. 91, May 19, 1927, p. 61.

[2] *Ibid.*, p. 62.

[3] *Ibid.*, p. 55.

In the meantime several other organizations have been formed to work in whole or in part for federal flood control. The Mississippi Valley Association, founded in 1920, was made up of hundreds of representatives from chambers of commerce, merchants exchanges, boards of trade, traffic clubs, shippers associations, etc. The announced purpose was to promote and to protect the commercial, agricultural and general interests of the valley.[1] The protection of the general interests of the valley certainly included flood control. The National Flood Prevention Bureau, similarly constituted, for the past few years has stood for handling the entire flood problem on a comprehensive basis.[2] Tri-state flood-control associations, inter-state flood-control associations, state and even district flood-control associations have been numerous, and have contributed somewhat toward creating a public demand for federal control.[3]

The various organizations coming into existence wholly or partly as flood-control organizations have by no means had to bear the entire burden of " education ". The local chambers of commerce and boards of trade in the valley cities have taken great interest and have spent much money in spreading propaganda for federal flood control.[4] In 1916 the New Orleans Association of Commerce urged Congress to declare by joint resolution that flood control constituted a national problem and an obligation of the Federal government.[5] In 1927 the Chicago Association of Commerce, composed of seven thousand of the city's leading business firms, urged construction and maintenance of flood-control works

[1] *House Committee on Flood Control, Hearings 1923*, p. 25.

[2] *Manufacturer's Record*, vol. 91, May 19, 1927, p. 62.

[3] *House Committee on Flood Control*, 70th Cong., 1st Sess., 1927-8, *Committee Doc.*, no. 1, p. 96.

[4] *House Committee on Flood Control, Hearings 1916*, p. 126.

[5] *Ibid.*, p. 129.

entirely at the expense of the United States.[1]   Congress has
generally been confronted by a long list of commercial associations urging it to appropriate money for Mississippi river
flood control.[2]   And not all of the organizations, by any
means, were local.   State associations in sections remote
from the valley showed great interest. The Chamber of Commerce of the State of New York has been one of the fore-
most fighters for many years.   In 1859 this association sent
a memorial to the President of the United States saying that
the Federal government should improve the Mississippi river,
because the effects of its floods extended all over the nation.[3]
Several memorials and resolutions have been sent to Congress at later dates taking the same position and urging immediate action.   The interest shown by the local and state
organizations quite naturally carried on to the national organizations.   The National Board of Trade in 1871 asked Congress to rebuild the levees because of the general effects of
floods on the nation's prosperity, either by the United States
government doing the work itself or by subsidizing a corporation to do the work.[4]   The United States Chamber of
Commerce has played an important role in securing legislation.   In 1922 by resolution it called on Congress to take the
necessary steps to control Mississippi floods.[5] It has strongly
urged business interests throughout the nation to support a
policy of federal control.[6]   Following the flood of 1927, the

[1] *House Committee on Flood Control*, 70th Cong., 1st Sess., 1927-8,
Committee Doc., no. 18, p. 7.

[2] *Mississippi River Levee Association, Public Sentiment on Flood
Protection as Expressed by Mayors and Commercial Organizations*,
1913, p. 1.

[3] *House Committee on Flood Control, Hearings 1916*, p. 12.

[4] *House Report*, no. 44, 42nd Cong., 2nd Sess., 1872, p. 16.

[5] *House Committee on Flood Control*, 70th Cong., 1st Sess., 1927-8,
Committee Document, no. 18, p. 24.

[6] New Orleans, *Times-Picayune*, September 24, 1927, p. 1.

United States Chamber of Commerce pledged its hearty co-operation in the effort to secure federal legislation to insure the Mississippi valley against further flood disasters.[1]   How well it lived up to that pledge will be shown in the next chapter.

The floods themselves cannot be overlooked as agents active in promoting the movement for federal control.   In spite of the volumes written about the materialism and selfishness of the people of the United States, they have shown that they have a real love for humanity by the way they have reacted toward calamities throughout the world.   " Immense losses and widespread suffering" of the delta people have made a lasting impression on the people of the whole nation.[2] It is very evident that floods have become increasingly important during the life of the Mississippi River Commission. While many have suggested the idea, the nation as a whole realizes that any plan of control must accept conditions as they are.   Civilization in the delta will not retreat.   Its people will not abandon much of our most fertile agricultural land.[3]

The people of the United States have finally realized that floods will continue to increase in importance.   The greatness of floods may be expressed in four ways; the area inundated, losses in life and property, height of gauge readings, and volume of water discharged.[4]   All of the standards of measurement have received attention from the public, but only the one standard of losses of life and property has made a lasting impression on the mind of the general public.   And the measurement of floods in that way makes their increasing

[1] New Orleans, *Times-Picayune*, May 6, 1927.

[2] New Orleans, *Times-Democrat*, April 19, 1882.

[3] Alvord and Burdick, *Relief from Floods*, p. 1.

[4] *Annals of the American Academy of Political and Social Science*, Jan., 1928, p. 1.

importance far more evident. Floods have not become more frequent, and measured by any other standard not so much worse. Secretary Hoover said that twenty-five years ago such a flood as that of 1927 would have wrought far less destruction, simply because there were far fewer people and far less property in the delta at that time.[1] As the levees grow higher and higher, due to the drainage of lands adjacent and the confinement of the water, and as population continues to increase, floods will become more and more destructive.[2] Property values and the density of population have already reached such a status that, in the words of Secretary Hoover, " No one can contemplate these millions of our fellow citizens living in such jeopardy without adequate and final protection ".[3] In 1880, outside of Memphis and New Orleans, the entire delta had a population of less than one-half million, and the value of farm property totaled less than $51,-000,000.[4] In 1927 the flood drove three-fourths of a million people from their homes and caused a direct property loss to farms of about one hundred million dollars.[5]

The *Washington Post* during the flood of 1897 proclaimed that it should teach Congress and the country that the Federal government would have to control floods to prevent tremendous losses and suffering from them.[6] Francis G. Newlands said that prior to the flood of 1913 the people of the country had felt that something ought to be done and perhaps would

[1] *House Committee on Flood Control*, 70th Cong., 1st Sess., 1927-8, *Committee Doc.*, no. 16, p. 13.

[2] *House Committee on Flood Control, Hearings 1916*, p. 13.

[3] *House Committee on Flood Control*, 70th Cong., 1st Sess., 1927-8, *Committee Doc.*, no. 16, p. 13.

[4] *House Report*, no. 300, 63rd Cong., 2nd Sess., pt. 2, 1914, p. 42.

[5] *Mississippi River Flood Control Association, Losses and Damages Resulting from the Flood of 1927*, p. 5.

[6] *Washington Post*, April 21, 1897.

be done in the future, but the great suffering and immense losses during 1913 had convinced the people of the United States that something had to be done, " and done at once ".[1] Certainly losses, suffering and appeals for aid have drawn the attention of our people to the need of and have created much sentiment for federal control, because the people have more and more come to believe that no power less than that of the nation could cope with the situation.[2]   Many import- ant witnesses have testified before Congressional Committees that floods had created much sentiment and much agitation for federal control.[3]   The statement that floods offer con- vincing proof that only the government of the nation can con- trol them has made frequent appearances during and im- mediately following great inundations.[4]   Many have gone so far as to state that floods have been blessings in disguise be- cause they aroused the nation to action to prevent future disasters.[5]

The lack of interest in federal control in periods when inundations have been few and small received confirmation by conditions from 1903 to 1912.   There were no serious floods during this period.   In the meantime the interest in the problem of control reached its lowest point since the Civil War.   Even the Mississippi River Commission almost con- cluded that no more money was needed for levees and that the Federal government could soon turn the entire task over to the local boards.[6]   In 1911 the Federal government spent

---

[1] *National Waterways*, vol. i, June, 1913, p. 316.

[2] St. Louis, *Globe-Democrat*, May 1, 1927.

[3] *House Committee on Flood Control*, 70th Cong., 1st Sess., 1927-8, *Committee Doc.*, no. 1, p. 137.

[4] *Scientific America*, February, 1928, p. 144.

[5] Memphis, *Commercial Appeal*, October 9, 1927.

[6] *House Report*, no. 300, 63rd Cong., 2nd Sess., pt. 2, 1914, p. 43.

only $130,000 for levees.[1]   Then the two great floods in successive years in 1912 and 1913 rekindled enthusiastic interest throughout the nation.

Certain phases of fighting a flood naturally tend to focus attention on the activities of the Federal government.   The Mississippi River Commission makes its power and presence felt on such occasions.   United States soldiers and sailors, airplanes, boats, army huts, army rations, public health officers and other agencies have active and visible parts in the fight.   The President issues proclamations, appoints Cabinet officials to supervise the work, and appeals to the people of the nation to give aid.   The Red Cross itself has been, unknowingly perhaps, an agency for creating public demand for Federal control.   The wide public appeal by thousands from the lowest to the President of the United States and the hundreds of proclamations by Mayors, Governors, and Presidents asking for aid and picturing the suffering have done much to create sympathetic public opinion.[2]   An appeal that could raise seventeen million dollars by voluntary contribution to relieve sufferers of one disaster must have a wide effect.[3]

The importance of the press as an agency for creating public sentiment for flood control would be hard to overestimate, although it is so obvious that it requires little discussion.   Of late years floods have been head-line events to be written up by star reporters of practically all of the nation's newspapers.   Flood disasters have been topics for editorials on thousands of occasions in hundreds of dailies in all sections.[4]   While a very few papers have opposed federal con-

[1] B. G. Humphreys, *Floods and Levees of the Mississippi River*, p. 58.

[2] *Commercial and Financial Chronicle*, vol. 124, April 30, 1927, p. 2540.

[3] *Mississippi River Flood Control Association, Losses and Damages Resulting from the Flood of 1927*, p. 5.

[4] *Literary Digest*, vol. 97, April 14, 1928, p. 11.

trol and several have insisted on local participation, the overwhelming sentiment has been for placing the entire burden
on the Federal government.   Magazines have joined the
newspapers in what has really amounted to a crusade.   A
regular deluge of articles by well-known authors has been
loosed upon the country.   Practically all have been favorable
to federal control, although they have differed in proposing
ways and means.[1]   The great suffering among the people of
the delta and the bad general effects of the floods have received especial attention from the press.[2]

Motion pictures have been important factors in spreading
propaganda.   They have shown thousands of reels depicting
floods and results of floods, generally with sub-topics friendly
to federal control.   The Chairman of the Board of Directors
of the American Picture Show Association, which controls
17,000 screens, submitted a resolution to the 70th Congress
urging the Federal government to pay the entire cost.   He
admitted that the great and powerful picture show association
had been spreading propaganda by showing flood scenes.[3]
The influence of the screen pictures on public opinion can
not very accurately be estimated.   Yet, it must have been
considerable, especially in a case where the humanitarian
spirit could be so easily roused as in the case of flood
pictures.

Also the radio must be given consideration as a vital factor
in influencing the public mind.   During the flood of 1927
several high-powered stations gave hourly reports on conditions.   At times during that flood as many as forty of the
nation's leading stations combined in hook-ups to broadcast
speeches of prominent men on the subject. Secretary Hoover
spoke on several occasions, and other prominent men spoke

[1] *Literary Digest*, vol. 94, April 6, 1927, p. 11.
[2] *Washington Post*, August 29, 1928.
[3] *Cong. Record*, 70th Cong., 1st Sess., pt. 8, 1928, p. 6161.

on the various programs.[1]   The speeches made appeals for
aid, described the conditions and suffering of the delta people,
stressed the effects of floods on the delta and on the whole
nation, and even made direct appeals for federal control.

The influence of political leaders could not be eliminated
from such a vast problem as flood control.   Members of
Congress from the delta have ever been prominent in unani-
mous support of flood-control legislation.   Garland, Alcorn,
Kellog, Gibson, Ransdell, Broussard, Humphreys, Wilson
and dozens of others have been leaders in securing legislation.
At home, in planning the actual control, such men as T. G.
Dabney have been great powers.[2]   But the political leaders
have not been confined to the delta.   President Tyler,
Thomas H. Benton, John C. Calhoun, Henry Clay, Abraham
Lincoln, Andrew Johnson, James A. Garfield, and Chester
A. Arthur have been listed as only a few of the early prominent men in politics who urged flood control.[3]   At a later
date William Jennings Bryan stressed the national duty of
solving the problem.[4]   At a time when the fight reached a
crucial stage Woodrow Wilson, William H. Taft, and Theodore Roosevelt pledged their support.[5]   Roosevelt considered
the problem of importance to the entire nation.[6]   President
Roosevelt and his contemporaries frequently referred to the
building of the Panama Canal as an example of the type of
organization and the method of handling a problem that
should be employed in managing the flood situation.   He
thought that the United States should provide funds and

---

[1] *Commercial and Financial Chronicle*, vol. 124, June 4, 1927, p. 3300.

[2] R. S. Taylor, *Mississippi River Improvement*, p. 7.

[3] *House Report*, no. 300, 63rd Cong., 2nd Sess., pt. 2, 1914, p. 9.

[4] B. G. Humphreys, *Floods and Levees of the Mississippi River*, p. 14.

[5] *House Committee on Flood Control, Hearings 1916*, p. 9.

[6] *Senate Committee on Commerce, Hearings 1904*, p. 29.

establish a policy for the whole river in one act " exactly as was done in the case of the Panama Canal ".[1]   Members of Congress often went so far as to suggest that the organization and machinery should be brought directly from Panama and put to work on the task of flood control.[2]   President Wilson requested his Secretaries of Agriculture, Commerce, and Interior to study the problem and to make recommendations to him.   They prepared a memorandum for him recommending a comprehensive plan to be financed largely by the sale of United States bonds.   However, they suggested that the existing plans for control on the lower Mississippi continue while investigations were being made, for the purpose of making more comprehensive plans.[3]

Politicians have their ears to the ground for all significant expressions of public opinion.   Even Congress hears the people speak.[4]   Thus, when legislatures both in and out of the delta sent resolutions to Congress asking for federal control politicians paid attention.[5]   When scores of mayors and various types of clubs added their requests they paid closer attention.[6]   The national platforms of the major parties could be expected to give the problem consideration.   Since 1892 the Democrat platform has embodied strong statements for control of the Mississippi river floods.[7]   In 1912, when the problem received the most attention in a national campaign, all three platforms (Republican, Progressive and

---

[1] *New York Times*, April 6, 1913.

[2] New Orleans, *Times-Picayune*, April 15, 1912.

[3] *House Committee on Flood Control, Hearings 1916*, p. 186.

[4] *Senate Committee on Commerce, Hearings 1904*, p. 67.

[5] *Cong. Record*, 64th Cong., 1st Sess., pt. 10, 1916, p. 8309.

[6] *Mississippi River Levee Association, Public Sentiment on Flood Protection as Expressed by Mayors and Commercial Organizations*, p. 1.

[7] K. H. Porter, *National Party Platforms*, p. 164.

Democrat) contained important clauses favoring Federal control.[1]

The favorable attitude of so many prominent leaders, the effects of so many resolutions and memorials from influential sources, and the endorsement of the major parties would surely reflect in the practical politics of Congress. Many of the leaders in the fight for flood-control legislation have from the beginning wanted the problem to stand alone on its own merits as a non-partisan measure. The conventions of the Mississippi Valley Association since 1845 have asked for the separation of flood control from all other problems because it touched the interests of the whole nation.[2] Many leaders have contended that such a good measure did not need to be linked up with any other cause, nor to have practical politicians bargain for it, as its own merits would carry it through.[3] But the majority of leaders appear to have been perfectly willing to engage in political bargaining. The most generally used method was to get the appropriations for flood control into the rivers and harbors bill in connection with many other projects scattered all over the country.[4] The rivers and harbors bill for years represented the greatest piece of pork-barrel legislation enacted by Congress. Yet, friends of flood control willingly took the chance of getting their project labeled as pork-barrel by allying themselves with other projects, undoubtedly pork-barrel, in order to secure federal funds. The persistence of the statement of the purpose to aid navigation in making appropriations for levees shows a distinct concession to practical politics. The friends of flood control knew that such a bill could get more votes than one that frankly admitted itself a flood-control

[1] K. H. Porter, *National Party Platforms*, p. 345.

[2] *Cong. Record*, 52nd Cong., 1st Sess., pt. 3, 1892, p. 2311.

[3] *Journal of the Association of Engineers*, vol. 49, Sept., 1912, p. 72.

[4] *Cong. Record*, 52nd Cong., 1st Sess., pt. 2, 1892, p. 1130.

bill.   So they saw to it that the purposes of the improvements always included the statement that they would aid the navigation of the river.   In 1917 the flood-control leaders for the first time proved willing to take a chance on a separate bill that frankly proposed control of the Mississippi for the protection of the delta.   Since that time all acts for flood control have been frankly delta-relief acts, and have been separated from all other projects.   However, much practical politics has been back of the later laws, because the members of Congress from the valley have always been willing to compromise on almost any other measure just to have their way on this one problem.

There appears to be something about the vast problem of the Mississippi that has caused those who have studied it to want to see the destructive work of floods.   Politicians have grasped this idea.   So they have often invited fellow members of Congress to tour the delta while the Mississippi spread itself like a yellow sea over wide areas.   Congressional parties of varying sizes have gone forth in boats on many occasions.[1]   The next session of Congress generally found all members of the touring party supporting legislation to control the unruly stream.   They have generally returned convinced that the people unanimously supported federal aid or federal control.[2]

Agencies created by Congress itself have become propagrandists for federal control.   Since 1822 numerous reports have been made by special commissions created by Congress or special details of engineers.   The reports have invariably suggested the advisability of federal control.   In 1898 a very strong commission, known as the Nelson Commission, made a lengthy report in which it stated " the burden of completing

[1] Memphis, *Commercial Appeal*, October 25, 1927.
[2] *The Outlook*, vol. 131, July 26, 1922.

the levee system is too great for local and state authority ".[1]
The Warren Committee of 1875 said only the Federal government could control it; the burden was too much for the states.[2] Hearings by various Congressional Committees on many occasions have proved to be great sources of propaganda for federal control. The testimony of some of the hearings has filled thousands of pages. It has come from prominent and influential men of all walks of life, and has practically all been favorable to federal control.[3] The Mississippi River Commission has also aided in creating favorable public sentiment by its annual and special reports, by the testimony of its members before Congressional Committees, and by numerous speeches delivered by its members in all parts of the country. The Commission has frequently stated that only federal aid could solve the problem, and that states and local districts could do little in the matter. And it has especially stressed the interstate nature of the problem, which has been a very strong point for federal participation.[4] It has also continuously contended that expenditures for flood control represented a good investment for the nation because they increased the wealth and prosperity of a large section of the country which in turn reflected itself throughout the nation.[5]

The speeches of many members of Congress have also strongly supported federal control. When delivered on the floors of Congress or printed in the extended remarks they have been given wide circulation.[6] And outside of Congress,

[1] *House Executive Document*, no. 127, 43rd Cong., 2nd Sess., 1875, p. 33.

[2] B. G. Humphreys, *Floods and Levees of the Mississippi River*, p. 54.

[3] B. G. Humphreys, *Floods and Levees of the Mississippi River*, p. 57.

[4] *House Committee on Flood Control*, 70th Cong., 1st Sess., 1927-8, *Committee Doc.*, no. 16, p. 7.

[5] *Ibid., Report to Accompany House Bill*, no. 8219, p. 91.

[6] Speech of James B. Aswell, House of Representatives, April 9, 1928, *Flood Control a National Obligation.*

the members have made many favorable speeches. Some have gone so far as to tour sections of the country on speaking campaigns avowedly in behalf of federal control.[1]   Any estimate of the forces that have made for federal control must give consideration to political leaders and practical politics as outstanding agencies.

[1] *Senate Committee on Commerce, Hearings 1904*, p. 69.

CHAPTER IX

THE FLOOD OF 1927 AND THE LEGISLATION OF 1928

THE people of the Mississippi delta have suffered as few others in the world from inundations. They have developed a fortitude in the face of floods that gives one of the world's best examples of how determined man's struggle with nature becomes when all his resources are needed. Many prominent engineers and many laymen feel that these people will continue to live in jeopardy of inundation every few years, even after all possible means of protection have been adopted.[1] This jeopardy from floods directly contradicts the statement in 1926 by the Mississippi River Commission that the end of the flood-control fight along the Mississippi was near. Now, even the Commission has admitted that the people of the delta will not be secure for several years, if ever. Although the rest of the people of the United States have known that inundations seem to be inevitabl in the lower Mississippi valley, the flood of 1927 so impressed them that it easily took first place in the list of important events in our national life during that year.[2]

The flood of 1927, measured by gauge readings, by volume of discharge, or by destruction, was the greatest since the formation of the Union. The Mississippi River Commission had established a provisional levee grade to give a freeboard margin of safety above the water line of three feet above the confined height of the greatest flood prior to 1927.

[1] *The Outlook*, vol. 146, June 8, 1927, p. 182.

[2] *The Annals of the American Academy of Political and Social Science,* vol. 135, January, 1928, p. 15.

This provisional grade called for 55.8 feet at Greenville and 60.5 at Arkansas City. The United States Chief of Engineers estimated that the 1927 flood confined would have been 62.8 feet at Greenville and 69 feet at Arkansas City.[1] The record-breaking gauge readings brought forth a recommendation of increases in levee heights by as much as nineteen feet in some places. It must be admitted that much of the height on the gauges came from confinement by the levees. The readings often went ten feet above those of corresponding points in the flood of 1882, which inundated practically the entire lower valley.[2] However, the volume of discharge shows that the gauge readings furnished a good standard of measurement and gave a good idea of the immensity of the flood.[3] The volume of confined discharge reached 1,800,000 second-feet at Cairo and 2,472,000 second-feet at Arkansas City.[4] The flood of 1828 had been considered one of the greatest in our history. The computed maximum discharge of that flood at Red River was 1,524,000 second feet.[5] The greatest previous discharge at Cairo occurred in 1858, reaching 1,420,000 second feet; and the flood of 1892 discharged 1,742,000 second feet at Arkansas City to establish the record for this station prior to 1927.[6]

A very heavy rainfall was experienced throughout most of the Mississippi valley during the fall of 1926 and early winter of 1926-7. The heavy rains filled the soil with water so that the extraordinary rains from January to April, 1927, found

[1] *Cong. Record*, 70th Cong., 1st Sess., pt. 6, 1928, p. 4247.

[2] *Ibid.*

[3] *American Railway Engineering Association Bulletin*, vol. 29, July, 1927, p. 51.

[4] *House Committee on Flood Control*, 70th Cong., 1st Sess., 1927, *Committee Doc.*, no. 3, p. 3.

[5] *Ibid.*, p. 33.

[6] *Ibid.*, no. 1, p. 13.

prompt discharge with a maximum run-off into the rivers.[1] The precipitation resulted directly from the moisture of the Gulf winds, and was especially heavy as far north as the Illinois river.[2]   At various times all of the several large tributaries sent down huge volumes of water to add to the floods already in the main stream.

As the floods rose higher and higher and as the rains continued to fall in various sections of the valley, the forecasts began to predict a record flood.   When it became apparent that the levees might break, the nation was appalled at the impending disaster.   Levees had about been completed to cope with the greatest flood prior to 1927, but they had never been planned to withstand a flood of such magnitude as then approached.[3]   The levee line had been constructed to provide safety from a flood slightly higher than those of 1912 and 1913, but it was hardly finished to that standard.   The flood of 1927 confined would have been four feet higher than these floods.[4]   By April 15, 1927 the inundation became a major disaster when 25,000 people were already forced from their homes.   The ever-ready Red Cross organization began work immediately.   As the crest of the flood moved slowly down the river and as heavy rainstorms on the lower tributaries made record heights certain and general conditions very unfavorable, the flooded area rapidly widened.[5]   By April 22nd, the number of flood refugees had reached 75,000 and was increasing very rapidly with unfavorable forecasts and bad con-

[1] *House Committee on Flood Control*, 70th Cong., 1st Sess., 1927-8, *Committee Doc.*, no. 1, p. 34.

[2] *Ibid.*, p. 34.

[3] *Ibid.*, p. 83.

[4] *American Railway Engineering Association Bulletin*, vol. 29, July, 1927, p. 91.

[5] *Editorial Research Reports, Economic Effects of the Mississippi Flood,* January 9, 1928, p. 10.

ditions for fighting floods still continuing.   " Sensing the enormity of the growing disasters," President Coolidge decided to take strong measures to meet the needs of the situation.[1]   On April 22, 1927, he appointed a committee of five Cabinet Members under the name of the Mississippi Flood Committee to co-operate with and to co-ordinate the work of the various flood-fighting and relief organizations. The members of that committee were the Secretaries of Treasury, War, Navy, Agriculture and Commerce.   Chairman Herbert Hoover immediately left for the scene of the disaster to take active direction of the work.   From time to time other members of the committee joined him but only Hoover remained constantly on the job.[2]

The increased levee heights caused a general realization that the danger from crevasses had been greatly enlarged.   If water piled so high should break through, it simply meant greater destruction.[3]   The destructiveness of the flood had been greatly increased by the rapid growth of population and property values behind the levees.[4]   With a record volume of water moving down the river under very bad weather conditions, with unfavorable forecasts from the Weather Bureau, and with the possibilities of greater damage due to a more dense population, increased property values and great height of levees, it became evident that the greatest fight in the history of Mississippi floods was about to take place.   The Mississippi River Commission, the Red Cross, the various military services of the states and of the nation, levee boards, municipalities, railways and other agencies entered the battle

[1] *The Congressional Digest*, February, 1928, p. 42.

[2] *Ibid.*, p. 41.

[3] I. M. Cline, *Floods in the Lower Mississippi Valley*, p. 17.

[4] *The Annals of the American Academy of Political and Social Science,* vol. 135, January, 1928, p. 15.

with fortitude and determination.[1]   The heroism of the victims, of the rescue parties, of the men fighting to hold the levees, of those working in the refugee camps and of thousands of others can be considered only a little, if any, less than that displayed by our soldiers in the World War.

The chief causes contributing to the breaking of the levees in 1927 were insufficient height, insufficient cross section and caving.[2]   More crevasses occurred than in any previous flood since 1882.[3]   The United States Weather Bureau listed forty important ones in Mississippi and tributary levees.[4]   Some authorities have listed as many as 225 crevasses.[5]   The breaks in the levees permitted about 18,000 square miles to be inundated.[6]

The number of people rescued from the inundated areas gave the Mississippi Flood Committee the " greatest piece of mass relief " that had ever been attempted in America.   The Chairman of the Committee divided the work of fighting the flood into four stages: the rescue of the people from their flooded homes; the care of the people while in the refugee camps; the reconstruction of the inundated areas; and flood prevention.[7]   The first part of the fight naturally received first consideration.   For that purpose Secretary Hoover and his associates collected the greatest rescue fleet this nation has ever known.   More than one thousand power boats and

[1] *The Mississippi River Flood Control Association, The Flood of 1927*, p. 1 *et seq.*

[2] *Journal of the Association of Engineers*, vol. 25, August, 1900, p. 89.

[3] *American Railway Engineering Association Bulletin*, vol. 29, July, 1927, p. 48.

[4] *House Committee on Flood Control*, 70th Cong., 1st Sess., 1927-8, *Report to Accompany House Bill*, no. 8219, p. 10.

[5] *Cong. Record*, 70th Cong., 1st Sess., pt. 6, 1928, p. 4251.

[6] *House Committee on Flood Control*, 70th Cong., 1st Sess., 1927-8, *Report to Accompany House Bill*, no. 8219, p. 3.

[7] *The Survey*, vol. 58, July 1, 1927, p. 357.

literally thousands of auxiliary craft of every description.[1]
The vastness of their task is shown by the fact that more than
700,000 people were driven from their homes and had to be
assembled in refugee camps or in places where they could be
cared for by the Red Cross and other agencies.[2]   How well
the work was done is shown by the fact that 330,000 people
were actually rescued from levee tops, trees, house tops, and
other points of temporary safety and that more than 607,000
were carried to Red Cross refugee camps.[3]   The actual loss
in life will never be known because of the large area inundated and the transient nature of much of the negro population of the delta.[4]   After the waters receded many human
bodies were found in some sections.[5]   However, the official reports show a total loss of life of less than 250.[6]   That
so many people could have been rescued from such precarious
places with such little loss of life was indeed remarkable.

When the officials began to check up the damages from this
inundation, which had surpassed the records of all previous
ones, they rightfully concluded that, in the words of Secretary Hoover, " this flood has been the greatest disaster of
peace times in our history ".[7]   And the press and public
apparently almost unanimously agreed that Secretary Hoover
had not at all overstated the calamity.[8]

[1] *The Congressional Digest*, February, 1928, p. 42.

[2] *House Committee on Flood Control*, 70th Cong., 1st Sess., 1927-8, *Report to Accompany House Bill*, no. 8219, p. 3.

[3] *Editorial Research Reports, Economic Effects of the Mississippi Flood*, p. 10.

[4] *Journal of Geography*, November, 1927, p. 298.

[5] *Cong. Record*, 70th Cong., 1st Sess., 1927-8, pt. 6, p. 4251.

[6] *House Committee on Flood Control*, 70th Cong., 1st Sess., 1927-8, *Report to Accompany House Bill*, no. 8219, p. 3.

[7] *Washington Star*, June 12, 1927.

[8] *The New Republic*, vol. 50, May 18, 1927, p. 343.

The Mississippi River Flood Control Association collected data from the various counties and parishes of the delta and published the compilation practically without comment in a booklet of 213 pages.[1]   The study went rather fully into a detail of property damages and loss of life.   The report placed the direct property damage at $236,334,414.06 and the loss of lives at 183.[2]   The United States Weather Bureau estimated the direct property loss at $363,533,154.00.[3]   This gigantic sum far surpassed the $78,188,000.00 for the flood of 1912 and $17,088,000.00 for 1922, which were the most destructive inundations prior to 1927.[4]   The terrible toll fell on farmers, business men, and people of all walks of life.   It affected rural districts, villages and cities both near and far. It scourged both white and black.   But of all classes the owners of land suffered most in property damages and the negro tenant farmers most in loss of lives.   The negroes more frequently than the whites lost all the property they had, but they owned practically nothing in most cases except very meager household furnishings.   The fare in the refugee camps and the supplies furnished by the Red Cross as they returned home seemed to satisfy most of them.

Yet, even the huge total, as estimated by the above agencies, does not by any means include all of the losses, not even the direct losses.   Just one illustration will show how far the direct losses extended.   The lower delta had become one of the leading fur-selling sections of the United States.   The muskrats alone in the state of Louisiana yielded 6,750,000 pelts annually prior to the flood of 1927.[5]   It will be many

---

[1] *Mississippi River Flood Control Association, Losses and Damages Resulting from the Flood of 1927.*

[2] *Ibid.,* p. 5.

[3] *Editorial Research Reports, Economic Effects of the Mississippi Flood*, January 9, 1928, p. 11.

[4] *Congressional Record*, 70th Cong., 1st Sess., pt. 6, 1928, p. 4252.

[5] *The National Geographic Magazine*, vol. 52, Sept., 1927, p. 264.

years before this industry will have reached its former position because the flood of 1927 took a terrible toll in all of the wild life of the lower valley.[1] It has been authoritatively estimated that 50 per cent of the animals in the inundated area perished.[2]

The indirect losses perhaps equaled or surpassed the direct losses. Certainly they totaled an enormous sum, but they were so intangible that they could not be calculated by the most skilled statisticians. Secretary Hoover estimated them at $200,000,000.00.[3] The estimate has been generally accepted as perhaps as good as any. The indirect losses extended to every one who was in any way affected by the unfavorable influence of the flood on business, including laborers, farmers and investors. The investors in securities of industries in the area, in securities of the levee boards and farm lands of the delta, and in industries closely connected with the lower valley suffered heavy indirect losses. The intangibility of these damages may be shown by a statement of Secretary Hoover in the summer of 1927 that " the greatest of all measures needed is prompt and effective flood control and quick legislation, for that will restore confidence and there will come a recovery in values in business ".[4] When one attempts to estimate the economic value of the business confidence of people in a section, he has assumed a rather difficult task. The ramifications of indirect losses may be illustrated by the dairy industry. Dairying had begun to gain a foothold in much of the inundated areas. The flood

---

[1] *Nature Magazine*, vol. x, July, 1927, p. 31.

[2] *Editorial Research Reports, Economic Effects of the Mississippi Flood,* p. 12.

[3] *Mississippi River Flood Control Association, Losses and Damages Resulting from the Flood of 1927,* p. 3.

[4] *Commerce and Finance,* vol. 16, July 27, 1927, p. 1495.

seriously delayed its development. The destruction of, or
serious injury to, an infant industry cannot be estimated as
the actual value of the property destroyed.[1] Another indirect loss that could scarcely be measured was the loss of
negro labor from the delta farms. Many negroes never returned to their former homes. Some sections lost as much
as one-third of their negroes. In a section of increasing
shortage of farm labor this was a serious blow, at least
temporarily.[2]

Thus, including both direct and indirect losses, the flood
of 1927 must have destroyed something less than 250 lives
and in the neighborhood of a half billion dollars of property
values. Judged on the basis of losses and damages, it was
the super-flood of our history, so much larger than any previous one that comparisons are difficult to make.

The Mississippi River Commission assumed charge of the
government funds to be spent in the emergency. The total
amount reached $6,806,574.00 of federal funds and $1,-
323,070.00 of local funds, in all $8,129,644.00 of public
money.[3] Just how that huge sum for emergency expenditure
became available forms an interesting example of an illegal
act that met the approval of all governmental agencies, and
apparently of practically all of the people. In the spring of
1927 the Mississippi River Commission had $5,000,000.00
on hand; but it could legally spend only about 60 per cent of
it because the locals could not raise their quotas. The Commission, if it could get the authorization, wanted to spend all
of the money to repair crevasses. The President and several
members of his official family wanted to use still additional
money from other funds in the hands of the government.

[1] *Manufacturers Record*, vol. 91, May 26, 1927, p. 67.

[2] *Congressional Record*, 70th Cong., 1st Sess., pt. 6, 1928, p. 4252.

[3] *House Committee on Flood Control*, 70th Cong., 1st Sess., 1927-8,
Committee Doc., no. 1, p. 87.

The Comptroller General was asked for a ruling concerning the use of the funds.[1] He ruled that the expenditure of the money in the hands of the Mississippi River Commission without local contribution and the diversion of other funds for purposes of flood relief would be illegal. Then, Chairman Martin B. Madden of the House Appropriation Committee publicly agreed with the Mississippi River Commission, President Coolidge and others that the funds ought to be illegally spent.[2] At the suggestion of President Coolidge, Mr. Madden and General H. M. Lord, Director of the Budget, conferred on what should be done under the existing conditions. Mr. Madden then wrote to the President expressing his willingness to share responsibility for using funds in a manner that the Comptroller General had declared would be a violation of the law. He also offered to assume full responsibility for replacing these funds when Congress met. With that understanding, the President authorized the Secretary of War to divert $2,000,000.00 that had been appropriated for river and harbor work. And the Mississippi River Commission spent $7,000,000.00 of Federal funds, about $4,000,-000.00 illegally, in the emergency work caused by the flood of 1927.[3] True to his promise, Mr. Madden succeeded in securing an emergency appropriation on December 22, 1927, of $7,000,000.00 to replace the money spent in the great emergency.

The flood of 1927, may be considered as having begun in August, 1926, when heavy general rains fell throughout the central valley. During September and October heavy rains continued to fall, even to the extent of serious floods in local areas. Thus, through a season of the year when the weather usually has been very dry the heavy rainfall soaked the earth

[1] *Congressional Digest*, February, 1928, p. 41.

[2] *Cong. Record*, 70th Cong., 1st Sess., pt. 1, 1927-8, p. 212.

[3] *Cong. Digest*, February, 1928, p. 41.

and filled the streams, which process continued during the usual heavy winter precipitation.[1]   The importance of the various drainage basins vary greatly in their contributions to floods on the lower Mississippi.   But one of the striking features of the flood of 1927 was that none of its major tributaries, with the exception of the Arkansas, could be charged with extreme flood conditions.   The flood on the main stream resulted from a co-ordination of floods from all of them.[2]   The co-ordination of floods piled up the water until in early April record heights were in prospect.   But April and May only brought more rains and more crevasses. The waters receded enough to permit many to rush back to their farms in the last of May and begin to plant their crops, which should have been planted before the inundation.   In June another rise poured through the levees and flooded most of the section again.   In considerable areas of Louisiana water stood over farming lands from this rise until late in July.[3]   On June 15, 1927, there remained in Red Cross refugee camps 63,378 persons and on July 15th 17,100. Even as late as September 15th, the Red Cross reported 2,667 in refugee camps.[4]   No other flood in history had approached this record for duration.

No account of the flood of 1927 could fail to report the work of the Red Cross.   No other peace-time task of similar size had ever been undertaken.   To care for more than 600,000 people by voluntary subscription looks like almost an impossible task.   The collection and wise expenditure of more than seventeen and a quarter million dollars show both

[1] *Cong. Digest*, February, 1928, p. 42.

[2] Lamar T. Beman, *Flood Control, Reference Shelf*, vol. v, no. 7, p. 52.

[3] *Editorial Research Reports*, January 9, 1928, *Economic Effects of the Mississippi Flood*, p. 10.

[4] *Mississippi River Flood Control Association, Losses and Damages Resulting from the Flood*, 1927.

the generosity of the American people and the efficiency of the Red Cross as a relief organization. To the people of the delta this organization in those dark hours was in fact the great Mother.[1]

The Red Cross rescue fleet seemingly sprang into existence over night. No one knows how many boats took part in the errands of mercy. But the official report of the Red Cross states that the fleet consisted of about 1,000 power boats, " and hundreds of small auxiliary craft, such as rowboats and launches ".[2] Boats of all descriptions came from the army, the navy, the coast guard, the Bureau of Lighthouses, the Mississippi River Commission, private corporations and hundreds of individuals.[3] From the Great Lakes to the Atlantic Seaboard and the Gulf of Mexico United States coast-guard boats rushed at full speed. Trainloads of small power boats poured into Memphis, Vicksburg, Baton Rouge and other river points. From the Gulf came scores of fishermen with their gasoline launches to volunteer for duty without pay. One Memphis factory built and donated fifty medium-sized craft in a single night and had them ready for duty with small motors and on the river the next day.[4] A large fleet of airplanes furnished by the state and Federal governments and by private owners became the eyes of the rescue fleet. Thirty United States planes inspected the flooded area twice daily, flying a total of more than 75,000 miles.[5] This motley fleet carried the many thousands of refugees to the Red Cross camps, which were kept under a

---

[1] *Cong. Digest*, February, 1928, p. 43.

[2] *House Committee on Flood Control*, 70th Cong., 1st Sess., 1927-8, *Report to Accompany House Bill*, no. 8219, p. 232.

[3] The Mississippi River Flood Control Association, *The Flood of 1927*, p. 24.

[4] *House Committee on Flood Control*, 70th Cong., 1st Sess., 1927, *Report to Accompany House Bill*, no. 8219, p. 233.

[5] *Ibid.*, p. 226.

semi-military discipline with the aid of state and local authorities and even soldiers. The homeless people were cared for in 149 refugee camps and in many public buildings.

While the flood inundated the lands the maintenance of the refugees and their livestock furnished the most expensive and the most important item. For this purpose the Red Cross spent about $6,500,000.00 and utilized the services of thousands of volunteer workers under the supervision of Red Cross workers of local authorities.[1] It should be noted that more than 200,000 head of livestock were rescued, taken to refugee camps, and cared for by the Red Cross.

Although the problem of maintenance required more money and more work, as far as the loss of lives was concerned, it soon became evident that the danger of disease was the greater menace. The Red Cross workers did not fear this problem so long as they had the refugees closely under supervision in the camps where cases of contagious diseases could be isolated, pure water furnished and sanitary measures carried out. On returning home, the refugees would become susceptible to various diseases the germs of which had been acquired in camp or were in the water or the unsanitary environment caused by the flood. While the Red Cross regarded the health work as supplementary, leaving the main responsibility on the United States Public Health Service and the State Boards of Health, its own work cost more than $600,000.00 and covered a wide range, including the inoculation of more than 410,000 persons against typhoid fever, the vaccinating of 141,229 persons against smallpox and the distribution of 25,000,000 grains of quinine to combat malaria.[2] The preventive work of the Red Cross went so far as to screen the houses of the returned refugees.

[1] *Cong. Digest*, February, 1928, p. 43.

[2] *House Committee on Flood Control*, 70th Cong., 1st Sess., 1927-8, *Report to Accompany House Bill*, no. 8219, p. 237.

This type of work led directly into the third phase of the flood problem as outlined by Secretary Hoover, that of reconstruction. The word reconstruction took on a new meaning to thousands of delta people as the refugees returned to their homes to be cared for until they could get back on their feet and earn their own living. The destruction of homes and crops, the loss of implements and livestock and in many cases the complete loss of all property made some plan of reconstruction absolutely necessary. The Red Cross furnished, at the expense of more than $6,500,000.00, food for people and feed for livestock and poultry, clothing, household furnishings, buildings, repairs, farm implements, livestock, seed, and whatever might be greatly needed by 565,000 people for varying lengths of time.[1]

An important phase of the work of reconstruction was the creation of Agricultural Finance Corporations for the purpose of furnishing credit to the farmers of the inundated area. In addition to the destitute, who were being aided by the Red Cross, Secretary Hoover and other leaders recognized that thousands of farmers would sorely need credit, which they could not obtain through ordinary channels, due to crop shortages and failures caused by the flood.[2] The bankers and business men of the South joined in forming in the states of Louisiana, Mississippi and Arkansas Agricultural Finance Corporations that would rediscount securities of the farmers to the extent of $7.50 per acre.[3] It soon became apparent that the three state corporations did not have sufficient capital to meet the urgent needs of the farmers. The entire situation was presented to President Coolidge by Secretary Hoover. The President by letter requested Lewis

[1] *Cong. Digest*, February, 1928, p. 43.

[2] *Editorial Research Reports, Economic Effects of the Mississippi Flood*, January 9, 1928, p. 15.

[3] *Commercial and Financial Chronicle*, vol. 124, June 4, 1927, p. 3301.

E. Pierson, a New York banker who had been selected by the Chamber of Commerce of the United States to lead in flood rehabilitation work, to call a conference of business men and to urge them to help out in the emergency. The bankers met in Washington with Secretary Hoover in attendence.[1] Within an hour the entire procedure had been finished. The bankers had formed a large holding company called the Flood Credits Corporation, with a capital of $2,000,000.00. Its subscribers received debentures against the Agricultural Finance Corporations of Louisiana, Mississippi and Arkansas. The officers were M. N. Buckner, Chairman of the Board of the New York Trust Company, President and S. W. Reyburn, President of Lord and Taylor, Vice-President. The directors came from the International Harvester Company, General Motors Corporation, General Electric Company, Duquesne National Bank of Pittsburg, and the Union Trust Company of Cleveland. The purpose of that corporation was solely to strengthen the stock of the corporations of the delta states.[2] The additional two million dollars in capital enabled the combination of credit corporation to secure twelve to fifteen million dollars from intermediate credit banks on a capital of three and one half million dollars.[3] In many sections the opinion was widely held that the expectation that this form of ordinary commercial credit would complete the work of reconstruction of the inundated areas was " excessively optimistic ".[4] But the fact that big business men of other parts of the country voluntarily risked $2,000,000.00 in the enterprise showed both that they had considerable faith in the ultimate success of the plan and

[1] *The Nation's Business*, vol. 15, July, 1927, p. 52.

[2] *Ibid*.

[3] *Ibid*.

[4] *Editorial Research Reports, Economic Effects of the Mississippi Flood*, January 9, 1928, p. 15.

that they felt that the problem definitely influenced the business conditions of the entire country.

" The immensity of the 1927 disaster was that touch of nature which established the kinship of the whole nation ".[1] There grew out of the terrible calamity a widespread feeling that it should be the last destructive flood. The people of the country, and especially the people of the delta, freely expressed the hope and the opinion that the Federal government would take ample steps to see that the world's greatest delta would not again suffer from an inundation.[2] Probably no peace-time disaster ever received such wide publicity. No greater public question in peace time ever had a more uniform demand for quick and decisive action. Magazines and newspapers almost without exception gave discussion of the 1927 flood prominent display. The very best reporters and writers wrote the flood reports. Many of the writers spent much time in the inundated area.[3] The very wide discussion of the gravity of such a great flood apparently almost universally aroused a sympathetic feeling for Federal control.[4] The wide publicity campaign had been prepared by special writers that had been sent to the flooded areas, by hundreds of moving-picture reels and by thousands of pictures that went to every hamlet in America.[5] Secretary Hoover said that the " one bright ray which comes out of the gloomy situation confronting the Mississippi valley " was the " realization that the 125,000,000 people of the United States " had been " awakened to the fact that this valley must

[1] Memphis, *Commercial Appeal*, April 26, 1928.

[2] *The Survey*, vol. 58, July 1, 1927, p. 277.

[3] *Literary Digest*, vol. 97, April 14, 1928, p. 10.

[4] *United States Daily*, October 28, 1927, p. 1.

[5] *House Committee on Flood Control*, 70th Cong., 1st Sess., 1927-8, *Report to Accompany House Bill*, no. 8219, p. 17.

be protected from future catastrophe ".[1]   He again urged the nation to take a lesson from the 1927 flood and to provide engineering works adequate to control, which would by no means cost as much as the flood loss of that year.[2]   The *Times-Picayune* of New Orleans sensed the situation when it stated that the entire population of the nation had apparently responded to the call of the inundated and stricken delta for aid in its great campaign for federal control.[3]

The response of the people to the great press campaign, in which a very large majority of both newspapers and magazines openly urged federal control of adequate and effective nature, caused the frequent statements from the press that the Federal government was duty bound to take ample measures to prevent a recurrence of such a disaster.[4]   Papers often urged flood control above all other matters for Congressional consideration.   The *Jersey City Journal* proclaimed that although the people of the nation greatly desired a reduction in taxation, they did not at all want any tax-reduction at " the expense of another disastrous flood in the Mississippi valley ".[5]   The press gave wide publicity to the results of a survey of American business that the United States Chamber of Commerce conducted to determine what business men considered the main problems confronting Congress.   The survey ranked flood control first, with taxation and agricultural relief following.[6]   This ranking apparently represented the consensus of opinion of American business men.   The *Cleveland Plain Dealer* concluded that the flood of 1927 had spoken louder than a five-foot shelf of engineers'

[1] *Cong. Record*, 70th Cong., 1st Sess., 1928, pt. 6, p. 4568.

[2] *Manufacturers Record*, vol. 91, May 12, 1927, p. 63.

[3] New Orleans, *Times-Picayune*, May 22, 1927, p. 9.

[4] *Detroit Free Press*, May 5, 1927, p. 6.

[5] *Literary Digest*, vol. 97, April 14, 1928, p. 11.

[6] *New York Times*, June 23, 1927, pt. 2, p. 27.

reports and resolutions by civic clubs and other organizations in calling attention to facts about floods.[1]

While the work of rescue was going on the campaign for
Federal control began with great enthusiasm and determination; and as the waters receded it continued with increased
momentum.   Every agency that had played any part in
securing Federal control contributed something to the great
campaign of 1927.   The Mississippi River Flood Control
Association obtained the services of nationally-known organizations to calculate the industrial losses.   It used Red Cross
chairmen and county and local officials in collecting and
checking a vast amount of data.   The data collected by the
experts and by the local people were published and given a
wide distribution.[2]   The Association also published a well-
prepared book of photographic views of many striking situations, which it dedicated to the Congress of the United
States.[3]   The deluge of resolutions from varied organizations appeared.   Fifteen years prior to 1927 the Mississippi
River Levee Association had collected and given publicity to
many resolutions from various types of organizations.   But
after the flood of 1927, Congress was deluged by resolutions
pouring forth apparently from every part of the country.
Banker's associations and business men's club with practically no dissenting voices memorialized the Federal government to control floods.[4]   As early as May 22, 1927, while
the flood still covered large areas, forty organizations, practically all of them national in scope, expressed a definite de-

[1] *Cleveland Plain Dealer*, April 18, 1927, p. 18.

[2] Mississippi River Flood Control Association, *Losses and Damages
Resulting from the Flood of 1927*, p. 3.

[3] Mississippi River Flood Control Association, *The Flood of 1927*,
p. 10.

[4] *House Committee on Flood Control*, 70th Cong., 1st Sess., 1927-8,
Committee Doc., no. 18, p. 63.

mand for federal control.[1]   And the period of resolutions
had only begun.   Before the meeting of Congress practically
all business, professional, civic and fraternal organizations
had fallen in line.   Even political organizations joined the
procession.   The National League of Women Voters unanimously indorsed Federal control.[2]   The Southern States
Republican Club adopted a very strong resolution for complete control by the United States.[3]   This club's membership
contained leading Republicans from all of the Southern states.
The American Federation of Labor by a letter from its
president, by resolution, and by official representation before
the House Committee on Flood Control stated in no un-
certain terms its position for complete control entirely at
federal expense.[4]   The American Legion went so far as to
send an urgent request to its members strongly urging them
to write to their members of Congress to support flood-control legislation.[5]   State conferences, tri-state conferences,
inter-state conferences and regional conferences composed of
business men, members of chambers of commerce, levee board
members, leaders of various organizations, politicians and
others met in many places, and seemingly all of the same
opinion and for the same purpose; to procure federal control.[6]
Such organizations as the American Farm Bureau Federation, the American Legion, the United States Chamber of
Commerce, the American Federation of Labor, the American
Investment Bankers Association, the American Bankers
Association, the Mississippi River Flood Control Associa-

[1] New Orleans, *Times-Picayune*, May 22, 1927, p. 9.

[2] *Ibid.*, October 25, 1927, p. 1.

[3] *House Committee on Flood Control*, 70th Cong., 1st Sess., 1927-8, *Committee Doc.*, no. 18, p. 118.

[4] *Cong. Record*, 70th Cong., 1st Sess., pt. 5, 1928, p. 3296.

[5] *Ibid.*, pt. 10, 1928, p. 7548.

[6] New Orleans, *Times-Picayune*, December 21, 1927, p. 14.

tion and others sent strong representations to Washington to work in behalf of legislation.[1] This great campaign of press, of platform, of resolutions and of lobbying grew larger and more enthusiastic throughout the summer and autumn months of 1927. Special trains carrying men urging Federal control again travelled to Washington.[2]

Two very notable examples of the creation of public sentiment by organized effort that should receive special attention occurred in the work of the United States Chamber of Commerce and in the activities of the Chicago Flood Control Conference. During the period of the flood the Board of Directors of the Chamber of Commerce of the United States appointed a special committee to study all phases of the problem that the committee considered " appropriate for Chamber action ".[3] The committee considered the relief and rehabilitation measures under the direction of Secretary Hoover's organization and the Red Cross as satisfactory. So, it turned its attention solely to the problem of formulating a program that would insure a permanent solution, as far as humanly possible, for the flood-control problem.[4] This committee was composed of fifteen well-known men of high rank in their various professions and business.[5] It made a thorough study of the floods over a long period of years, the losses resulting from them and the fight made to control them.[6] Then the committee submitted a short and well-prepared report setting forth its findings. Based on those

[1] *Cong. Record*, 70th Cong., 1st Sess., pt. 7, 1928, p. 5547.

[2] Memphis, *Commercial-Appeal*, December 5, 1927.

[3] *Annals of the American Academy of Political and Social Science,* vol. 135, January, 1928, p. 27.

[4] *Annals of the American Academy of Political and Social Science,* vol. 135, January, 1928, p. 28.

[5] *Ibid.*, p. 27.

[6] *Ibid.*, p. 25.

findings, the Chamber then submitted on October 31, 1927, four recommendations to the entire membership for a referendum by letter ballot.[1] The balloting closed midnight December 15, 1927. The various organizations could cast as many votes as they were entitled to delegates to the annual meeting of the Chamber, which depended upon the size of the organization, but in no case was the vote to be below one or more than ten. The response to the referendum was immediate and very widespread. A total of 1,053 organizations from every state in the Union, the District of Columbia, Alaska, Cuba, Hawaii, Brazil and Germany voted in what proved to be a very one-sided and an exceedingly large vote.[2] The first proposition submitted stated that the Federal government should pay the entire cost of building and maintaining adequate flood-control works on the lower Mississippi river. The vote on that proposition was 2131 in favor of and 512 against it. The second recommendation said that the United States government should assume full responsibility for locating, constructing and maintaining flood-control works. The vote of 2581 for and 240 against proved more one-sided than that on proposition number one. Proposal number three favored adequate appropriations " to insure efficient, continuous, and economic work, the funds to be available as needed ". On it the vote stood 2657½ for and 156½ against. The final recommendation stated that the Mississippi river should be separated from all other projects or undertakings and dealt with by legislation wholly on its own merits. A vote of 2629½ for and 231½ against plainly showed the business men's view on this point. Thus, by an overwhelming vote the Chambers of Commerce of the United States went very definitely on record in favor of complete

[1] *Chamber of Commerce of the United States, Referendum number fifty-one, Special Bulletin,* January 6, 1928, p. 1.

[2] *Ibid.*

control of Mississippi floods at federal expense. Such a referendum of the business organizations very forcibly impressed Congress and the public. The men who had cast this one-sided vote would pay most of the bill if the Federal government should follow their recommendations. As a result of the referendum Frederick Delano, Chairman of the Committee, and other prominent members of the Committee officially stressed before the House Committee on Flood Control the urgent demand and the great necessity for the United States government to finance flood control on the lower Mississippi in its entirety, and for the immediate beginning of the work of construction.[1] In listing the influences which brought about the legislation of 1928, the activities of the Chamber of Commerce of the United States must be given a prominent place.

The other notable event that deserves special mention was the Chicago Flood Control Conference. While the flood was raging, William Hale Thompson, the famous " Big Bill " of Chicago, went down the river to New Orleans on a " victory pilgrimage ". He announced to the world that Chicago stood willing and ready to join hands with New Orleans and with anybody else in the valley to secure immediate and adequate flood control entirely at federal expense.[2] He promised to do all in his power to present flood control before Congress in the most impressive manner. Faithful to his promise, Mayor Thompson secured the meeting of a large number of the Members of Congress at Peoria, Illinois on May 6 and 7, 1927, receiving the cooperation in that enterprise of Representative Martin B. Madden, Chairman of the Appropriations Committee of the House.[3]

[1] *Cong. Record*, 70th Cong., 1st Sess., pt. 6, 1928, p. 4567.

[2] New Orleans, *Times-Picayune*, April 25, 1927.

[3] New Orleans, *Times-Picayune*, May 3, 1927.

In the meantime Mayor O'Keefe of New Orleans joined hands with " Big Bill " of Chicago and Mayor Miller of St. Louis in planning and calling a general flood conference to meet at Chicago in June. This great conference met on June 2, 3 and 4, 1927, in the home town of Mayor Thompson. To it came more than 2,000 people — governors, mayors, members of the House, Senators, Cabinet Members, politicians, engineers, representatives of business organizations and other powerful organizations.[1]   Mayor Thompson's plans moved according to schedule, when he severely indicted the United States government for permitting the great disaster of 1927 as the opening shot of the conference.[2] Whatever one may think of Mayor Thompson, one must admit that "Big Bill" has been a first-class showman. From the time of his " victory pilgrimage " down the Mississippi to his appearance before the Congressional Committee on November 7th, he constantly kept his show going, but the Chicago Conference represented his greatest triumph.   The program prepared for the occasion contained the names of many prominent men in various professions.   President Coolidge sent as his representative Secretary of War, Dwight Davis.   The sentiment of the group seemed unanimously for control of the Mississippi floods.   There appeared some differences as to the nature of the plan and some criticism of the work of the Mississippi River Commission and of Congress.   Secretary Davis's speech proved interesting, especially because he represented the views of the administration. He argued that flood-control was a national problem, but that the nation should first get a workable plan that was sound in both engineering and economic aspects.[3]   His expression

[1] *House Committee on Flood Control*, 70th Cong., 1st Sess., 1927-8, *Committee Doc.*, no. 1, p. 250.

[2] *New York Times*, June 3, 1927, pt. 1, p. 9.

[3] New Orleans, *Times-Picayune*, June 4, 1927, p. 8.

calling for a plan caused some criticism of the Mississippi River Commission for not already having one. Throughout the conference some one occasionally referred to the bureaucracy or to the narrow-mindedness of the Commission.[1] But on the whole the meeting reminded Representative J. J. Cochran of Missouri, who seemed in good Missouri style to scent something suspicious in the proceedings, " of a meeting of a mutual admiration society ".[2]   Whatever happened, Mayor Thompson had star reporters from all of the great newsgathering agencies ready to give the public the side of the question favorable to federal control.   The other side could look out for itself so far as the Mayor was concerned. " Big Bill " simply had a group of publicity experts to tell the world about his show.[3]   Papers in all parts of the country gave prominent and ample space to many strong articles in favor of federal control.

Just how much influence the conference had no one could say, but it was undoubtedly a factor in formulating a favorable opinion.   Several members of Congress from the conference platform and through the press established themselves as strong supporters of federal control.   The President, through his Secretary of War, again went on record in favor of control by the United States government.[4]   Also, much real education came from the conference.   Most of the country had remained marvelously ignorant on the subject in spite of the efforts of the valley people to get their problem before the public.[5]

The Chicago conference requested President Coolidge to call a great nation-wide conference of army engineers, civilian

---

[1] *Manufacturers Record*, vol. 92, July 21, 1927, p. 83.

[2] *Cong. Record*, 70th Cong., 1st Sess., pt. 8, 1928, p. 6248.

[3] *Manufacturers Record*, vol. 91, June 9, 1927, p. 59.

[4] *Commercial and Financial Chronicle*, vol. 124, June 4, 1927, p. 3301.

[5] *Manufacturers Record*, vol. 91, June 9, 1927, p. 59.

engineers, conservationists, geologists, financiers and other experts " to formulate a policy of flood prevention " as a basis for legislation by the next session of Congress.[1] While the resolutions submitted no definite plan of control, the proposal for a meeting of such a diverse group of experts from various professions suggested the idea of a comprehensive scheme.[2]   They plainly urged the nation's duty immediately to " attack the flood problem in a broad and comprehensive way ".[3]   They declared the control of the Mississippi was the sole responsibility of the Federal government, which alone could adequately solve the problem, and that additional means besides levees would have to be employed.   The resolutions were submitted to President Coolidge on June 10, 1927, and apparently received very favorably by him.[4]

The great campaign continued until it seemed that Congress had never received a more universal demand on any question than it had in the demand for immediate and adequate action to control floods on the Mississippi.[5]   Secretary Hoover said : " I believe the whole of the United States is unanimous in that we must undertake such engineering works as will give security not only now but for the future ".[6] The apparent unanimity caused many Congressmen to agree with Representative Luther A. Johnson that one very good reason for the Federal government's controlling floods on the

---

[1] *Manufacturers Record*, vol. 92, July 21, 1927, p. 83.

[2] *New York Times*, June 5, 1927, p. 24.

[3] *House Committee on Flood Control, Committee Doc.*, no. 1, 70th Cong., 1st Sess., 1927, p. 134.

[4] *Ibid.*, p. 259.

[5] *House Committee on Flood Control*, 70th Cong., 1st Sess., 1927, *Report to Accompany House Bill*, no. 8219, p. 5.

[6] *Annals of the American Academy of Political and Social Science*, vol. 135, January, 1928, p. 16.

Mississippi was " because it was the will of the American people ".[1]   And to one who investigates the subject it certainly seems that an overwhelming majority of the American people actually wanted Congress to enact legislation for adequate protection of the delta of the Mississippi.

As the campaign for federal control went on, the question of a special session of Congress to enact flood-control legislation became one of the most controversial questions before the public.   The interest of the public in preventing the recurrence of any disaster has always decreased as the space of time beyond the disaster increased.   The fear of a decreased public interest caused many friends of flood control to desire a special session so that they could present the question to Congress on the wave of public enthusiasm.[2]   To those who wanted the special session, it seemed that President Coolidge had determined to have Congress in session as little as possible, and that he would not heed the demand of a large majority of the American people.[3]   The President's refusal and the flood-control forces' demand caused a widespread debate on the question and much disappointment in many cases.   Many people sincerely felt that the problem justified a special session, if any occasion ever justified one in peace time.[4]   They followed the usual procedure and began to work on their representatives in Congress.   They had little trouble in gaining the support of a large number of Congressmen, several of whom favored the special session of their own accord.   Many members actively campaigned for an extra session.   Senator James A. Reed of Missouri took an active part, sending a telegram to every member of Congress urging

[1] *Cong. Record*, 70th Cong., 1st Sess., pt. 7, 1928, p. 5547.

[2] *Review of Reviews*, vol. 75, p. 567.

[3] *Manufacturers Record*, vol. 92, August 4, 1927, p. 79.

[4] *Commerce and Finance*, vol. 16, June 1, 1927, p. 1102.

the special session.[1]   Reed proved to be the usual hard
fighter.   The *New York Times* said that he was like a parrot
in that he constantly repeated the demand for a special session.[2]   Senator K. D. McKellar of Tennessee also strove
hard for a special session, and several other senators joined
him.[3]

The *Manufacturers Record* polled the sentiment of
members of Congress and found most of them in favor of a
special session.   This magazine took the President to task
for his stand, saying that the South had been sorely disappointed.[4]   The reason that several Congressmen offered
for favoring the special session, according to the poll of the
Manufacturers Record, furnished an interesting sidelight on
the ways of politicians.   Several stated that they wanted to
be back in their home districts by June, 1928.   They feared
that the regular session could not dispose of flood-control
legislation by that time.   Therefore, they favored the special
session to insure them that they would be at home in time for
the political campaign of 1928.[5]   Other papers and magazines aided in the fight.   The main argument of those who
favored the special session was that the work of re-building
the levees should be done before or during the winter of
1927-8 to meet the possible danger of another great flood in
the spring of 1928.[6]   Some members of Congress claimed
that politics played a prominent part in preventing the special
session.   They maintained that politics prevented the Chicago
Conference from passing a resolution asking for a special
session " to appropriate money for the relief of the starving

[1] *Cong. Record,* 70th Cong., 1st Sess., pt. 7, 1928, p. 5497.

[2] *New York Times,* June 2, 1927, pt. 3, p. 24.

[3] *United States Daily,* May 17, 1927, p. 1.

[4] *Manufacturers Record,* vol. 92, August 4, 1927, p. 78.

[5] *Ibid.,* p. 79.

[6] *Commerce and Finance,* vol. 16, May 11, 1927, p. 938.

and the destitute and to pave the way for flood-prevention work ".[1]   Senator LaFollette issued a statement urging public opinion to force the President to call Congress together.[2]   He could see plainly that President Coolidge was playing politics, but he in turn was accused by many of playing politics himself.[3]

As President Coolidge continued to stand out against the special session several members of Congress defended him and others attacked him for his stand.[4]   Then, much of the press of the country, including leading delta papers, defended his position.[5]   According to a telegraphic query sent out by the *New York Times,* a majority of bankers, security owners, engineers and scientists of the delta area in the last part of May were opposed to a special session.[6]   The chief arguments of the opponents of the special session offered strong rebuttals to the contentions of the proponents.   They claimed that a special session would open the way to wrangling and controversies on a varied group of topics far removed from flood control, a condition which the public considered a bad situation and of doubtful advantage even to flood-control legislation.[7]   They further maintained that the Red Cross had relief and necessary rehabilitation of the victims well in hand; that the Mississippi River Commission could close the gaps caused by crevasses before another flood time came; that another great flood in 1928 was very unlikely; and even if one should come a special session could do little to control

[1] *Manufacturers Record*, vol. 92, July 21, 1927, p. 83.

[2] *United States Daily*, May 5, 1927, p. 1.

[3] *The Detroit Free Press*, May 11, 1927.

[4] New Orleans, *Times-Picayune*, May 19, 1927.

[5] New Orleans, *Times-Picayune*, May 19, 1927.

[6] *New York Times*, May 23, 1927, p. 1.

[7] *The Indianapolis Star*, May 18, 1927, p. 6.

it.[1]   Then, the strongest argument was that the 1927 flood
had made new engineering plans an absolute necessity, which
situation meant that the engineers would have to have several
months in which to study the problem before they could spend
any money that Congress might appropriate.   Congress
might as well wait for the regular session and let the engineers
work in the meantime.[2]   The result finally came to something
of a compromise when Senator Joseph Robinson of Arkansas
and Senator Charles Curtis of Kansas agreed that perhaps the
wise thing to do was to call the appropriate Congressional
Committee together for an extensive investigation before the
time for the regular session of Congress, so that when Congress met at the fixed time the committee would have the
project in definite shape, which would enable early action by
Congress.[3]

While the flood was still raging President Coolidge called
on the Mississippi River Commission for a report on the
special problems that would need to be solved as a part of a
comprehensive plan for control of the Mississippi floods.
At the same time he called for a similar report from the Chief
of Engineers of the United States army.[4]   The Secretary of
War directed the Mississippi River Commission to hold public hearings at New Orleans, Vicksburg, Memphis and St.
Louis.[5]   These hearings really represented a part of the investigation into public sentiment and ideas.   Scores of the
leaders of all classes of the South appeared as witnesses.   The
Flood Control Committee of the House of Representatives,
with Frank R. Reid as chairman, met on November 7, 1927,

[1] New Orleans, *Times-Picayune*, May 19, 1927.

[2] *Detroit Free Press*, May 7, 1927, p. 6.

[3] *New York Times*, June 2, 1927, pt. 3, p. 24.

[4] New Orleans, *Times-Picayune*, May 4, 1927, p. 1.

[5] *House Committee on Flood Control*, 70th Cong., 1st Sess., 1927-8,
Committee Doc., no. 1, p. 1.

for hearings on the problem.   This was one of the most extensive investigations ever held by a Congressional Committee.   The committee was in session sixty-three days. More than 300 witnesses appeared before it, and more than 5,000 pages of testimony were taken.[1]   Chairman Reid soon gave indications on numerous occasions of the determination that he was to show in the investigation.   He thoroughly understood the immensity of the problem before the committee in planning for the greatest piece of internal improvement in all of our history.[2]   And the witnesses themselves seemed to appreciate the fact that they were participating in a great investigation.   Chairman Reid declared that it was doubtful whether so many citizens and so many prominent men had ever attended hearings or had given testimony on a single national problem.[3]   As a result of that extensive investigation by the House Flood Control Committee and the work of the Mississippi River Commission and the Corps of Engineers, Congress had at its disposal an abundance of official materials.   Besides the testimony of more than 5,000 pages there had been published upward of 30 bulletins, some of them long and technical.   The special report of the Mississippi River Commission, published as House Flood Control Committee Document No. 1, contained 334 pages.   The report submitted by Chairman Frank R. Reid to accompany House Bill No. 8219 contained 407 pages.   Others were more moderate in length.   House Report No. 1100 on Flood Control on the Mississippi River and Tributaries contained 109 pages, while a few were merely short pamphlets.   The total represented a collection of official literature that fully considered every phase of the problem.

[1] *Cong. Record*, 70th Cong., 1st Sess., pt. 6, 1928, p. 4026.

[2] *House Committee on Flood Control*, 70th Cong., 1st Sess., 1927-8, *Committee Doc.*, no. 18, p. 1.

[3] *Cong. Record*, 70th Cong., 1st Sess., pt. 8, 1928, p. 5853.

The trend of public opinion and the statements of officials from the President down left little doubt about the enactment by Congress of flood-control legislation. The only question to be answered was the nature of the plan. That no shortage of plans existed was shown by the fact that more than 300 were presented to the committee.[1] They ranged all the way from wholly ridiculous ones to the most colossal and accurately worked-out engineering plans ever presented to Congress. In the hearings the advocates of spillways, reservoirs, levees, and the comprehensive, or combination, plans of control all had their innings. The people who wanted a broad comprehensive plan for the entire valley, including the tributaries, especially made a splendid fight. The Mississippi Flood Control Association, which consisted of all the levee boards, recommended a plan for spending $100,-000,000.00 annually in the entire valley.[2] Several of the leading valley papers urged the President to have such a plan drawn up by a commission of experts.[3] The Flood Commission of Pittsburgh requested the President to select a commission to draw up recommendations for a very comprehensive scheme.[4] In the opinion of the *Pittsburgh Post* such a commission should have used all available flood remedies.[5] The proponents of reservoirs found themselves severely handicapped by the official report of a board of engineers on the control of floods on the Mississippi by reservoirs. This report had been published in 1927 as House Committee on Flood Control Document No. 2 and gave very adverse findings. The only bright spot in the report for the supporters of reservoirs concerned sites on the Arkansas and White

[1] *Cong. Record*, 70th Cong., 1st Sess., pt. 8, 1928, p. 5853.
[2] *New York Times*, August 21, 1927, p. 13.
[3] *St. Louis Globe-Democrat*, May 5, 1927, p. 18.
[4] *United States Daily*, May 6, 1927, p. 1.
[5] *The Pittsburgh Post*, May 5, 1927, p. 6.

rivers on which according to the estimate reservoirs could be built for $242,000,000.00 that would lower heights five feet at Red river and eight feet at Arkansas City.[1] The arguments for other uses of reservoirs, such as hydro-electric power and irrigation, could not overcome the engineering committee's report on their high cost.[2] Thus, the people who favored control at the sources of the tributaries and by reservoirs along the streams joined the forces urging a plan that would make use of all remedies. Those who favored forests as an aid in stream control did likewise. They frankly admitted the necessity of levees and other engineering works, but maintained that reforestation would help, especially in preventing erosion.[3] When the group that wanted all remedies combined in one plan could make no headway, it became evident that the supporters of two other theories would fight for a measure to suit them. The " levees only " people still could muster a mighty army of supporters. But New Orleans, Cairo and other localities had entrenched themselves to fight to the finish for spillways and diversion channels. Secretary Hoover's report to the President had given them much comfort. It had recommended higher and wider levees, some type of diversion to lower flood heights and possibly other measures.[4] The supporters of outlets also received much encouragement from the fact that the Governor of Louisiana, with the permission and advice of the Mississippi River Commission, had dynamited the levee at Poydras, Louisiana during the flood of 1927 to create an outlet to relieve flood conditions at New Orleans.[5] This act was heralded as the

[1] *House Committee on Flood Control*, 70th Cong., 1st Sess., 1927-8, *Committee Doc.*, no. 2, p. 1.

[2] *New York Times*, May 29, 1927, pt. 6, p. 1.

[3] *United States Daily*, June 18, 1927, p. 2.

[4] *Commerce and Finance*, vol. 16, July 27, 1927, p. 1495.

[5] *Engineering News Record*, vol. 98, April 28, 1927, p. 705.

" most significant move " in the history of flood control.[1]
The faith of New Orleans in the remedy was shown by the
city's agreement to pay all damages. The Mississippi River
Commission at first apparently took the position that its advice to cut the levee did not constitute a recognition of the
spillway or diversion principle. However, on May 6, 1927,
this body, which had previously stood like the Rock of Gibral-
tar for levees only, gave out a statement admitting that diversion plus levees might be more feasible than levees only.[2] In
the opinion of Gifford Pinchot, the Corps had been shaken by
the proposal of the probable addition of spillways to levees,
but that it had not been shaken much because the suggestion
of the addition of any other means besides levees and spillways remained "evidence of moral turpitude".[3] But the concession by the Mississippi River Commission greatly pleased
the advocates of diversion. Their position received much additional strength from the official report of the board of
engineers appointed to investigate the feasibility of flood control by diversion channels. The report estimated that in
providing protective works of the size demanded by the new
situation created by the flood of 1927 the construction of
diversion channels on the lower Mississippi to aid levees
would furnish the same protection at a saving of $135,-
000,000.00.[4] Those facts seemed to assure the diversion
channels a prominent place in any plan that would have a
chance to pass in Congress.

Although the citizens of New Orleans and other cities
stood almost to a man for spillways, those who knew the situation realized that levees would again receive the major con-

---

[1] *Manufacturers Record*, vol. 91, May 5, 1927, p. 73.

[2] *Ibid.*, p. 63.

[3] *The Survey*, vol. 58, July 1, 1927, p. 367.

[4] *House Committee on Flood Control*, 70th Cong., 1st Sess., 1927-8,
Committee Doc., no. 3, p. 11.

sideration.[1]   After every flood in recent years that seriously threatened to overtop the levees, the Mississippi River Commission has only recommended and built stronger and higher levees.   And always the people of the delta have looked upon the great barriers of earth between them and the Mississippi with approval.   They have seen and have understood them.[2] The people who have suffered from inundations by the Mississippi would likely vote ten to one for levees and revetments against any other or all other methods of control.[3]   Many of the leaders in formulating public opinion maintained that lack of money and not lack of engineering ability or plans was responsible for the existing conditions.   They held that the engineers had known for many years just how to control the river.[4]   In their opinion, stripped of its technicalities, hobbies and nonsense, flood control " is a matter of money and earth, each in sufficient volume and properly applied ".[5]   Secretary Hoover and General Edgar Jadwin, Chief of Engineers of the United States army, gave out a joint report upholding the levee system while the flood was in progress, except for the modification including diversion channels.   The report might have been issued to prevent a lot of hasty and uncalled-for criticism of the Mississippi River Commission that could be expected after such a flood.   But it certainly added security to the position of the advocates of control by levees.[6] Thus, the new plan could be expected to carry provision for levees of increased height and size as the main protective works, with some kind of diversion channels as a supplementary means of control.

[1] *World's Work*, vol. 54, August, 1927, p. 414.
[2] *The New Republic*, vol. 50, May 18, 1927, p. 344.
[3] *The Outlook*, vol. 146, June 8, 1927, p. 183.
[4] *Baltimore Sun*, April 17, 1927, p. 8.
[5] *Commerce and Finance*, vol. 16, June 1, 1927, p. 1102.
[6] *New York Herald-Tribune*, May 2, 1927.

From the beginning of the work of the Mississippi River Commission there has been the question whether protective works should be built to protect against the great floods that come at long intervals, or only against ordinary floods that come frequently.[1] The question was whether complete control was worth the price, and, if not, what degree of control would be reasonable.[2] The opinion seems to have been generally held that the new plan should aim high enough to protect against the greatest flood, in the estimation of the experts, likely to come.[3] J. Russell Smith thought that the plan should provide for any and all emergencies.[4] The Secretary of War, Dwight Davis, said that it had become evident that the country had to adopt a new and enlarged project to protect against great floods.[5] The Mississippi River Commission certainly took a definite stand for protection against the greatest probable flood when it suggested protection against a flood twenty-five per cent larger than that of 1927.[6] In fact, there appeared to be few dissenting opinions to the suggestion to provide protection against the greatest flood.

With these major points of engineering settled as far as getting a measure through Congress was concerned, it became rather apparent that only plans providing complete protection by levees and diversion channels would be considered. The feeling generally prevailed among the governmental officials that no one could solve the problem without prolonged study and patient effort under actual field conditions.   Since

[1] B. G. Humphreys, *Floods and Levees of the Mississippi River*, p. 45.

[2] *House Committee on Flood Control*, 70th Cong., 1st Sess., 1927-8, *Committee Doc.*, no. 1, p. 84.

[3] *American Railway Engineering Bulletin*, vol. 29, July, 1927, p. 95.

[4] *The Survey*, vol. 58, July 1, 1927, p. 370.

[5] *House Committee on Flood Control*, 70th Cong., 1st Sess., 1927-8, *Committee Doc.*, no. 16, p. 14.

[6] *Ibid.*, no. 1, p. 46.

only the Mississippi River Commission and the Army Engineers had had such experience, the plans for the new project could be expected to come from them.[1]　Of all the more than three hundred plans that were submitted only two received any serious consideration.　One of them came from the Mississippi River Commission.　The other came from the Chief of Engineers of the United States army.　Both, therefore, represented to a large extent the experience and the ideas of the Corps of Engineers.　The plan submitted by the Mississippi River Commission will be called the Commission plan and that submitted by the Chief of Engineers of the United States army will be called the Jadwin plan.

The Mississippi River Commission discarded the policy of levees only and really drew up quite a comprehensive plan, but levees still provided the major means of protection.　In forming its plan the Commission based it on a combination of maximum discharges, which were possible but very unlikely, of the various tributaries according to the information from the Weather Bureau.　On this basis, it estimated the probably greatest future flood at twenty-five per cent greater than the flood of 1927.[2]　The estimate suggested a possible flood of 2,250,000 second-feet at Cairo and 2,850,000 second-feet at Arkansas City.[3]　The comprehensive plan submitted by the Commission provided for complete protection against such a flood.　The first line of defense provided was a levee system that would provide a free-board safety margin of five feet above the estimated greatest flood, which would be approximately twelve feet above the flood of 1927, with a greatly increased cross section of 1 on 4 on river side and 1

[1] *Saturday Evening Post*, vol. 200, July 9, 1927, p. 108.

[2] *House Committee on Flood Control*, 70th Cong., 1st Sess., 1927-8, *Committee Doc.*, no. 1, p. 46.

[3] *Ibid.*, p. 47.

on 4 to 1 on 6½ on land side with a crown of 12 feet.[1]   The
next item of protection provided for a diversion channel at
Cypress Creek to carry 600,000 second feet, a diversion channel through the Atchafalaya to carry 1,000,000 second feet,
and spillways at Bonne Carre and Caernavon to carry 250,000
second feet each, which outlets were expected to reduce the
flow past New Orleans to 1,400,000 second feet and to reduce
flood heights at New Orleans to a maximum of 20 feet.[2]
Further protection was suggested by safety-valve spillways
to prevent overtopping or breaking of levees, possibly by
diversion through the St. Francis Basin, and possibly by
reservoirs in the White and Arkansas river basins.[3]   But
these features would require intensive study, which should
await a thorough economic survey that should precede an
undertaking of such magnitude.[4]   To stabilize the channel
and protect the levees, extensive dredging operation and revetment of banks to cost $172,000,000 were provided for.[5]
For presentation to Congress the plan was divided into two
parts.   The first part, designated as the essential features,
included the increase in levee height and section, the floodways through Cypress Creek and the Atchafalaya, the spillway at Bonne Carre above New Orleans and the channel
stabilization works.   This part of the plan was recommended
for immediate adoption.   The cost was estimated at $407,-
500,000.00.[6]   The other features of the plan could await

[1] *House Committee on Flood Control*, 70th Cong., 1st Sess., 1927-8,
Committee Doc., no. 11, p. 1.

[2] *Ibid.*

[3] *Cong. Digest*, February, 1928, p. 49.

[4] *House Committee on Flood Control*, 70th Cong., 1st Sess., 1927-8,
Committee Doc., no. 1, p. 89.

[5] *Cong. Digest*, February, 1928, p. 49.

[6] *House Committee on Flood Control*, 70th Cong., 1st Sess., 1927-8,
Report to Accompany House Bill, no. 8219, p. 74.

long and patient study and an economic survey, but if adopted would probably raise the total cost of protection to $775,000,000.00.[1]

The Commission plan provided for the payment of all damages and the purchase of rights of way and flowage rights for floodways. It also provided for ample levees to confine the waters to the proposed diversion channels and to tributaries affected by the Mississippi floods.[2] The plan called for the expenditure of $25,000,000.00 the first year and $40,-000,000.00 annually thereafter.[3] The local interests would pay one-third of the cost of raising the levees to the 1914 Mississippi River Commission grade, which part of the cost was estimated at $15,440,367.00.[4] The Federal government would bear the remaining expense, which included two-thirds of the cost up to the 1914 grade, all of the levee cost above the 1914 grade, all of the cost of dredging and revetment, and all diversion channel and spillway costs and damages.[5]

The Jadwin plan presented much of the fundamental principles of the Commission plan. It was drawn to provide protection against the same estimated greatest future flood. It provided for levees slightly above the grade of the predicted flood, instead of the five feet proposed by the Mississippi River Commission.[6] It provided for the diversion of 900,000 second feet through Cypress Creek and 1,500,000 second-feet through the Atchafalaya, as compared to 600,000 and 1,000,-000 respectively by the Mississippi River Commission. It

[1] *Cong. Digest*, February, 1928, p. 49.

[2] *House Committee on Flood Control*, 70th Cong., 1st Sess., 1927-8, *Report to Accompany House Bill*, no. 8219, p. 74.

[3] *Cong. Digest*, February, 1928, p. 70.

[4] *House Committee on Flood Control*, 70th Cong., 1st Sess., 1927-8, *Report to Accompany House Bill*, no. 8219, p. 74.

[5] *Ibid., Committee Doc.*, no. 11, p. 2.

[6] *Ibid., Report to Accompany House Bill*, no. 8219, p. 74.

proposed a spillway of 250,000 second feet at Bonne Carre, but not one at Caernarvon.[1]

But the similarity of the two plans in engineering features ended there. For further protection the Jadwin plan provided a riverside floodway seventy miles long from Birds Point, Missouri to New Madrid, Missouri, very largely for the protection of Cairo, Illinois.[2] This protection would be accomplished by lowering by five feet the present river-bank levee between these points. Then, five miles back a higher and stronger levee would be built to protect against the great floods that would overtop the river-bank levee. The area between the two levees would form a huge storage basin, or create a riverside floodway.[3] Then the Jadwin plan proposed to build fuse-plug sections in the levees just above New Madrid, Missouri, in the vicinity of Arkansas City and on both sides of the Atchafalaya at its head.[4] This simply meant purposely weakened sections designed to break, at a point about three feet below the top of the new grade proposed by the plan, before the levee in general was threatened.[5] Thus, the Jadwin plan provided to send diverted water through uncontrolled outlets into virtually uncontrolled diversion channels; whereas the Commission plan provided controlled concrete spillways to send the water into protected diversion channels.[6]

The cost of the Jadwin plan of control was estimated at $296,400,000.00.[7] But the plan contained no provision for

---

[1] *House Committee on Flood Control,* 70th Cong., 1st Sess., 1927-8, *Committee Doc.,* no. 11, p. 1.

[2] *Ibid., Report to Accompany House Bill,* no. 8219, p. 73.

[3] *House Doc.,* no. 90, 70th Cong., 1st Sess., 1927-8, p. 29.

[4] *House Committee on Flood Control,* 70th Cong., 1st Sess., 1927-8, *Report to Accompany House Bill,* no. 8219, p. 82.

[5] *House Doc.,* no. 90, 70th Cong., 1st Sess., 1927-8, p. 28.

[6] *House Committee on Flood Control,* 70th Cong., 1st Sess., 1927-8, *Report to Accompany House Bill,* no. 8219, p. 82.

[7] *House Doc.,* no. 90, 70th Cong., 1st Sess., 1927-8, p. 32.

the payment of damages, flowage rights, or for building levees in and along the floodways.[1]   This fact stood out strikingly in the estimates of the costs of the Cypress Creek diversion channel.   The Jadwin plan placed the cost of this protection at $7,700,000.00, while the Mississippi River Commission placed it at $107,000,000.00.[2]   The argument of the Jadwin plan for not paying damage for floodway rights was that the floodways were natural outlets that had been appropriated by man, who must suffer the servitude imposed, and, therefore, could not except damages when the flood waters were turned upon him.   The plan recommended the expenditure of $25,000,000.00 the first year and $30,000,000.00 annually for nine years thereafter.[3]   The Federal government would pay all cost of revetment and four-fifths of the cost of flood-control works, with the exception of special levees, which would be built on a fifty-fifty basis.   The local interests would bear all other costs and damages.[4]   The special levees were provided for the purpose of protecting populous centers by enclosing them wholly or partially by encircling embankments.[5]   The Jadwin plan did not provide alternatives in the way of other diversions and reservoirs, as the Mississippi River Commission plan did.

An interesting phase of the presentation of these plans appeared in the apparent friction that had developed between the Mississippi River Commission and the Chief of Engineers.   The Commission felt that its dignity had been somewhat offended by the Chief of Engineers when he failed to

[1] *House Committee on Flood Control*, 70th Cong., 1st Sess., 1927-8, *Committee Doc.*, no. 8, p. 2.

[2] *Ibid.*, no. 11, p. 36.

[3] *House Doc.*, no. 90, 70th Cong., 1st Sess., 1927-8, p. 32.

[4] *House Committee on Flood Control*, 70th Cong., 1st Sess., 1927-8, *Committee Doc.*, no. 1, p. 2.

[5] *House Doc.*, no. 90, 70th Cong., 1st Sess., 1927-8, p. 25.

present its plan to the Flood Control Committee of the House. All official reports had to pass through the hands of the Chief of Engineers. General Jadwin simply withheld the report containing the Commission plan until he received a request for it from the House Committee. Then he contended that it had been necessary for him to prod the Mississippi River Commission to get a definite recommendation, and that he reminded it that it had had forty-eight years in which to study the Mississippi river and that a report suggesting further study was not sufficient.[1] But General Jadwin had previously said much in praise of this organization.[2] In the official report submitting his plan and before the Congressional Committees he was not very complimentary.[3] The Commission plainly thought General Jadwin had usurped its power by submitting his plan. The act of 1879 creating it provided that the Mississippi River Commission should " take into consideration and mature such a plan or plans and estimates " that would " prevent destructive floods " and submit them to the Secretary of War but not necessarily through the Chief of Engineers.[4] General Jadwin based his authority for making the plans on the Rivers and Harbors Act of January 21, 1927. This act had authorized him to make surveys of the Mississippi and other rivers to ascertain the feasibility of the development of water power and for the purpose of controlling floods.' The House Flood Control Committee agreed with the Mississippi River Commission that the act of 1927 in no way repealed or superseded the act of 1879, and,

[1] *Cong. Record*, 70th Cong., 1st Sess., pt. 8, p. 5884.

[2] *American Railway Engineering Association Bulletin*, vol. 29, July, 1927, p. 91.

[3] *House Doc.*, no. 90, 70th Cong., 1st Sess., 1927-8, p. 33.

[4] *House Committee on Flood Control*, 70th Cong., 1st Sess., 1927-8, *Report to Accompany House Bill*, no. 8219, p. 47.

[5] *Ibid., Committee Doc.*, no. 18, p. 127.

therefore, that General Jadwin had gone beyond his authority.[1] The Committee on Flood Control had nothing to do but to consider the Jadwin plan because it had been submitted directly by President Coolidge, after it had received the approval of Secretary of War Davis.

Naturally, serious differences of opinion arose concerning the two plans and the proper legislation. The differences of opinion might be divided into three classes; concerning respectively the engineering features of the plan, the administrative features of the proposed legislation, and the economic phases of the problem. There was little doubt that the engineers could draw up a plan and agree upon it more easily than they could get Congress and the public to accept the plan after it had been formulated.[2] The differences of opinion concerning the two plans generally concerned the adequateness or inadequateness of the Jadwin plan, or more specifically, objections to the Jadwin plan. The engineering feature most severely criticized was the uncontrolled floodways.[3] J. E. Kemper, C. E., stating the case for New Orleans, claimed that the Jadwin plan would inundate one million acres of land, 250 miles of railway, 400 miles of highway and several towns, and would completely cut New Orleans off from the West.[4] The second point of criticism of the engineering phases of the plan was in the matter of fuse-plug levees. The fear of serious difficulties arising from an uncontrolled mass of water flowing through a crevasse made in a chosen place was freely expressed. Crevasses have

[1] *House Committee on Flood Control*, 70th Cong., 1st Sess., 1927-8, *Report to Accompany House Bill*, no. 8219, p. 47.

[2] *World's Work*, vol. 54, August, 1927, p. 417.

[3] *House Committee on Flood Control, Committee Doc.*, no. 10, 70th Cong., 1st Sess., 1927-8, p. 1.

[4] *House Committee on Flood Control*, 70th Cong., 1st Sess., 1927-8, *Committee Doc.*, no. 10, p. 1.

had the habit of digging out great lakes or new channels and depositing much sand. Also, no one could predict how much water would flow through crevasses.[1] Many feared anything short of controlled concrete spillways.[2] A third engineering point often criticized was the river-side floodway between Birds Point and New Madrid, Missouri for the protection of Cairo, Illinois. The claim was advanced that the return of the water at New Madrid would cause a piling-up which would reduce the slope and velocity of the river and, therefore, the carrying capacity. The reduction in volume of discharge would fail to relieve Cairo, although 144,000 acres of fine land would have been inundated by the new floodway.[3] The factor of safety that the plan provided was severely criticized simply as being inadequate to insure protection.[4] These represent the major criticisms against the Jadwin plan. However, others were made, including the general one that the whole plan had been based on insufficient data and that it was generally not dependable.[5] A perusal of the hearings shows that, including the engineers, perhaps ninety-five per cent of the witnesses had some criticism of the Jadwin plan as an engineering project.

Two phases of the administrative problem caused some discussion and some disagreement. The question of a conflict between state and federal authority received some attention. The Jadwin report suggested that the states should be required to enact appropriate legislation for accepting the conditions and responsibilities of the act before any money

[1] *House Committee on Flood Control, Hearings 1927*, p. 2365.

[2] *House Committee on Flood Control*, 70th Cong., 1st Sess., 1927-8, *Committee Doc.*, no. 22, p. 7.

[3] *House Committee on Flood Control*, 70th Cong., 1st Sess., 1927-8, *Report to Accompany House Bill*, no. 8219, p. 16.

[4] *Ibid.*

[5] *Ibid.*

should be spent within their borders, unless the absence of such legislation would delay the initiation of work of " far-reaching benefit ", especially where another state was concerned.[1]   Former Senator William Lorimer regarded this requirement as a great hindrance to the progress of flood control.   He wondered how Missouri would feel about paying heavy damages for protecting Cairo in Illinois, when the Governor, the Attorney General and members of Congress asserted Missouri would not pay for Cairo's protection.[2] Senator Ransdell of Louisiana expressed a very general opinion when he asserted that flood control should in no way depend on state legislation or local levee boards, but that it should be under one power with absolute authority.[3]   However, this topic never assumed much importance because it appeared that the states of the delta had definitely concluded to co-operate heartily in any reasonable plan.

An administrative problem that received considerable attention concerned the constitution of the agency that would carry out the program to be adopted.   The Mississippi River Commission had been the agency that had carried out the flood-control construction programs of the past.   It had also been the agency that had made plans for flood control.   But the Commission had been most severely criticized during and following the flood of 1927, as it frequently had been at intervals since its creation.   The Commission plan said nothing at all about the agency of administration, which, of course, meant that it expected the Commission to continue to administer.   The Jadwin plan saw great evils and inefficiency in administration by a board.   So, it suggested that the program should be administered by the Chief of Engineers, with the

[1] *House Committee on Flood Control*, 70th Cong., 1st Sess., 1927-8, *Committee Doc.*, no. 13, p. 9.

[2] *Ibid.*, no. 26, p. 9.

[3] *Ibid.*, no. 1, p. 94.

Mississippi River Commission serving in an advisory capacity, maintaining that the United States government and corporations were efficiently managed because they had one-man governments.[1]

It was its domination by the Corps of Engineers that brought forth so much criticism of the Commission. So General Jadwin could hardly expect to obtain absolute domination. Gifford Pinchot stated the case for many when he accused the Corps of Engineers of never abandoning an opinion that it had once expressed, a condition which meant that any agency dominated by the Corps would try to justify a policy of "levees only," or would draw a conclusion and then try to make plans to prove it. He also asserted that after fifty years of " active and responsible dealing with the river " the Commission had asked for more time to formulate its plan, a fact which afforded enough evidence to condemn it to abolishment. If people thought he was too harsh, he pointed to the Corps' attempt to prove that the Eads Jetties had failed " long after the ships were actually using the deep waterway they had made ".[2] Many magazine writers and newspaper correspondents urged reform of the agency of administration.[3] Some members of Congress took up the criticism. Senator Lynn J. Frazier of North Dakota said that General Jadwin had tried to prove the value of his own ideas and had shut his eyes to all others. He seriously doubted the ability of the Corps of Engineers to carry out such an extensive program.[4] But, at the hearings, the opponents of the Mississippi River Commission and of the Corps could not get together on any type of agency or commission. Some suggested an absolutely independent organization

[1] *Cong. Record*, 70th Cong., 1st Sess., pt. 5, 1928, p. 3571.
[2] *The Survey*, vol. 58, July 1, 1927, p. 369.
[3] *Cong. Record*, 70th Cong., 1st Sess., pt. 11, 1928, p. 8508.
[4] *Ibid.*

similar to the Interstate Commerce Commission.[1] Some favored a board composed of the various Members of the Cabinet whose departments had reason to be interested, a position which had been a hobby of Francis G. Newlands.[2] Some wanted a commission that would contain experts on all methods of flood control and that would be dominated by civilians.[3] The sizes of the agencies proposed varied considerably. Representative G. E. Campbell of Pennsylvania proposed a commission of 13 : three from the Corps of Engineers, six civilian engineers and four business men.[4] The Reid bill, which sponsored the Commission plan, provided for abolishing the Mississippi River Commission and substituting for it the Mississippi Valley Flood Control Commission of seven members, four of whom should be engineers, either army or civilian.[5] Such an organization was very little different from the Mississippi River Commission as it then existed. One of the surprising facts about the hearings was the little organized opposition to the Mississippi River Commission in comparison with the vast amount of criticism that had filled the press only a few months before. Most witnesses seemed to be content, so far as they were concerned, to urge federal control and to let the matter of the agency take care of itself. [6] So the question of the composition of the board of administration apparently did not present such a difficult problem.

The activities of Congress had not gone very far until it became apparent that the main fight over the proposed legis-

[1] *House Committee on Flood Control*, 70th Cong., 1st Sess., 1927-8, *Committee Doc.*, no. 18, p. 30.

[2] *House Committee on Flood Control, Hearings 1927*, p. 3852.

[3] *Ibid.*, p. 3467.

[4] *Ibid.*, p. 2713.

[5] *Cong. Record*, 70th Cong., 1st Sess., pt. 8, 1928, p. 5854.

[6] *House Committee on Flood Control*, 70th Cong., 1st Sess., 1927-8, *Committee Doc.*, no. 18, p. 31.

lation would come neither on the engineering nor on the administrative phases of the problem, although the engineering phases presented some problems that would have to be adjusted. It became quite evident that the real fight would center around the economic aspects of the problem.

Two bills had appeared around which the factions could center their arguments. House of Representatives bill No. 8219, known as the Reid bill, had come from the Flood Control Committee with a strong favorable majority report. Senate bill No. 3740, called the Jones bill, had come from the Senate Committee on Commerce. The House bill presented the views very largely of the Mississippi River Commission plan; whereas the Senate bill accepted most of the Jadwin plan. However, on economic phases of the problems both bills failed to follow either plan on some important points.

The first controversy in considering the economic phase of the problem arose in trying to decide how much money would be provided for the project. The Jadwin plan had proposed the least, with an estimate of $296,400,000.00.[1] The Mississippi River Commission plan had proposed the expenditure of $407,500,000.00 for the immediate project and $775,-000,000.00 for the comprehensive project.[2] Other plans with wide endorsement proposing to spend a billion dollars had been presented but they did not get serious committee consideration.[3] The Jones bill provided for the expenditure by the United States of $325,000,000.00. The Reid bill called for the expenditure of $473,000,000.00.[4] The Jones bill, however, provided for surveys, which obviously might lead to

[1] *House Doc.*, no. 90, 70th Cong., 1st Sess., 1927-8, p. 32.

[2] *House Committee on Flood Control*, 70th Cong., 1st Sess., 1927-8, *Report to Accompany House Bill*, no. 8219, p. 74.

[3] *United States Daily*, October 28, 1927, p. 1.

[4] *House Committee on Flood Control*, 70th Cong., 1st Sess., 1927-8, *Report to Accompany House Bill*, no. 8219, p. 128.

great additional costs, as the author of the bill himself frankly admitted.[1]   But the center of the economic storm did not come on this point, for all seemed to realize that Senator Wesley L. Jones of Washington, author of the Senate bill, had reached the crux of the matter when he said that Congress would from time to time appropriate the amounts it thought necessary to carry out the program.[2]   This statement was obviously true, for no group of engineers, or Congressmen, could work out a plan for the solution of such a colossal problem extending over a period of ten years so that the estimates of ultimate cost would approximate correctness.

The second controversial point on an economic phase came in considering the damages that would result from the floodways that would carry the waters diverted from the main river.   These floodways would inundate large areas of agricultural lands, much railway trackage, several towns and whole communities.   The areas in the proposed floodways contained more than 100,000 people and perhaps 3,000,000 acres of land.[3]   The Jadwin plan proposed no payment for damages to these areas, on the ground that the floodways were originally natural overflow channels that had been appropriated by men, who must have accepted the servitude imposed by the river at flood.[4]   The minority report, which was signed by six of the twenty-one members of the House Flood Control Committee, agreed with General Jadwin that these people had been subject to such servitude ever since they settled the lands.[5]   The Commission plan, on the other hand, proposed to pay damages in full.   The Commission argued

[1] *Cong. Record*, 70th Cong., 1st Sess., pt. 8, 1928, p. 3688.

[2] *Ibid.*, p. 3687.

[3] *House Committee on Flood Control*, 70th Cong., 1st Sess., 1927, *Report to Accompany House Bill*, no. 8219, p. 82.

[4] *House Doc.*, no. 90, 70th Cong., 1st Sess., 1927-8, p. 28

[5] *Cong. Record*, 70th Cong., 1st Sess., pt. 8, 1928, p. 6160.

that the floodways offered more benefits to other states than to the territory adjacent to them.   Therefore, Louisiana should not bear the burden of protecting Mississippi and other states.[1]   Then, as one would naturally expect, there arose the inevitable question of the confiscation of private property. General Jadwin's proposal to let the states meet the bill did not satisfy the opinions of many Congressmen and laymen.[2]

One point that caused very bitter strife in this connection arose in regard to paying railways for relocating and raising tracks.   The Commission plan provided for paying the railways for the changes made necessary by the proposed programs.[3]   But the Jadwin plan, which had the support of the administration, did not provide for paying any such damages.[4]   The railways marshaled all of their influence to prevent such an expense being forced upon them, which they officially estimated at $71,835,000.00.[5]   The engineering departments of the various delta roads prepared a brief, which was published as Committee Document number 23.   It strongly argued the case of the railways.   Other private property interests for whom no damages were provided rushed to the aid of the railways, and the fight on this point became rather heated, with widely varying ideas both as to the responsibility of the Federal government and as to the amount of damages the roads would incur.

Some discussion arose over the method of paying for the protective works.   Those who want bonds for most everything apparently have always been active in politics.   So a few wanted a bond issue.[6]   Even so powerful an association

[1] *House Committee on Flood Control*, 70th Cong., 1st Sess., 1927-8, *Committee Doc.*, no. 11, p. 38.

[2] *Ibid.*, no. 26, p. 6.

[3] *Ibid.*, no. 11, p. 24.

[4] *Ibid.*, no. 14, p. 1.

[5] *Ibid.*, no. 23, p. 8.

[6] *United States Daily*, October 28, 1927, p. 1.

as the Mississippi River Flood Control Association came to support a bond issue.[1] Although those who favored a bond issue totaled a considerable number, those who favored payment out of current revenues stood firmly against the bonds.[2] This point of difference caused some discussion, but really delayed the action of Congress very little.

The greatest point of controversy developed in considering what part of the expenses of the program should be paid for by the Federal government. Some took the rather extreme position that the Federal government should go so far as to give indemnity to the delta section to cover the flood losses.[3] Another group, considerably larger than the above one, wanted the Federal government to pay all future bills and to assume the obligation for payment of all outstanding bonds of the levee boards.[4] But these extremists did not represent any considerable portion of Congress. It soon became evident that those who wanted the Federal government to pay the entire bill for carrying out the program that was being formulated and those who believed that local interests should pay a portion of the cost formed two important groups that would fight before either would yield. Thus, the question of local contribution became the most controversial point of all.

In the matter of numbers, those who favored the entire payment from federal funds far surpassed those who favored local participation among the witnesses appearing before the Flood Control Commitee. In fact, with the exception of the army engineers, practically all of the three hundred witnesses urged that the United States should pay the whole cost.[5] These witnesses gave several reasons why

[1] New Orleans, *Times-Picayune*, June 23, 1927.

[2] *House Committee on Flood Control, Hearings 1927*, p. 443.

[3] *The Survey*, vol. 58, July 1, 1927, p. 357.

[4] *Commerce and Finance*, vol. 16, June 1, 1927, p. 1101.

[5] *Cong. Record*, 70th Cong., 1st Sess., pt. 8, 1928, p. 6159.

the control of floods on the Mississippi constituted an obligation of the Federal government.[1]   The weakening effect of
a program being executed under two jurisdictions, which
must occur when the local boards share the expense, appealed
to many as a most important consideration.[2]   The inseparable problems that make districts interdependent could not be
overlooked.   The President of the Mississippi River Commission admitted spending funds in 1927 contrary to law,
because some districts that did not pay formed a part of a
system that simply had to be maintained as a whole, if the
levee system had any value.[3]   Many of these problems were
interstate.   With all the pressure the Mississippi River
Commission could exert, the weak local districts that could
not furnish their quotas of funds seriously hindered the
work of construction, perhaps causing the Commission to
work three years behind schedule.[4]

The strongest argument for the Federal government bearing all the cost was based on the poor financial condition of
the various levee boards and the very heavy sacrifices they
had already made to protect themselves.   Senator Arthur
Capper of Kansas stated the idea of many when he said in
regard to the delta people, " They are bled white in their
battles with recurring floods; they are mortgaged and taxed
to their limit and they are financially unable to meet any
additional charges ".[5]   The total indebtedness of the levee
districts on January 1, 1928 was $819,642,576.00.[6]   This

[1] *House Committee on Flood Control*, 70th Cong., 1st Sess., 1927-8,
Report to Accompany House Bill, no. 8219, p. 21.

[2] *Ibid.*, no. 13, p. 6.

[3] *Ibid.*, no. 18, p. 127.

[4] *House Committee on Flood Control, Hearings 1927-8*, p. 3041.

[5] New Orleans, *Times-Picayune*, January 19, 1928, p. 3.

[6] *House Committee on Flood Control*, 70th Cong., 1st Sess., 1927-8,
Report to Accompany House Bill, no. 8219, p. 27.

amount far exceeded the assessed valuation of the districts. Some districts had outstanding public bonds and real-estate mortgages for more than two hundred per cent of their assessed valuation.[1] Of this large total, only about $44,000,-000.00 had been spent fighting floods.[2] The larger part of the debt had been accumulated through drainage and general improvements. Nevertheless, the flood of 1927 dealt the levee boards a staggering blow. They had burdened themselves with all kinds of taxes and the people simply could pay no more, the ordinary farm-land tax being a total of $4.00 per acre.[3] The only way possible for the levee boards to secure money would have been through a loan from some source. An abundance of expert opinion said the majority of them could not get loans from anybody.[4] The very districts that could not get loans were the ones that needed protective works most, and the ones that affected the whole system very adversely. Investment bankers who handled the levee-board bonds stated that heavy defaults in these securities had depressed the market until they could not be sold.[5] Such facts caused most Congressmen to feel that it was absolutely impossible for the local levee boards to bear any of the expense, beyond their expenses of rehabilitation. Secretary Hoover joined those who did not believe the locals could pay more, and urged the Federal government to pay all.[6] The House Committee on Flood Control, which very thoroughly investigated every phase of the problem, said that it

[1] *House Committee on Flood Control*, 70th Cong., 1st Sess., 1927-8, *Report to Accompany House Bill*, no. 8219, p. 26.

[2] *Mississippi River Flood Control Association, Losses and Damages Resulting from the Flood of 1927*, p. 195.

[3] *House Committee on Flood Control, Hearings 1922*, p. 44.

[4] *Cong. Record*, 70th Cong., 1st Sess., pt. 7, 1928, p. 5547.

[5] Memphis, *Commercial Appeal*, November 30, 1928.

[6] *Commerce and Finance*, vol. 16, July 27, 1927, p. 1495.

" was forced finally to the conclusion that it was not practical " to place any part of the expense on the locals and that such an effort would nullify any legislation.[1]

The people of the delta received quite a disappointment in the two plans that Congress took up for serious consideration. The Jadwin plan suggested that the Federal government pay all costs of channel stabilization and eighty per cent of the cost of protective works, and that the locals furnish the rights of way, pay damages from floodways and twenty per cent of the cost of construction of protective works.[2] The Commission plan provided for the locals to furnish rights of way and to pay one-third of the cost of raising the levees to 1914 standard.[3] The Federal government was to bear all other costs. The Commission plan, therefore, left much less of the burden to the local interests.

Those who supported local contribution maintained that if the Federal government paid the whole cost it might tend to cause it to have " to pay for every project such as reclamation ".[4] They also stressed the point of special benefit for those behind the protective works.[5] The Mississippi River Commission insisted on local control for a unique reason. It held that locals should contribute not because they received special benefits but because of the " belief that without a local sharing in the costs, the Commission, as an agent of the Federal government disbursing Federal funds, will be confronted by inordinate demands for flood-control work not needed nor justified ".[6]

[1] *Cong. Record*, 70th Cong., 1st Sess., 1927-8, pt. 8, p. 5848.

[2] *Cong. Digest*, February, 1928, p. 48.

[3] *House Committee on Flood Control, Committee Doc.*, no. 1, 70th Cong., 1st Sess., p. 81.

[4] *New York Times*, January 24, 1928, p. 29.

[5] *House Doc.*, no. 90, 70th Cong., 1st Sess., 1927-8, p. 4.

[6] *House Committee on Flood Control*, 70th Cong., 1st Sess., 1927-8, *Committee Doc.*, no. 1, p. 81.

President Coolidge threw consternation into the camp of the delta people when he came out squarely for the Jadwin plan, local contributions and all.   In submitting the Jadwin plan to Congress, the President maintained that the people of the delta would receive special benefits and that the states should share the expense.[1]   He strongly opposed paying damages caused by the construction of flood-control works.[2] It soon became quite evident that a large majority of both houses of Congress stood in favor of the Federal government bearing the entire expense and the army engineers, a few administration leaders and President Coolidge demanded some local contribution.   Representative Frank R. Reid sounded the warning that no policy of economy would satisfy the people on this question.[3]   But those who favored local contribution showed that a mere warning would not cause them to abandon their position.

Congress demonstrated that it would fight when both the Reid bill from the House and the Jones bill from the Senate provided no local participation, except furnishing rights of way on the main river.   The House bill sponsored the Commission plan in general, while the Senate bill sponsored the Jadwin plan, but neither bill pleased the administration.   The Jones bill suited the President far better than the Reid bill, but the President criticized it because it did not estimate the final cost of the project and because it provided for no local contribution.[4]   As time went on it became evident that any bill that embodied so comprehensive a plan as that proposed by the Mississippi River Commission had no chance of

[1] *House Doc.*, no. 90, 70th Cong., 1st Sess., 1927-8, p. 2.

[2] *House Committee on Flood Control*, 70th Cong., 1st Sess., 1927-8, *Committee Doc.*, no. 13, p. 5.

[3] *New York Times*, April 29, 1928.

[4] *Cong. Record*, 70th Cong., 1st Sess., pt. 8, 1928, p. 6162.

approval by the President.[1]   In the meantime the delta people
were becoming afraid that a political issue might develop.
The warning had been frequently sounded by the press that
the question should be kept clear of politics, and for some
time it appeared that it would be fought out on a non-partisan
basis.[2]   The delta people plainly wanted flood-control to be
considered wholly on its own merits.[3]   Thus, when members
of Congress on the Republican side began to demand that
the Democrats cease to play politics with the revenue bill by
demanding big cuts, and to insinuate that retaliations might
take place, the proponents of federal control began to take
notice.[4]   The matter became a little more complicated when
members of Congress showed some resentment against the
President's interference in legislation by a threat of veto,
saying the real issue had become the " integrity of Congress ".[5]   Representative Martin B. Madden of Illinois
warned that the President's veto could kill any measure that
had been proposed.[6]   Madden originally had favored local
contribution, but since Congress had assembled he had
changed to favor federal control entirely.[7]   Fearing that
Madden's warning might prove true, the delta supporters of
the Commission plan began to desert the Reid bill and support
the Jones bill, which very largely carried out the Jadwin
plan.[8]   In March, 1928, the Tri-State Flood Control Committee, consisting of powerful representations from Louisiana, Mississippi and Arkansas, urged the immediate passage

[1] *Cong. Record*, 70th Cong., 1st Sess., pt. 7, 1928, p. 5500.

[2] *United States Daily*, October 13, 1927, p. 1.

[3] *New York Times*, November 27, 1927.

[4] Memphis, *Commercial Appeal*, April 30, 1928.

[5] *Cong. Record*, 70th Cong., 1st Sess., pt. 10, 1928, p. 7319.

[6] *Ibid.*, p. 7318.

[7] *Ibid.*, p. 6162.

[8] New Orleans, *Times-Picayune*, January 29, 1928, p. 1.

of the Jones bill. The Committee accepted the bill in principle but suggested some amendments to provide for controlled spillways, to clarify the language so that the bill would clearly provide for compensation for property damages from protective works and to state clearly that jurisdiction of the Mississippi River Commission on tributaries would not be curtailed.[1]

When the leaders for federal control began to show a tendency to accept most of the Jadwin plan, the tension lessened noticeably. Compromise then became the order of the day. The President won his point against paying compensation to the railways for damages in the floodways.[2] He also won a point in the provision for the local's furnishing rights-of-way on the main river, although it was of minor importance.[3] He further won, to an undetermined extent, the adoption of the Jadwin plan as opposed to the Commission plan. The Jones bill adopted the engineering features of the Jadwin plan, which might be considered a Coolidge victory. But the supporters of the Commission plan received some consolation in the creation of a board consisting of the Chief of Engineers, the President of the Mississipp River Commission and one civil engineer to be appointed by the President, to consider the engineering features of the Commission plan and of the Jadwin plan with the authority to adopt the best features of both plans.[4] The fact that the composition of this board gave the President and the Corps of Engineers complete domination of it made it pretty much a victory for the administration. The President yielded his point in regard to an estimate of the final cost and permitted the bill to go through with provisions that opened the way

[1] Memphis, *Commercial Appeal*, March 16, 1928.

[2] *Cong. Record*, 70th Cong., 1st Sess., pt. 10, 1928, p. 7295.

[3] *Ibid.*, p. 7298.

[4] *Ibid.*, p. 7316.

for huge projects. But the most important concession by the President was in regard to local contributions. This had been by far the most controversial point, and the one on which the President had been feared most.[1] He held out until the end for the principle of local contribution. So the bill was drawn to declare that the principle of local contribution was sound and that it had not been abandoned. But, in view of the fact that the local interests had already paid $292,000,-000.00 for flood protection, whereas the Federal government had only paid $71,000,000.00 [2] the United States would comply with the principle of bearing its just share by bearing the whole expense of the new project.[3] The army engineers were satisfied because it left the Mississippi River Commission in charge and left the Corps still in a position to dominate.

Thus, the Jones-Reid bill, as the amended bill was known, very speedily passed the Senate and the House by overwhelming votes. The President approved it on May 15, 1928. The non-partisan character of the measure was shown by the fact that both Senator Charles Curtis of Kansas and Senator Joseph Robinson of Arkansas, the leaders of the Republican and Democrat parties in the Senate, favored it. Senator Joseph E. Ransdell of Louisiana thanked almost everybody in behalf of the people of the valley, and all seemed happy that the problem had been settled for the time being.[4]

[1] *New York Times*, February 24, 1928, p. 1.

[2] *House Committee on Flood Control*, 70th Cong., 1st Sess., 1927-8, *Report to Accompany House Bill*, no. 8219, p. 344.

[3] *Congress of the United States, Public Document*, no. 391, 70th Cong., 1st Sess., 1928.

[4] *Cong. Record*, 70th Cong., 1st Sess., pt. 8, 1928, p. 5695.

CHAPTER X

Results of the Jones-Reid Act to November, 1929

THE people of the delta showed great enthusiasm over the enactment of the Jones-Reid bill. The New Orleans *Times-Picayune* said that by signing the bill President Coolidge " rendered the greatest national service of his career " by initiating " a national undertaking " that would make his administration forever memorable.[1] This paper went on to say that, in time, the accomplishment of the flood-control program would be accounted by history as almost as epochal as the Louisiana Purchase. Robert R. Ellis, a leading business man of Memphis and Vice President of the Chamber of Commerce of the United States, placed a full-page advertisement in the *Memphis Commercial Appeal* painting the future of the delta in glowing terms and declaring that the flood-control legislation would have a far-reaching effect. In his language: " The Great Fathers of Waters has at last found its master ".[2] Another leading Memphis firm in a full-page advertisement paid its respects to the Federal government and made glowing predictions for the future. It said, among other enthusiastic remarks: " The Mid-South, with Uncle Sam backing up the line, is now in an enviable position. The Father of Waters has been harnessed; monies will soon be rushing in, and we of the Mid-South shall benefit ".[3] Real-estate men considered the Jones-Reid bill

[1] New Orleans, *Times-Picayune*, May 16, 1928, p. 10.

[2] Memphis, *Commercial-Appeal*, May 17, 1928.

[3] *Ibid.*, May 19, 1928.

the greatest piece of legislation that ever came before a peace-time Congress. They maintained that the restoration of credit and confidence would carry the delta area on to a long period of prosperity and that delta lands would continue to go higher on that basis.[1] Greenville, Mississippi, a city suffering heavier losses than any other similar area from the 1927 flood, celebrated the approval of the bill whole-heartedly and enthusiastically. Its people showed a revived spirit because they said that they would never again be called upon to make such sacrifices as they had so bravely made in 1927, for the levees would never again be overflowed.[2] The same spirit and enthusiasm swept over the entire delta and gave a marked contrast to the spirit of depression that had been very noticeable after the great disaster and heavy sacrifices of 1927.

Two appropriations had been made that bore directly on flood-control before the Jones-Reid bill passed. On December 22, 1927, a deficiency appropriation measure was enacted to restore the $7,0000,000 that the Mississippi River Commission had spent in emergency work during and following the flood of 1927.[3] Two million dollars reverted to the War Department to replace funds diverted from allotments for work on rivers and harbors, and the remainder became available for the use of the Mississippi River Commission for the construction of protective works. Then, on January 16, 1928, another law was enacted that dealt with the rehabilitation program. The various county agricultural extension agents were paid principally by the various counties in which they were employed. The flood of 1927 so depleted the county treasuries that they could not meet their shares of the expenses. The Federal government provided $500,000 to

[1] Memphis, *Commercial-Appeal*, May 22, 1928.

[2] *Ibid.*, May 24, 1928.

[3] *Cong. Digest*, Feb., 1928, p. 41.

carry on the work, because it was felt that the activities of these agents formed a valuable part of the program of reconstruction.[1] The funds necessary to meet the provisions of the Jones-Reid act for the year of 1928-29 were provided by an appropriation of $24,000,000, of which Secretary of War Davis alloted $21,228,000 for immediate use.[2] The Mississippi River Commission then had funds for the construction of levees rapidly and for carrying out other provisions of the act.

A very important change occurred in the personnel of the Mississippi River Commission in June, 1928. Colonel Charles L. Potter during the hearings preceding the enactment of the Jones-Reid bill, as President of the Commission, had presented a much more comprehensive plan of control than General Edgar Jadwin, the Chief of the United States Army Engineers, had presented. Colonel Potter had criticized General Jadwin's plan and activities and in turn had had his plan and activities criticized by General Jadwin. President Coolidge apparently supported General Jadwin in the dispute. So it was not surprising that Colonel Potter was soon succeeded as President of the Commission by Colonel T. H. Jackson. The change seemed to please the people of the delta, who regarded Colonel Jackson as a capable and forward-looking man.[3] Then reorganization of the Commission took place to meet the new conditions. The Commission had formerly designated certain of its members as officers in charge of work in given districts. In November 1928 the direction of the program was turned over to one man as Director of the Flood Control Project. Major Paul S. Reinecke became the first director.[4] The change

[1] *Cong. Digest*, Feb., 1928, p. 41.

[2] *World Almanac*, 1929, p. 160.

[3] New Orleans, *Times-Picayune*, June 13, 1928.

[4] *World Almanac*, 1929, p. 160.

left the work under the Commission but placed one man in charge of the entire program instead of several individuals in their own districts as formerly.

The supporters of the Commission's plan forced through a clause in the Jones-Reid act providing that the Flood Control Board should adjust the engineering differences between the two plans by adopting or rejecting features of either plan.[1] The composition of the board received considerable criticism. It consisted of the Chief of Engineers of the United States Army, the President of the Mississippi River Commission and a civilian engineer to be selected by the President. The criticism offered was that the creation of such a board really meant turning the program over to the Corps of Engineers and practically to insure the adoption of the Jadwin plan, since President Coolidge favored that plan and would likely make appointments of men favorable to it.[2] The people who fought for tributary control especially felt keen disappointment, for they knew that all of the administration forces opposed their ideas of the proper method of flood control.[3] The appointment of Colonel T. H. Jackson to succeed Colonel C. L. Potter as President of the Mississippi River Commission naturally removed the strongest supporter of the Commission plan from the Flood Control Board. To complete the Board, President Coolidge appointed C. W. Sturtevant of New York.

The Board had formulated its plan and prepared its report early in August 1928. General Jadwin visited temporary executive offices at Superior, Wisconsin, and presented the report to President Coolidge. The President approved it; and it was made public by the Department of War on August

[1] Memphis, *Commercial Appeal*, April 25, 1928.

[2] *Cong. Record*, 70th Cong., 1st Sess., pt. 11, 1928, p. 8508.

[3] *Ibid.*, pt. 8, 1928, p. 5691.

16th.[1] It should have occasioned little surprise that the Jadwin plan had been unanimously adopted in practically all points.

The Board had traveled through the alluvial areas and had held public hearings at various places to give the local interests opportunities to set forth their positions on their problems.[2] The large amount of data that had been compiled by the Mississippi River Commission during its entire lifetime was used, and some additional surveys were made before the official report was made. Under the law that created it, the Board had been given the duty of making recommendations to the President in regard to the engineering differences between the Jadwin plan and the Mississippi River Commission plan. Except to make the necessary surveys to adjust the engineering differences between the two plans, the Board had no other function.[3]

It should be noted that in a large measure, perhaps in 75 per cent of the items, the two plans had a rather close agreement as to engineering principles, and in most other phases there was a partial agreement. Both plans called for levees supplemented by diversion channels to carry the flood waters up to given heights and then to divert the surplus.[4] But, where the important differences occurred in regard to controlled or uncontrolled spillways, in regard to the floodway below Cairo and in regard to the Cypress Creek and Atchafalaya diversions, the Jadwin plan received approval in all cases.

In its conclusions the Board made one very interesting observation, especially in the light of present conditions. The project adopted proposed to permit the water to go into

[1] *United States Daily*, August 17, 1928, p. 1.
[2] *Ibid.*, p. 2.
[3] *Ibid.*
[4] *Ibid.*, p. 1.

natural low areas in some cases, which would increase the areas subject to inundation from backwater. The local interests naturally wanted these areas protected. The Board cautioned that space could not be continually taken from the river without allowing it space elsewhere, "either vertically or horizontally".[1] Thus, it would be highly inconsistent to shut the waters out of additional areas before the proposed works had been completed. In the future, the prediction said that possibly enough land in the floodways would be cleared to increase the velocity and discharge capacity enough to reduce flood heights so that additional land might be cleared. This statement put the Board on record against shutting the river out of low areas that might be reclaimed and put into cultivation, at least until the completion of the present project.

Although the decision of the Board in favor of the Jadwin plan should have been expected, its announcement aroused a storm of protest in some quarters. The section lying within the proposed Cypress creek floodway especially considered the plan an outrage. Nine Louisiana parishes and two Arkansas counties did all they could to enlist support for their opposition to this part of the Jadwin plan.[2] They wanted controlled spillways as proposed by the Mississippi River Commission; they further wanted the diversion channel and the spillway on the Atchafalaya completed before the water should be turned into the Boeuf basin floodway.[3] The one plainants had strong support in their contentions. The one redeeming feature of the report of the Board came in the form of a suggestion that changes might be made in the floodways as the project finally developed.[4] The official report said that the project permitted such modifications of the plans as,

[1] *United States Daily*, August 17, 1928, p. 6.

[2] Memphis, *The Commercial Appeal*, August 18, 1928.

[3] *Ibid.*

[4] New Orleans, *Times-Picayune*, August 17, 1928, p. 1.

in their discretion, "the Secretary of War and Chief of Engineers may deem advisable ", so that any change that should be shown to be expedient might be made.[1]   This little loophole seemed to be the only hope of the people who wanted controlled spillways.

On one point the report of the Board left the matter in such a condition as to cause a great deal of discussion and controversy.   The greatest difference in cost estimates of the Jadwin plan and the Commission plan came in the matter of damages and flowage rights.   The Jadwin plan considered the flowage rights a natural servitude in most of the area to be inundated by the floodways, because of the fact that floods in the natural state flowed through them.[2]   The Commission plan proposed to pay all damages and flowage rights on the ground that floods affected all other states of the delta and were interstate.[3]   The Jones-Reid act appeared to the people of the delta to provide for compensation for damages in the floodways.   It plainly said that the United States should provide flowage rights, but that benefits resulting from the construction of protective works should reduce the compensation to be paid.[4]   The statement in the act did not sound complicated, but the Flood Control Board took the position that the purchasing of flowage rights needed legal interpretation.[5]   However, the report made it clear that any necessary legal interpretation would not stand in the way of the actual speedy construction of the protective works.   At the semi-annual meeting of the Mississippi River Flood Control Association at Memphis in November 1928, several members of

[1] *United States Daily*, August 17, 1928, p. 6.

[2] *Cong. Record*, 70th Cong., 1st Sess., pt. 8, 1928, p. 6160.

[3] *House Committee on Flood Control*, 70th Cong., 1st Sess., 1927-8, *Report to Accompany House Bill*, no. 8219, p. 136.

[4] *Cong. Record*, 70th Cong., 1st Sess., *Public Document*, no. 391, p. 2.

[5] *United States Daily*, August 17, 1928, p. 6.

Congress, including Senators Joseph E. Ransdell of Louisiana and K. D. McKellar of Tennessee and Representatives W. J. Driver of Arkansas, Riley J. Wilson of Louisiana and W. M. Whittington of Mississippi, stated their beliefs that the flood-control act provided compensation for flowage rights.[1] Senator Ransdell said that it was " inconceivable that the government would take the property of its citizens to benefit other citizens without giving full compensation ".[2] During the autumn months of 1928 many meetings of property owners protested that part of the program. They apparently had not decided whether to take their fight to Congress or to the Federal Courts. But the complainants made it rather clear that if they did not go to Congress they would call upon the Federal Courts to pass upon the question of taking property without just compensation.[3] They wanted the government to purchase their property outright instead of buying flowage rights for a flood that was supposed to come once in twelve years, but that might come any year or any series of years.

While protests have been going on and while the legal interpretation of the question of compensation for flowage rights has been in abeyance, the work of construction on the main levees has proceeded rapidly and apparently satisfactorily. The work of the Mississippi River Commission and of the Army Engineers was receiving very little criticism. But, in the meantime, the people of northern Louisiana had taken their case over flowage damages to the Federal courts and the people of Missouri were preparing to go to court to stop construction of the Birds Point floodway. It appears very likely that the United States Supreme Court will have to

[1] Raleigh, *News and Observer*, November 14, 1928.

[2] Raleigh, *News and Observer*, November 14, 1928.

[3] *New York Times*, December 9, 1928, Sec. E, p. 2.

render a decision on these points.[1]   The work of acquiring rights of way and the condemnation of property for the flood-ways and the spillway above New Orleans (Bonne Carré) formed a part of the program of work for the year 1929-30. The War Department appropriation bill, passed in January, 1929, provided the annual budget of $30,000,000 to carry on the program under the Jones-Reid bill.   The rapid execution of levee building and the general progress in carrying out the project apparently have met general approval despite strenuous local protests against the forced sale of flowage rights.   The autumn of 1929 found the levees in condition to offer more protection than ever before.   The completion of the program provided by the Jones-Reid bill will give to the delta protection that was thought wholly unnecessary prior to the flood of 1927 and that seems adequate according to available data on that flood.

[1] *New York Times*, Sept. 30, 1929, p. 1.

APPENDIX

DOCUMENTS OF THE UNITED STATES GOVERNMENT

Alcorn, James L., *Mississippi River Levees*, Washington, Government Printing Office, 1873.

Aswell, James B., *Flood Control a National Obligation*, Washington, Government Printing Office, 1928.

Frankenfield, H. C., *The Floods of the Spring of 1903 in the Mississippi Watershed*, Washington, Weather Bureau Bulletin M, 1904.

Humphreys, Andrew A. and Abbot, Henry L., *Report upon the Physics and Hydraulics of the Mississippi River*, Washington, War Department, 1861.

Lewis, Barbour, *Levees of the Mississippi*, Washington, Government Printing Office, 1874.

Louisiana, *Mississippi River Levees, Memorial of Citizens of the State of Louisiana in Favor of Nationalizing the Levees of the Mississippi River*, House Miscellaneous Document No. 41; 42nd Cong., 3rd Sess., 1873.

Townsend, C. McD., *Elements of Flood Control, Address at St. Louis in 1913*, House Document 51, 63rd Cong., 1st Sess., 1913.

——, *Flood Control of the Mississippi River, Speech at Memphis in 1912*, Senate Document 1094; 62nd Cong., 3rd Sess., 1912.

United States Congress. *Congressional Globe*, 28th Cong., 1st Sess., 1833-4; 29th Cong., 1st Sess., 1846; 34th Cong., 1st Sess., part 3, 1855; 40th Cong., 2nd Sess., part 5, 1868; 42nd Cong., 1st Sess., part 2, 1871; 42nd Cong., 2nd Sess., part 1, 1871; 42nd Cong., 3rd Sess., part 3, 1873.

United States Congress. *Congressional Record*, 43rd Cong., 1st Sess., part 4, 1874; 43rd Cong., 1st Sess., part 5, 1874; 43rd Cong. 2nd Sess., part 2, 1875; 44th Cong., 1st Sess., part 2, 1876; 45th Cong., 3rd Sess., part 1, 1879; 45th Cong., 3rd Sess. part 2, 1879; 45th Cong., 3rd Sess., Appendix, 1879; 46th Cong., 1st Sess., Part 1, 1879; 46th Cong., 1st Sess., part 2, 1879; 47th Cong. 1st Sess., part 2, 1882; 47th Cong., 1st Sess., part 3, 1882; 47th Cong., 1st Sess., part 4, 1882; 51st Cong., 1st Sess., part 6, 1890; 52nd Cong. 1st Sess., part 2, 1892; 52nd Cong., 1st Sess., part 3, 1892; 55th Cong., 1st Sess., part 1, 1897; 55th Cong., 1st Sess., part 2, 1897; 59th Cong. 1st Sess., part 10, 1906; 63rd Cong., 2nd Sess., part 19, 1914; 64th Cong., 1st

Sess., part 2, 1916; 64th Cong., 1st Sess., part 6, 1916; 64th Cong., 1st Sess., part 9, 1916; 64th Cong. 1st Sess., part 10, 1916; 64th Cong., 1st Sess., part 11, 1916; 64th Cong. 2nd Sess., part 6, 1917; 67th Cong., 4th Sess., part 7, 1923; 70th Cong., 1st Sess., part 1, 1927; 70th Cong., 1st Sess., part 3, 1928; 70th Cong., 1st Sess., part 4, 1928; 70th Cong., 1st Sess. part 5, 1928; 70th Cong., 1st Sess., part 6, 1928; 70th Cong., 1st Sess., part 7, 1928; 70th Cong., 1st Sess., part 8, 1928; 70th Cong., 1st Sess., part 10, 1928; 70th Cong., 1st Sess., part 11, 1928.

United States Congress. House. Committee on Flood Control, *Hearings on Mississippi River Floods*, 64th Cong., 1st Sess., 1916; 67th Cong., 4th Sess., 1922; 68th Cong., 1st Sess., 1924; 70th Cong., 1st Sess., 1927.

United States Congress. House. Committee on Flood Control, *Abstract of Hearings before the Committee on Flood Control*, Committee Document No. 18; 70th Cong., 1st Sess., 1928.

United States Congress. House. Committee on Flood Control, *Analysis of Plans of Army Engineers and Mississippi River Commission by L. T. Berthe*, Committee Document No. 11; 70th Cong., 1st Sess., 1928.

United States Congress. House. Committee on Flood Control, *Bibliography on Flood Control Prepared by the Division of Bibliography*, Library of Congress; Committee Document No. 4; 70th Cong., 1st Sess., 1927.

United States Congress. House. Committee on Flood Control, *Brief of Hearings before the Committee on Flood Control*, Committee Document No. 24; 70th Cong., 1st Sess., 1928.

United States Congress. House. Committee on Flood Control, *Brief Submitted by Oscar Johnson on Plan of Army Engineers*, Committee Document No. 22; 70th Cong., 1st Sess., 1928.

United States Congress. House. Committee on Flood Control, *Brief Submitted by John E. Martineau on Plan of Army Engineers*, Committee Document No. 9, 70th Cong., 1st Sess., 1928.

United States Congress. House. Committee on Flood Control, *Brief Submitted by Governor O. H. Simpson of Louisiana on Plan of Army Engneers*, Committee Document No. 19; 70th Cong., 1st Sess., 1928.

United States Congress. House. *Message from the President of the United States Transmitting, with Favorable Recommendation, the Plan of the Army Engineers*, House Document No. 90; 70th Cong., 1st Sess., 1927.

United States Congress. House. Committee on Flood Control, *Report of Committee of Chief Engineers of Railroads Operating in Mississippi Valley on Plan of Army Engineers*, Committee Document No. 23; 70th Cong., 1st Sess., 1928.

United States Congress. House. Committee on Flood Control, *Report on the Control of Floods of the Mississippi River by Means of Diversion Channels*, Committee Document No. 3; 70th Cong., 1st Session, 1927.

United States Congress. House. Committee on Flood Control, *Report on the Control of Floods of the Mississippi River by Means of Reservoirs*, Committee Document No. 2; 7th Cong., 1st Sess., 1927.

United States Congress. House. Committee on Flood Control, *Report Submitted by Hon. Frank R. Reid to Accompany S. 3740*, House Report No. 1100; 70th Cong., 1st Sess., 1928.

United States Congress. House. Committee on Flood Control, *Report Submitted by Hon. Frank R. Reid to Accompany House Bill 8219*, Report not numbered; 70th Cong., 1st Sess., March, 1928.

United States Congress. House. Committee on Flood Control, *Report on Diversion Channel through St. Francis Basin*, Committee Document No. 25; 70th Cong., 1st Sess., 1928.

United States Congress. House. Committee on Flood Control, *Report on Improvement of Mississippi River for Navigation*, Committee Document No. 6; 70th Cong., 1st Sess., 1928.

United States Congress. House. Committee on Flood Control, *Report Submitted by Several Engineers at Request of Governor Len Small of Illinois*, Committee Document No. 20; 70th Cong., 1st Sess., 1928.

United States Congress. House. Committee on Flood Control, *Reports on the Ohio and Mississippi Rivers by General S. Bernard and Col. Jos. G. Totten in 1822, Charles Ellet, Jr. in 1852 and Gen. A. A. Humphreys in 1866*—Reprint, Committee Document No. 17; 70th Cong., 1st Sess., 1928.

United States Congress. House. Committee on Flood Control, *Special Report of the Mississippi River Commission on Revision of Plans for Improvement of Navigation and Flood Control of the Mississippi River*, Committee Document No. 1; 70th Congress, 1st Sess., 1927.

United States Congress. House. Committee on Flood Control, *Statement of Hon. Frank R. Reid in Regard to House Bill 8219*, Committee Document No. 7; 70th Cong., 1st Sess., 1927.

United States Congress. House. Committee on Flood Control, *Statement of Former Senator William Lorimer of Illinois*, Committee Document No. 26; 70th Cong., 1st Sess., 1928.

United States Congress. House. Committee on Levees and Improvements of the Mississippi River, *Improvement of the Mississippi River*, House Report No. 714; 45th Cong., 2nd Sess., 1878.

United States Congress. House. Committee on Levees and Improvement of the Mississippi River, *Levees of the Mississippi River*, House Miscellaneous Document No. 127; 51st Cong., 2nd Sess., 1891.

United States Congress. House. Committee on Levees and Improvements of the Mississippi River, *Mississippi River Improvements,* Hearings 1906.

United States Congress. House. Committee on Rivers and Harbors, *Floods and Levees of the Mississippi River,* Report 300, Part 2; 63rd Cong., 2nd Sess., 1914.

United States Congress. House. Select Committee on the Mississippi Levees, *Report of April 12, 1872,* House Report 44; 42nd Cong., 2nd Sess., 1872.

United States Congress. Senate. Committee on Commerce. *Hearings on the Prevention of Floods on the Mississippi River,* 1904, 1910, 1912, 1914, 1917, 1928.

United States Congress. Senate. Committee on Improvements of the Mississippi River, *Hearings on Levees of the Mississippi,* 1888.

United States. Engineer Department, *Report of the Board of Engineers on the Ohio and Mississippi Rivers, Made in the Year 1821 by General S. Bernard and Col. J. G. Totten,* House Document No. 35; 17th Cong., 2nd Sess., 1823.

United States. Inland Waterways Commission, *Preliminary Report,* Senate Document No. 325; 60th Cong., 1st Sess., 1908.

United States. Mississippi River Commission. *Official Annual Report,* 1881, 1882, 1883, 1884, 1888, 1892, 1897, 1911, 1912, 1913, 1916, 1921, 1922, 1923.

United States. Mississippi River Commission, *Contributions by Districts or Localities Benefitted by the Construction of Levees on Mississippi River,* House Document No. 645; 69th Cong., 1st Sess., 1916.

United States. Mississippi River Commission, *Separation of the Red and Atchafalaya Rivers from the Mississippi River,* House Document No. 841; 63rd Cong., 2nd Sess., 1914.

United States National Waterway Commission, *Final Report,* Senate Document 469; 62nd Cong., 2nd Sess., 1912.

United States. Treasury Department, *Levees—Mississippi and Other Rivers,* House Document 11; 24th Cong., 1st Sess., 1835.

United States. War Department, *Letter of the Secretary of War, Communicating a Copy of Gen. A. A. Humphreys' Report on the Levees of the Mississippi,* Senate Executive Document No. 8; 40th Cong., 1st Sess., 1866.

United States. War Department, *Letter from the Secretary of War, Relative to the Improvement of the Ohio River,* House Executive Document No. 127; 43rd Cong., 1st Sess.

United States. War Department, *Report of the Secretary of War, Communicating Reports in Reference to the Inundations of the Mississippi River,* Senate Document No. 20; 32nd Cong., 1st Sess., 1852.

United States. War Department, *Report of the Secretary of War, Communicating Reports in Reference to the Inundations of the Mississippi River*, Senate Executive Document No. 49; 32nd Cong., 1st Sess., 1852.

United States. Weather Bureau, *Floods of the Mississippi River*, Weather Bureau 1897, Weather Bureau Publication No. 143.

United States. Weather Bureau, *Destructive Floods in the United States in 1913*, Water Supply Paper 96.

West, Charles H., *Improvement of the Mississippi River*, Senate Document No. 600; 62nd Cong., 2nd Sess., 1912.

OTHER DOCUMENTS

Chamber of Commerce of the United States, *Referendum No. 51 on the Report of the Committee on Mississippi Flood Control*, Washington, 1927.

Interstate Mississippi River Improvement and Levee Association, *Proceedings of the Convention of 1890 at Vicksburg*, Vicksburg, 1890.

Kemper, J. P., *Proposed Plan for Flood Control below the Arkansas, etc.; A Report to the Safe River Committee of 100*, New Orleans, 1925.

Klorer, John *Report of the Engineers' Committee of the Safe River Committee of 100*, New Orleans, 1923.

Louisiana. General Assembly. Senate. Committee on Levees, *Report of March 21, 1850*, New Orleans, 1853.

Mississippi River Improvement Convention, *Official Report of the Proceedings of the Convention Held in St. Louis in 1881*, St. Louis, 1881.

Mississippi Flood Control Association, *Losses and Damages Resulting from the Flood of 1927*, Memphis, 1927.

Mississippi River Levee Association, *Public Sentiment as Expressed by Mayors of Cities and Commercial Organizations*, Memphis, 1916.

Mississippi River Levee Association, *Letters from Prominent Bankers Favoring Legislation by Congress to Prevent Floods*, Memphis, 1913.

Pittsburgh Flood Commission, *Report Containing Results of Surveys, etc.*, Pittsburgh, 1912.

BOOKS AND PAMPHLETS

Alvord, John W. and Burdick, Charles B., *Relief from Floods*, McGraw-Hill, New York, 1918.

Bock, Carl A., *History of the Miami Flood Control Project*, Dayton, Ohio, 1918.

Beman, L. T., *Flood Control*, H. W. Wilson, New York, 1928.

Channing, Edward, *The Jeffersonian System*, New York, 1906.

Cline, I. M., *Floods in the Lower Mississippi Valley*, New Orleans, 1927.

DuPratz, Le Page, *History of Louisiana, 1774*, An Early History of Louisiana, London, 1774.

Darby, William, *Geographical Description of Louisiana*, Publisher and Date not given.

Editorial Research Reports, *Economic Effects of the Mississippi Flood of 1927*, Washington, 1928. Mimeographed.

Ellet, Charles, *The Mississippi and Ohio Rivers: Containing Plans for the Protection of the Delta from Inundation*, Philadelphia, 1853.

Flint, Timothy, *History and Geography of the Mississippi Valley*, Cincinnati, 1832.

Forshey, Caleb G., *The Delta of the Mississippi: the Physics of the River, etc.*, Cambridge, 1873.

Fox, John A., *The Mississippi River Flood Problem; How Floods Can Be Prevented*, Washington, 1914.

Haupt, Herman, *The Problem of the Mississippi, Reprint from the Gulf Ports Marine Journal*, New Orleans, 1905.

Henry, Alfred J., *Floods in the Ohio River, 1870-1913*, Washington, 1913.

Humphreys, Benjamin G., *Floods and Levees of the Mississippi River*, Washington, 1914.

McMaster, John B., *History of the People of the United States, Vols. 1 and 2*, New York.

Mississippi River Flood Control Association, *The Flood of 1927*, Memphis 1927.

Morgan, Arthur E., *The Miami Valley and the 1913 Flood*, Dayton, Ohio, 1917.

Moses, Barnette E., *The Problem of the Mississippi*, Washington, 1914.

New York World. The World Almanac, 1929.

Ogg, Frederic A., *The Opening of the Mississippi*, New York, 1904.

Parker, Walter, *Why Flood Control and River Regulation Are Essential to the Economic Welfare of the Mississippi Valley and the Nation*, New Orleans, 1925.

Pickles, George W., *Drainage and Flood Control Engineering*, New York, 1925.

Porter, K. H., *National Party Platforms*, New York, 1924.

Randall, Henry S., *Life of Thomas Jefferson*, 3 vols., New York, 1858.

Reynolds, Robert V. R., *Grazing and Floods*, Washington, 1911.

Richardson, James D., *Messages and Papers of the Presidents*, vols. 2, 3, 5, 6 and 7.

Rightor, Henry, *Standard History of New Orleans*, Chicago, 1890.

St. Francis Levee District of Arkansas, *Report of the Officers, 1924-5*, Memphis, 1925.

Safe River Committee of 100, *Report of the Engineering Committee*, New Orleans, 1922.

Saxon, Lyle, *Father Mississippi*, New York, 1927.

Stoddard, Ames, *Sketches of Louisiana*, Mathew Carey, Philadelphia, 1812.

Taylor, Robert S., *Mississippi River Improvement; Collected Speeches and Magazine Articles*, Washington, 1921.

Tompkins, Frank H., *Riparian Lands of the Mississippi River*, Chicago, 1901.

Magazine Articles

American Railway Engineering Association, "Series of Articles on Various Phases of the Flood of 1927," *Bulletin*, July, 1927, V. 29: 1-96.

Bell, Stephen, "Untamed Mississippi," *Commerce and Finance*, April 27, 1927, V. 16: 838-9.

Blake, E. E., "Flood Control by Flood Prevention," *Manufacturers' Record*, June 9, 1927, V. 91: 63-4.

Brown, Robert M., "Notes on the Mississippi River Flood of 1903 and on the Floods of Other Years," *American Geographical Society Bulletin*, February, 1906, V. 38: 131-4.

"Can Floods Be Prevented?" *New Republic*, May 18, 1927, V. 50: 344 f.

Child, Richard W., "After the Flood Is Over," *Saturday Evening Post*, July 2, 1927, V. 200: 8-9.

Chittenden, H. M., "Detention Reservoirs, with Spillway Outlets, As an Agency in Flood Control," *American Society of Civil Engineers*, Sept., 1917, V. 43: 43 and 1425—44 and 2009—15 and 2467-70.

Cockrill, W. R., "A Plan to Drain the Lower Mississippi Valley," *De Bow's Review*, V. 8: 1850.

"Congressmen Discuss the Pros and Cons of a Special Session of Congress," *Manufacturers' Record*, May 19, 1927, V. 91: 53-9.

"Control *v.* Prevention," An Imposing Array of Opinions of Prominent Engineers, Scientists and Business Men. *Cassier's Monthly*, V. 44, July, 1913: 35 ff.

Dabney, A. L., "Success of the Mississippi River Levees in the Flood of 1922," *American Society of Civil Engineers, Proceedings*, August, 1923, V. 49: 1149-54.

Davis, Henry P., "And the Waters Prevailed," *Nature Magazine*, July, 1927, V. 10: 31-3.

Delano, Frederic A., "The Report of the Committee on Mississippi Flood Control Appointed by the United States Chamber of Commerce," *Annals of the American Academy of Political and Social Science*, January, 1928, V. 135.

"Economic Consequences of the Mississippi Flood," *The Nation's Business*, V. 15: 52.

Edmonds, Richard W., "This Flood Could Have Been Prevented; Others Must Be," *Manufacturers' Record*, June 2, 1927, V. 91: 79-80.

Ely, Richard T., "Farm Relief and Flood Control," *American Review of Reviews*, November, 1927, V. 76: 487 f.

Fauntleroy, Thomas, " Lord, Plant My Feet on High Ground," *Independent*, June 4, 1927, V. 118: 580-6.

" First Effects of the Mississippi Flood," *Literary Digest*, June 18, 1927, V. 93: 8-10.

" Flood Control Fight in Congress," *Literary Digest*, Dec., 24, 1927, V. 95: 8.

" Four Stages of the Flood," *The Survey*, July 1, 1927, V. 58.

Fox, John A., " Prevention of Mississippi River Floods A National Duty," *Rand-McNally Bankers' Monthly*, Feb., 1915, V. 32: 13-18.

Freeman, John R., " Taming the Mississippi," *Outlook*, June 8, 1927, V. 146: 182-6; *Outlook*, June 15, 1927, V. 146: 219-22.

Garner, George, " A Great River Conference at Chicago," *Manufacturers' Record*, June 9, 1927, V. 91: 59-62.

——, " The Time Has Come to Demand and Command Action," *Manufacturers' Record*, July 21, 1927, V. 92: 83 f.

Goins, Craddock, " Congress Must Translate Neglect into Action, etc.," *Manufacturers' Record*, May 12, 1927, V. 91: 63 f.

——, " Picture Story of the Mississippi Valley Flooded Area," *Manufacturers' Record*, May 26, 1927, V. 91: 65-8.

Gray, George W., " When the Flooded Mississippi Rushes Downward to the Sea," *American Magazine*, December, 1926, V. 102: 52-5.

Greeley, W. B., " The Part of Forestry in Flood Control," *American Forests and Forest Life*, July, 1927, V. 33.

Hardee, William J., " High Water Protection Methods on the Lower Mississippi River," *Journal of the Association of Engineering Societies*, August, 1900, V. 25: 85-106.

Harrington, D. V., " Financial and Business Effects of the Mississippi Flood," *Magazine of Wall Street*, June 18, 1927, V. 40: 282-5.

Harris, L. O., " The Battle for the Delta," *Independent*, May 14, 1903, V. 55.

Hart, Albert B., " Mississippi Floods," *Current History*, June, 1927, V. 26: 458-9.

" Hoover's Flood Control Plan," *Commerce and Finance*, July 27, 1927, V. 16: 1495 f.

Hoover, Herbert, " Greatest Peace-time Calamity," *Commercial and Financial Chronicle*, June 4, 1927, V. 124: 3301-3.

——, " The Improvement of Our Mid-West Waterways," *Annals of the American Academy of Political and Social Science*, Jan., 1928, V. 135.

Horton, A. H., " The Effects of the Conservation of Flow in the Ohio Basin on Floods in the Lower Mississippi," *Engineering News*, June 11, 1908, V. 59.

" How Hoover's Forces Fought the Flood," *Literary Digest*, July 30, 1927, V. 94: 37, 40, 42.

Irwin, Will, "The Aftermath of Mud and Money," *The Survey*, July 1, 1927, V. 58: 358.

——, "Can We Tame the Mississippi," *World's Work*, Aug., 1927, V. 54: 405-15.

Jadwin, Gen. Edgar, Small, Len, *et al.*, "Should States of Mississippi Flood Area Share Costs of Flood Control Projects.", *Congressional Digest*, February, 1928, V. 7: 49.

Kellogg, Arthur, "Up from the Bottom Lands," *The Survey*, July 1, 1927, V. 58: 360-6.

Kerr, F. M .,"Red and Atchafalaya Rivers with Relation to Their Separation from the Mississippi River," *Journal of the Association of Engineering Societies*, March, 1911, V. 46: 185-206.

"Law of the River," *Outlook*, May 25, 1927, V. 146: 104-5.

Martineau, John E., "Government Control," *Century*, Sept., 1927, V. 114: 639.

——, "Why Investors Should Be Interested in Flood Control of the Mississippi and Its Tributaries," *Commercial and Financial Chronicle*, Oct. 15, 1927, V. 125: 2074-6.

"Mississippi—Father of Waters," *Nation*, May 11, 1927, V. 124: 518.

"Mississippi Flood Control Plan Submitted to President Coolidge by Secretary Hoover," *Commercial and Financial Chronicle*, July 30, 1927, V. 125: 600.

"Mississippi Flood Four Hundred Years Ago," *Literary Digest*, July 30, 1927, V. 94.

"Mississippi Flood of 1927," *The Congressional Digest*, Feb., 1928, V. 7: 42.

"Mississippi Record Flood Crest Passes Memphis," *Engineering News-Record*, April 28, 1927, V. 98: 702-7.

"The Mississippi Will Quickly Rebuild," *Manufacturers' Record*, May 5, 1927, V. 91: 73 f.

Monette, John W., "The Mississippi Floods," *Publications of Mississippi Historical Society*, 1903, V. 7: 427-478.

Moore, Willis L., "Forests and Floods," *American Review of Reviews*, Aug., 1927, V. 76: 199-200.

Morgan, Arthur E. and Bock, C. A., "History of Flood Control in Ohio," *Ohio Archeological and Historical Quarterly*, Oct., 1925, V. 34: 474-505.

Morgan, Arthur E., "A Policy for the Mississippi," *The Annals of the American Academy of Political and Social Science*, Jan., 1928, V. 135.

Newell, F. H., "Mississippi River Floods," *American Review of Reviews*, June, 1927, V. 75: 592-600.

Newlands, Francis G., "How Floods May Be Prevented," *National Waterways*, June, 1913, V. 1: 316-24.

"Newspaper Editorials on Mississippi Floods," *Public Opinion*, April 1, 1897, V. 22 : 393.

Oakes, J. C., "Flood Prevention and Protection from the Point of View of the Federal Government," *Engineering and Contracting*, March 18, 1914, V. 41 : 338-41.

"Operating Results Show Floods' Effect on Railroads," *Railway Age*, Aug. 6, 1927, V. 83 : 272.

Parker, John M., "After the Flood," *Outlook*, June 1, 1927, V. 146 : 148-9.

——, "Louisiana Looks to Washington," *Survey*, July 1, 1927, V. 58 : 359.

Parker, Walter, "The Problem of the Mississippi," *Commerce and Finance*, May 11, 1927, V. 16 : 938.

Payne, John Barton, "Review of Red Cross Relief Activities in Mississippi Flood Areas," *Congressional Digest*, Feb., 1928, V. 7 : 42.

Pickett, William D., "The Floods of the Mississippi Delta; Their Cause and Suggestions as to Their Control," *Proceedings of the American Society of Civil Engineers*, Nov., 1908, V. 34 : 1232-51.

Pinchot, Gifford, "Prevention First," *Survey*, July 1, 1927, V. 58 : 367-9.

——, "Some Essential Principles of Water Conservation as Applied to Mississippi Flood Control," *Annals of the American Academy of Political and Social Science*, Jan., 1928, V. 135.

Potter, Charles L., "How the Mississippi River Is Regulated," *Engineering News-Record*, April 2, 1925, V. 94 : 508-14 and 556-9.

——, "Levees on the Mississippi Tend to Lower River Bed," *Engineering News-Record*, Feb. 14, 1924, V. 92 : 280-2.

"Recent Great Flood: What May Be Done to Prevent Such Inundations in the Future," *Scientific American*, April 12, 1913, V. 108 : 336-7.

Ricker, Samuel, "The Crevasses of Louisiana," *De Bow's Review*, Feb., 1851, V. 10.

Seddon, James A., "Reservoirs and the Control of the Lower Mississippi," *Journal of the Western Society of Engineers*, Aug., 1900, V. 5 : 259-91.

Sherman, E. A., "What Forests Can Do for the Mississippi River," *The Annals of the American Academy of Political and Social Science*, Jan., 1928, V. 135.

Simons, P. T., "Flood Probability," *Engineering News-Record*, April 29, 1926, V. 96 : 704.

Simpich, Frederick, "Great Mississippi Flood of 1927," *National Geographic Magazine*, Sept., 1927, V. 52 : 243-89.

"Sinking of Land as a Cause for the Mississippi Floodss," *Science*, N. S., June 3, 1927, V. 65, Supp : 10-12.

Smith, J. Russell, "Plan or Perish," *Survey*, July 1, 1927, V. 58 : 370-7.

——, "Wealth from Mississippi Mud," *Survey*, Nov. 1, 1927, V. 59 : 127-31.

Spears, R. S., " Real Problem of the Mississippi," *Scientific American,*
Feb. 15, 1913, V. 108: 155.

" Steps Taken by the Federal Government for Mississippi Flood Relief,"
Congressional Digest, Feb., 1928, V. 7: 41.

Stone, A. H., " And the Waters Prevailed," *Commerce and Finance,*
June 1, 1927, V. 16: 1101-2.

Sullivan, H. G., " Credits in the Flood Area," *Credit Monthly,* June,
1927, V. 29: 19-20.

Sullivan, Mark, " President's View of Extra Session Vexing to South,"
Manufacturers' Record, Aug. 4, 1927, V. 92: 78.

" Summary of Plans of Army Engineers and the Mississippi River
Commission," *Congressional Digest,* Feb., 1928, V. 7: 49.

" Suspicion of Pork in the Flood Control Bill," *Literary Digest,* April
14, 1928, V. 97: 10.

Surain, G. F., " The Influence of Forests on Climate, Floods and Erosion,"
Engineering News, April 14, 1910, V. 63: 427-9.

Sweinhart, H. L., " Mastering the Mississippi; Interview with J. E.
Ransdell," *Outlook,* July 26, 1922, V. 131: 518-9.

Switzer, J. E., " A Trip to the Mississippi-Yazoo Flood District,"
Journal of Geography, Nov., 1927.

" Symposium on the Flood's Lesson: Burton, Theodore; Caldwell, A. S.;
Hill, James J.; Cox, James M.," *Review of Reviews,* June, 1913,
V. 47.

" Taming the Father of Waters," *Journal of Forestry,* May, 1927, V.
25: 507-9.

Taylor, Harry, " Problems of Flood Control," *Scientific Monthly,* April,
1923, V. 16: 352 f.

" Telephone in the Mississippi Flood," *Literary Digest,* Aug. 20, 1927,
V. 94: 21.

Thomas, Lewis F., " Basic Factors in Flood Frequency in the Lower
Mississippi River," *The Annals of the American Academy of Political and Social Science,* Jan., 1928, V. 135.

" To End Floods," *World's Work,* May, 1913, V. 26: 22-4.

Tolman, Charles F., " When the Waters Break Loose," *Nature Magazine,*
April, 1925, V. 5.

Townsend, Curtis McD., " Levee Construction on the Mississippi and
Its Effect on River Section," *Engineering and Contracting,* Jan. 14.
1920, V. 53.

——, " The Problem of Flood Control," *National Waterways,* June,
1913, V. 1.

——, " Why the Spillways will not Solve the Mississippi Problem,"
Engineering News-Record, Jan. 4, 1923, V. 90.

Walker, J. Bernard, " Curbing the Mississippi," *Scientific American,*
Feb., 1928, V.

" Washington, Webster and Roosevelt on the Mississippi Valley," *Manufacturers' Record*, June 2, 1927, V. 91 : 68.

White, O. P., "And the Floods Came," *Collier's Weekly*, July 9, 1927, V. 80 : 5-6.

White, Walter, "The Negro and the Flood," *Nation*, June 22, 1927, V. 124 : 688-9.

"Why Flood Experts Disagree," *Literary Digest*, July 2, 1927, V. 94 : 21-2.

Williams, Frank E., "The Geography of the Mississippi Valley," *Annals of the American Academy of Political and Social Science*, Jan., 1928, V. 135.

Winter, T. G., "Man-Made Floods," *Outlook*, May 18, 1927, V. 146 : 88.

Zon, Raphael, "Do Forests Prevent Floods?" *American Forests and Forest Life*, July, 1927, V. 33.

NEWSPAPERS

Baltimore Sun, April 17, 1927.

Chicago Tribune, April 12, 1882; April 22, 1882; April 24, 1882; April 25, 1897; April 18, 1927.

Cleveland Plain Dealer, April 18, 1927.

Detroit Free Press, May 5, 1927; May 7, 1927; May 11, 1927.

Indianapolis Star, May 13, 1927.

Jacksonville Times-Union, April 4, 1897.

Kansas City Daily Star, April 27, 1927.

Memphis Commercial Appeal, May 4, 1897; April 4, 1913; April 20, 1913; May 7, 1927; Oct. 9, 1927; Oct. 21, 1927; Oct. 25, 1927; Nov. 7, 1927; Nov. 22, 1927; Dec. 5, 1927; Mar. 16, 1928; April 25, 1928; April 26, 1928; April 30, 1928; May 17, 1928; May 22, 1928; May 23, 1928; May 24, 1928; June 20, 1928; August 18, 1928; Nov. 30, 1928.

Memphis News Scimitar, May 12, 1913; Jan. 12, 1914; Dec. 2, 1914.

New Orleans States, April 18, 1897.

New Orleans Times-Democrat, April 5, 1882; April 10, 1882; April 17, 1882; April 19, 1882; April 22, 1882.

New Orleans Times-Picayune, April 6, 1912; April 15, 1912; April 25, 1913; April 30, 1913; May 19, 1913; May 4, 1922; May 8, 1922; May 23, 1922; April 25, 1927; May 3, 1927; May 4, 1927; May 6, 1927; May 19, 1927; May 22, 1927; June 4, 1927; June 23, 1927; July 10, 1927; Sept. 24, 1927; Oct. 16, 1927; Oct. 18, 1927; Oct. 25, 1927; Dec. 6, 1927; Dec. 9, 1927; Dec. 21, 1927; Jan. 19, 1928; Jan. 26, 1928; Jan. 29, 1928; May 16, 1928; June 13, 1928; August 17, 1928.

New York Herald Tribune, May 2, 1927.

New York Times, April 21, 1882; April 22, 1882; April 6, 1913; May 19, 1927; May 23, 1927; May 29, 1927; June 2, 1927; June 3, 1927; June

5, 1927; June 23, 1927; July 13, 1927; August 21, 1927; Sept. 18, 1927; Nov. 27, 1927; Jan. 24, 1928; Jan. 29, 1928; Feb. 24, 1928; Feb. 26, 1928; April 19, 1928; April 29, 1928; Dec. 9, 1928; Sept. 30, 1929.

New York World, April 26, 1927; April 24, 1927.

Pittsburgh Post, May 5, 1927.

Raleigh News and Observer, Nov. 14, 1928; Jan. 27, 1929.

St. Louis Globe-Democrat, April 7, 1897; May 1, 1927; May 5, 1927.

San Francisco Chronicle, April 7, 1897.

United States Daily, May 5, 1927; May 6, 1927; May 17, 1927; June 4, 1927; June 18, 1927; Sept. 20, 1927; Sept. 28, 1927; Oct. 7, 1927; Oct. 13, 1927; Oct. 19, 1927; Oct. 28, 1927; Nov. 18, 1927; August 17, 1928.

Washington Post, April 21, 1897; Feb. 17, 1928; Aug. 29, 1928.

Washington Star, June 12, 1927.

Hartford Daily Courant, May 30, 1897.

INDEX